WITHOUT
PRECEDENT

WITHOUT PRECEDENT

The Story of the Death of McCarthyism

JOHN G. ADAMS

W·W·NORTON & COMPANY·NEW YORK·LONDON

The text of this book is composed in VIP Times Roman, with display type set in Times Roman.
Composition and manufacturing by Maple-Vail Book Manufacturing Group.

Library of Congress Cataloging in Publication Data
Adams, John Gibbons, 1912–
    Without precedent.
Bibliography: p.
Includes index.
1. Internal security—United States.   2. McCarthy,
Joseph, 1908–1957.   3. Subversive activities—
United States.   I. Title.
E743.5.A64 1983   973.921′092′4   82–14112

ISBN 0-393-01616-1

W. W. Norton & Company, Inc., 500 Fifth Avenue, New York, N.Y. 10110
W. W. Norton & Company Ltd., 37 Great Russell Street, London WC1B 3NU

2 3 4 5 6 7 8 9 0

Truth crushed down to earth shall rise again.

—*Bryant*

Contents

III   WINTER 1954

IV   SPRING 1954

V   ENDINGS

〔 I 〕

BEGINNINGS

CHAPTER I

Tail Gunner Joe

Joe McCarthy was almost born in a log cabin. His parents moved out of one into a white clapboard farmhouse outside Appleton, Wisconsin, shortly before he was born in 1908. McCarthy was a rambunctious, loud, extroverted child, though some friends noticed a nervous giggle and a certain awkwardness. He left school after the eighth grade and became first a successful chicken farmer and then manager of a grocery store while still a teenager.

At twenty McCarthy went back to school, completing a full four-year high school course in one year. He then entered Marquette University and earned a law degree in 1935 at age twenty-six. He immediately set up practice in Northern Wisconsin. As a lawyer he was not a success. Steady fees were hard to come by for a young country lawyer in the depths of the depression. In later years, he liked to brag that he supported himself primarily by winning at poker.

In 1938 McCarthy decided to seek a more secure job, so he ran for state circuit judge. Lacking other qualifications for the job, he made age the issue of the campaign. McCarthy was 29, and Judge Edgar V. Werner, the incumbent who had a long and distinguished record, was 66. McCarthy decided to make his opponent a little older, so in his speeches and campaign literature he added seven years to the judge's age, making him 73. On occasion, he advanced that to 89. In his speeches he often referred to "my senile opponent." Meanwhile McCarthy subtracted a year from his own age, so he would be the youngest circuit judge in Wisconsin history, if he won. His campaign slogan was "Justice is Truth in Action."

McCarthy did win. It was an early lesson in the power of lies.

As a judge, McCarthy was known mostly for granting fast divorces; he could dissolve a marriage in less than five minutes. He was also caught destroying judicial records that showed him abusing a local lawyer from the bench; for this he was reprimanded by the Wisconsin Supreme Court.

When World War II broke out, McCarthy asked the Marine Corps for a direct commission, and he was appointed as a first lieutenant. He would later say that he had enlisted in the Marines as a buck private and had won his commission on the battlefields of the South Pacific. Actually he was a ground intelligence officer stationed on an island well to the rear. From time to time he liked to sit in the tail gunner's seat of a parked airplane and shoot coconuts off the trees.

In 1944, while the Pacific war was still raging, McCarthy wrangled a four-month leave from duty and returned to Wisconsin to run for the Senate. He was able to get this unusual wartime leave because he had not resigned from the bench when he entered the Marines, and he contended that he was "needed at home" for his judicial duties.

Wearing his Marine uniform, he campaigned in the Republican primaries through the spring of 1944 against the incumbent senator, advertising himself as Tail Gunner Joe. He claimed a combat wound, and liked to say that he carried around in his leg ten pounds of shrapnel, which caused the slight limp he affected when he thought of it. The "wound" was from falling down a ship ladder during an equator-crossing party. He had broken his ankle.

McCarthy lost to Senator Alexander Wiley, but he managed to cover the entire state and meet all the Republican leaders, thus laying the groundwork for the next election. Less than a year later, and many months before the war was over, he resigned from the Marines and went back to Wisconsin to run again for the Senate.

This time McCarthy's primary opponent was Robert M. LaFollette, Jr., the son of the great Progressive, and himself a twenty-four-year Senate veteran. LaFollette was quiet, thoughtful, and full of high-minded purpose. He was chairman of the Senate Civil Liberties Sub-committee, and had only recently been voted by newsmen as "the best U.S. Senator." But he was also remote and out of touch with his state, and he narrowly lost to McCarthy. Seven years later, when McCarthy was at the peak of his power, LaFollette shot himself.

CHAPTER II

The Worst U.S. Senator

The first time I met Joe McCarthy, he hugged me. It was at a Republican luncheon at the Schroeder Hotel in Milwaukee, in the spring of 1946. I was doing some organizational work for the Republican National Committee. McCarthy was running hard for the Senate, pressing the flesh from table to table. Before long he reached mine.

We were both wearing the "ruptured duck," the lapel pin given to World War II veterans. He grinned as he fingered my lapel and asked me where I had served. I said I had been in the Army, stationed in Europe most of the time. He said he had been in Marine aviation in the South Pacific. With a wry smile and a slightly rueful but brave tone, he patted the leg he was favoring from time to time as he walked. "I was luckier than most of the guys," he said. "Just a little flak."

On leaving us he put his arm around my shoulder and gave me a friendly bear hug. As he moved to the next table it was clear to me that he was a perfect candidate; a rural upbringing, a half-Irish, half-German Catholic in a predominately German and Catholic state, a self-made lawyer and judge, and a legitimate, wounded war hero. I did wonder, however, why he wasn't wearing the purple lapel bar insignia denoting the Purple Heart, the medal awarded to all battle wounded. Too modest, I guessed.

My roots were not very different from Joe McCarthy's. I grew up in South Dakota, graduating from the state university Law School in 1935, the same year Joe McCarthy graduated from Marquette Law School. I went to work in the criminal branch of the South Dakota attorney general's office, but within a year my father died and I took over the family oil distributorship, which like all other small businesses of the era, was struggling to survive. I also got involved in politics, first by helping a law school classmate in his campaign for county prosecutor, and then by becoming actively involved in the local Republican party. I did it more as a hobby than out of political ambition. In South Dakota, there wasn't much else to do in the bottom of the depression. The movie changed only twice a week, and the bird-shooting season lasted only a few weeks. But I liked politics. I took the two-day train trip to the 1940 Republican Convention in Philadelphia just to see what it was like.

When World War II came to America I went overseas as a first lieutenant. I participated in five campaigns and waded ashore in two landing operations, once at H-hour (North Africa), but spent most of my time as a staff officer in various field headquarters where I saw many of the wartime leaders.

Although some of them were pompous, I admired most of them. I had a sufficiently high opinion of the Army so that when I was discharged, I stayed on in the Army reserve until I had completed a full thirty years of active reserve service, which was in 1964. I was proud of what the Army had done in the overseas theaters in which I had served, and I particularly admired some of the leaders such as Generals Dwight D. Eisenhower, Omar M. Bradley, Matthew B. Ridgway, J. Lawton Collins, and Maxwell Taylor.

After the war, I married a pretty WAVE named Margaret Williams, a sweet and gentle Virginia girl, and soon got a job as staff director of the Senate Armed Services Committee. The senator who hired me was Chan Gurney of South Dakota, who had just become chairman of the committee. I had worked in Gurney's election campaign in South Dakota in 1938 and I liked him and shared many of his political likes and dislikes.

The Senate was a slower, more intimate place in those days. This was before the age of huge staffs, and one could meet and come to know many senators on a first-name basis, and could wander down the aisle of the Senate floor and sit beside them during debates. Every morning, you could see Clyde Hoey step off a trolley car in his cut-away coat, or Felix Frankfurter and Dean Acheson walking along "P" Street, with Acheson's State Department limousine gliding along behind. Secretary of Defense James Forrestal would walk across Memorial Bridge on the way home from the Pentagon, possibly brooding on his eventual suicide.

There were still great orators in the Senate—men like Alben Barkley and Carl Hatch, President Truman's old poker buddies. Often they would go off the Senate floor to the well-stocked office of the secretary of the senate, otherwise known as "Les Biffle's Watering Hole," and, after a suitable time, emerge to make resounding speeches. There was also a lot of good-natured horseplay. Truman's drinking companions once tried to bribe a pageboy to climb up into the Senate gallery with a fishing rod and cast for a senator's toupee while he spoke. One of their more sober colleagues put a stop to that plot.

Another popular congressional pastime in those postwar years was chasing Communists. The House Un-American Activities Committee had been sniffing around for subversives since the late 1930s, and after World War II the Republican right wing took up the chase. There was a lot of hot talk—Congressman Richard Nixon of California, for instance, flatly stated that the Democrats were responsible for the "unimpeded growth of the Communist conspiracy in the United States," while Senator William Jenner of Indiana called General George C. Marshall "a front man for traitors" and a "living lie," who along with President Truman and Secretary of State Dean Acheson ("this criminal crowd of traitors and Communist appeasers") was "selling America down the river." Jenner said that it was Acheson—the Red Dean—and his crowd of "egg-sucking phony liberals," "Communists and queers" who had "sold China into atheistic slavery." But the Red hunters were hard put to find any Reds in government. They compiled a few lists but they never really came up with an authentic, card-carrying Communist in the upper echelons of government.

Then Alger Hiss arrived on the scene.

Hiss was a Baltimore patrician, Phi Beta Kappa, Harvard Law, law clerk to the great justice Oliver Wendell Holmes, special adviser to President Franklin Delano Roosevelt at Yalta, Secretary General of the international conference at San Francisco, which established the United Nations, favorite of Secretary of State Acheson, and a recent appointee of John Foster Dulles as president of the Carnegie Foundation for International Peace. Lean, tanned, and well tailored, Hiss was the epitome of the liberal Eastern Eastablishment, the Brahmin New Dealer.

He was also a Communist, charged Whittaker Chambers. Chambers himself had been a Communist, a courier carrying stolen secrets to the Soviets. He claimed that Hiss had given him some of these secrets, and testified that Hiss represented "the concealed enemy."

Chambers had been, by his own admission, a scoundrel; he was also proven to be a liar and a thief. However, he was able to produce scores of classified documents, some allegedly in Hiss's own handwriting and some from his typewriter. Chambers said that Hiss had given the papers to him in the 1930s when Hiss had been a high State Department official.

Chambers also had Richard Nixon on his side—a dogged, relentless prosecutor determined to expose the pink underside of the liberal "Establishment." If he could show that someone like Hiss had worked for the Russians, then who was to say that the State Department wasn't full of such phony liberals, quietly stealing State secrets?

Indicted for perjury for denying Chambers's allegations, Hiss was tried in the summer of 1949. The jury was hung, 8 to convict, 4 to acquit. He was tried a second time in the early winter; this time, in January 1950, he was convicted.

In between the trials, China fell to the Communists, the Red Army suppressed the last shreds of democracy in Eastern Europe, and Russia exploded its first atom bomb. The cold war got colder, and at home, Red-baiting became shriller and more paranoid.

At the time I did not take it very seriously. As a young man learning about politics in the 1930s, I had seen a great deal of the tactics of Karl E. Mundt, an ambitious speech teacher and windbag from my own congressional district. His persistent Red-baiting, beginning in about 1936, was considered pretty much of a joke by most of my Sioux Falls friends. But he was a true political survivor, shrewd at self-advancement. His 1936 congressional platform was "A Fair Chance for a Free People," a slogan he was still using when he ran for a third Senate term in 1966. I got along well enough with Mundt, but hard as I tried I just couldn't take his Red Scare preaching seriously.

In later years my Democratic friends liked to joke that Mundt was running against Stalin in every election, and that Stalin's death in 1953 was a Russian dirty trick on Mundt, because now he didn't have anybody to run against.

I thought the Red-baiters of Washington in the late 1940s were equally shallow; the China lobby was mostly nonsense, and I never

thought the House Un-American Activities Committee was doing anything but dragging the same old tired people over the coals. In general,
I didn't care much for the right wing of the Republican party, and I
did not admire their leader, Bob Taft. Like Taft, his followers tended
to be self-righteous and intolerant.

However, I was not exactly a flaming liberal. Mostly, I was a moderate Republican staff member who did his work and got along in the
small postwar world of Washington, D.C.

During his first three years in the Senate, Joe McCarthy didn't pay
much attention to the Red Menace, either. He was too preoccupied
with less global concerns. His early Senate career was undistin-
guished, to put it mildly. "Tail Gunner Joe" became better known by
reporters covering Congress as "Pepsi-Cola Joe"; a Pepsi bottling
company official gave McCarthy a $20,000 unsecured loan. McCarthy
was also given $10,000 by the Lustron Corporation, makers of prefab-
ricated houses, when the company was looking for funds from the
Reconstruction Finance Corporation. In neither case could any clear
quid pro quo be proved, and McCarthy apparently labored honestly to
remedy the postwar housing shortage. But he was not taken very seriously as a senator. He was perhaps a more familiar figure in night spots
and race tracks than on the Senate floor.

McCarthy made headlines only once in those early years, and he
picked an odd cause to embrace. During the 1944 Battle of the Bulge,
73 Nazi SS Troopers from the charmingly named "Blow Torch Bat-
talion," had massacred 100 captured American soldiers at Malmedy,
Belgium. In 1949, perhaps to placate Wisconsin voters who were fifty
percent German, McCarthy decided to rescue the 43 troopers who had
been convicted by a U.S. Army war crimes trial. He had made the
bizarre charge that the Army had "tortured" the SS troopers to extract
their confessions. There was nothing to support his allegation, just a
batch of meaningless papers he waved about. But he got his first big
headlines: MCCARTHY HITS BRUTALITY: MCCARTHY HINTS
AT MYSTERY WITNESS: MCCARTHY CHARGES WHITE-
WASH. The style was to become very familiar.

I saw little of McCarthy in those early years, and when I did, he
invariably gave me a grin and a big hello. I had a friend, however,
who had a different experience with McCarthy.

Joe Chambers was a staff member of the subcommittee that had

Raymond E. Baldwin, Republican senator from Connecticut, was described by Herbert Hoover in 1944 as a Republican governor well suited to be president. Baldwin resigned the Senate in 1949, saying that McCarthy's attack on him and his handling of the Malmedy hearings had been the "last straw" in his decision to give up politics. COURTESY WIDE WORLD PHOTOS.

looked into McCarthy's Malmedy massacre charges. One day in 1949, Chambers told me about the beating he had taken from McCarthy during the course of the inquiry. McCarthy had heaped abuse on Chambers for no particular reason, and Chambers was dumbfounded. They were both Catholics and both ex-Marines; Chambers had won the Medal of Honor at Iwo Jima, and McCarthy often spoke of that award in a complimentary manner; and they had been friends until McCarthy suddenly turned on him. Chambers added that McCarthy was even rougher on the subcommittee chairman, Raymond E. Baldwin. McCarthy had so brutally attacked Baldwin that the Senate felt it necessary to pass an extraordinary resolution expressing full confidence in Baldwin's honor and integrity. A few months later Baldwin resigned from the Senate and accepted an appointment as a judge on the highest court in Connecticut. He told the New York *Times* that in deciding whether to give up his political career, McCarthy's abuse had been the last straw.

Shortly thereafter, in December 1949, in a poll of Senate correspondents, McCarthy was voted the worst U.S. senator.

CHAPTER III

The Gold Strike
at Wheeling

As the decade closed McCarthy did not have much to show for his three years in the Senate. Moreover, he had put his political donations into soybean futures and lost his shirt. He desperately needed an issue, something that would put him in the public eye and get him reelected in 1952.

On January 7, 1950, he discussed his problem at a dinner at the Colony Restaurant with Father Edmund Walsh, dean of the Foreign Service School at Georgetown University; Charles Kraus, a Georgetown political science professor; and William Roberts, a Washington lawyer—what McCarthy and this trio had in common was Roman Catholicism. McCarthy announced that he needed a cause. The others urged him, as a young Roman Catholic senator, to take something seriously.

They suggested the St. Lawrence Seaway. McCarthy wasn't interested. Old age pensions? No to that, too. Then Father Walsh suggested communism.

"That's it!" exclaimed McCarthy. "The government is full of Communists. We can hammer away at them."

First, however, he had to find some Communists. He called up the Chicago *Tribune* reporter—Willard Edwards—and asked if he knew of any. Edwards told him of an old congressional investigation that had looked at the files of 108 State Department employees suspected as bad security risks. As of 1948, 57 still worked for the department. McCarthy also checked in with Congressman Richard Nixon's office. He was referred to an issue of the *Congressional Record* where he learned that in 1946 the State Department had recommended against the permanent employment of 284 wartime employees. Of these, 79 had been discharged. McCarthy subtracted 79 from 284 and got the magic number of 205.

His research complete, McCarthy needed a platform from which to launch his new career as a Communist hunter. The Republican National Committee had invited him to speak at three Lincoln Day dinners, one before the Ohio Valley Women's Republican Club in Wheeling, West Virginia, another at Reno, and a third at Salt Lake City. The Red Menace would be his subject. He was still clipping together items lifted from speeches of others when his plane landed at Wheeling. McCarthy's speech to the Republican women that night of February 9, 1950, was mostly a rehash of an old Nixon speech made two weeks earlier.

William Manchester compared them in his book, *The Glory and the Dream:*

NIXON IN CONGRESS (1/26/50)	MCCARTHY IN WHEELING (2/9/50)
The great lesson which should be learned from the Hiss case is that we are not just dealing with espionage agents who get 30 pieces of silver to obtain the blueprint of a weapon . . . but this is a far more sinister type of activity, because it permits the enemy to guide and shape our policy.	One thing to remember in discussing the Communists is that we are not dealing with spies who get 30 pieces of silver to steal the blueprint of a new weapon. We are dealing with a far more sinister type of activity because it permits the enemy to guide and shape our policy.

McCarthy did add at least one paragraph of his own. Waving a wad of papers above his head, he exclaimed: "I have in my hand a list of 205 card-carrying Communists who are now employed in the State Department and whose identities are well known to the State Department as being members of the Communist party."

It was pure fiction, of course, and the Republican women didn't seem much impressed by it. However, a West Virginia newspaper story about the speech was picked up by the wire services, and by the time he got to Denver, there was a reporter waiting to ask him if he really had a list of 205 Communists who worked in the State Department.

McCarthy was a bit taken aback, but pleased. "Why, certainly, right here in my briefcase," he said, thinking fast. After making a great show of fumbling through the partitions he said, "I guess it's in my other bag in the cargo compartment of the plane." The next morning, the Denver *Post* ran a picture of McCarthy anxiously peering into his battered briefcase.

By the time he returned to Washington and to the furor the Wheeling charges had created McCarthy realized he had struck gold.

McCarthy was not entirely new to Red-baiting. He had charged his opponents in the 1946 primary and general elections with Communist leanings, thereby provoking the scorn of the Madison *Capital Times*. McCarthy then turned on the state capitol newspaper, steadily describing it as a pink sheet and its writers as fellow travelers. Most of the major Wisconsin newspapers continued to headline his charges against the *Capital Times* without first authenticating their accuracy, and then gave very short notice to the *Capital Times* answers when they came later. McCarthy was shrewd enough to discover this institutional weakness of the press; it was a weakness he would exploit again and again in the years ahead.

But McCarthy had not realized the potential that Red-baiting held for a demagogue of truly national stature. The Wheeling speech thus was a revelation.

His timing couldn't have been better. The Hiss conviction a month earlier had proved that high-level Communists were not a myth. And over the next few months a far more chilling story of Communist spying was to unfold.

In 1945, Julius Rosenberg, an electrical engineer in the employ of the U.S. Army, and his wife, Ethel, had persuaded her brother, David Greenglass—a soldier at the atomic research labs at Los Alamos—to sketch blueprints of the atom bomb. The information was fed into an elaborate spy network and sent on to Russia which enabled the Soviets to catch up to the United States and build their own bomb.

In the spring of 1950, the story began to seep out as a member of the spy ring confessed. Shortly after the FBI arrested the Rosenbergs one night as they sat in front of their television watching the *Lone Ranger,* the full extent of their perfidy became clear. Because of the treachery of some native-born Americans, the Russians had the bomb far sooner than they might have had. So there were real spies out there after all. The "concealed enemy" was not just the fantasy creation of right-wing fanatics.

America was ripe for Joe McCarthy. But in March of 1950, there were still some senators who were willing to challenge McCarthy's imagination. On the very first day he appeared back in the Senate after the Wheeling speech, the Democratic floor leader, Scott Lucas of Illinois, was waiting with a simple question: Where did McCarthy get his list of 205 Communists in the State Department?

McCarthy had come prepared, in his own fashion. This time his briefcase bulged with documents. A staff member of the House Appropriations Committee named Robert E. Lee, had provided him with the folders on 108 State Department employees collected by Lee's committee staff a couple of years before. It was the same old list Willard Edwards had told McCarthy about back in January, when he was "researching" his Wheeling speech. Only 40 of the 108 still worked for the State Department, and in any case, *all* of them had been cleared after thorough security reviews.

None of that bothered McCarthy. He reached into his bag and pulled out 81 dossiers, which he stacked on his desk on the Senate floor. It was only when he began reading from them that it became clear that he had never looked at them before. Some of them didn't even work for the State Department, and clearly none of them were spies. Number nine was the same as number 77. Number 14 ("primarily a morals case") appeared in the folder of number 41. McCarthy didn't have much information on number 40, he announced, "except that there is nothing in his files to disprove his Communist connections."

And so it went, all day and into the night, even past midnight, as McCarthy doggedly blustered on. Even the most powerful Republican, Robert A. Taft, was forced to admit that McCarthy's was a "perfectly reckless performance." Thinking they smelled blood, the Democrats called for a full hearing to explore McCarthy's allegations of disloyalty in the State Department. They chose Senator Millard Tydings, for twenty-four years a dominating and aggressive patrician in the Senate, to chair the special investigating subcommittee. Said he: "Let me have McCarthy for three days in public hearings and he will never show his face in the Senate again." Tydings was to rue that remark.

Throughout the spring and into the summer of 1950, McCarthy conducted a leisurely forage for Communists. He kept up a running war of words with Tydings while he continued to make false accusations—always while on the senate floor, or at one of Tydings's hearings, where he was immune from libel suits. Among his targets were a New York woman judge, a news correspondent long stationed in China, two astronomers, a pair of foreign service officers whose careers he ruined, and Owen Lattimore, a Johns Hopkins professor McCarthy identified as "the biggest . . . of all," upon whose guilt McCarthy would "stand or fall."

McCarthy never proved that Lattimore, or anyone else for that matter was a Communist. The ingredients of McCarthyism began to emerge. It began with a senator's privilege to make accusations without fear of libel actions. This would then be spread through the medium of the bold-faced headline, where it would reach a huge and receptive audience, drawing strength from a deep well of suspicion, fear, and hate.

McCarthy was supposed to be the accused in the Tydings hearings. Instead, he became the accuser, exploiting Tydings's arbitrary and careless handling of the hearings in order to launch attacks. For nearly three months, he lashed out at former and present State Department officials; U.S. foreign policy, past and present and his own colleagues in the Senate. And he got headlines.

In July, the Tydings committee reported to the Senate that McCarthy's charges were a "fraud and a hoax." Tydings blistered McCarthy in a two-hour speech, accusing him of "whitewashing with mud, whitewashing with filth, whitewashing with the dregs of publicity," and putting on "the most nefarious campaign of half truths in the history of this republic." When he finished, dripping with perspiration, he was surrounded by fellow Democrats who pounded him on the back and showered him with congratulations McCarthy sat impassively on the floor through the whole speech, plotting his revenge.

During those weeks of the Tydings hearings, McCarthy's brutal

Secretary of State George C. Marshall and his undersecretary Dean G. Acheson, who succeeded him as secretary when Marshall retired. General of the Army Marshall, as Army chief of staff during World War II, was called by many the "architect of victory." President Truman regularly referred to him as "the greatest living American." The Marshall Plan to revive shattered Europe after World War II was developed during his incumbency at the State Department and earned him the Nobel Peace Prize in 1953.

To the radicals of the far right, however, he was "a front man for traitors" and his life "a living lie." Acheson served four years as secretary of state, and when he retired, President Truman wrote him, "I would place you among the greatest of the Secretaries of State this country has ever had." The radical right called him the "Red Dean," and one said his crowd of "egg-sucking liberals" was "selling America down the river." COURTESY PHOTOWORLD (F.P.G.).

attacks and accusations against present and past Democratic leadership and its policies, were widely applauded within the right wing of the Republican party, regardless of their lack of foundation in fact.

Shortly after the Tydings committee report to the Senate, the Mid-

west and Rocky Mountain Republican state chairmen met the GOP
national chairman to draw up strategy for the forthcoming off-year
elections. The Truman administration was to be criticized for getting
the United States involved in the Korean War, and then for bungling
it. Next, they wanted to oust both Secretary of State Acheson and
Secretary of Defense Louis Johnson (the one to be blamed for the
"loss" of China, the other for the inadequate state of American forces).
And finally, they wanted McCarthy's charges of communism in the
government to be made a major campaign issue, and to use McCarthy
as a prime campaign speaker in as many states as possible.

Only eight months after he had been voted the "worst U.S. Senator," McCarthy had achieved international notoriety and the staunch
support of the Republican Right, the dominant wing of the party.

The press, too, began to take notice of this "tough new kid in the
block." Even the liberal press began to take him seriously. In mid-
June 1950, the *New Republic* said that at that moment McCarthy was—

> . . . the most formidable figure to hit the Senate since Huey Long . . .
> Coolly calculating, fully aware of what he is doing, gambling for the
> highest stakes, bold and daring and elusive and slippery . . . McCarthy
> is as hard to catch as a mist, a mist that carries lethal contagion.

A strange media machine began to gear up, fueled by hot air and
printer's ink. It rumbled about the government and academe, while
randomly running over people. Out spewed the headlines: MCCAR-
THY CHARGES . . . Rebuttals were rare; when they did appear, they
were buried on the inside pages. It was a magnificent device for a
demagogue, and McCarthy used it expertly.

Many Americans appeared to take these headlines seriously indeed.
The Soviets had the bomb, and one hundred twenty thousand Korean
Communist troops were about to drag America into another war. The
post World War II peace was a sham and a lot of people wanted to
know why. They were looking for scapegoats, and McCarthy offered
them Communists. Wrote William F. Buckley: "McCarthyism is a
movement around which men of good will and stern morality will close
ranks." At the Daughters of the American Revolution rallies and
American Legion Halls they began to sing: "Nobody Loves Joe but
the Pee-pul." Many of the people started sending Joe money, and
some of them were Texas oil men. The crumpled five-dollar bills as

well as large checks, began arriving at McCarthy's office. The money went into the Joseph R. McCarthy Special Fund in the Riggs National Bank, and then into the soybean futures market and other dubious ventures. Money was not all that McCarthy received. An underground network sprang up—McCarthy called it his "Loyal American Underground"—to feed him bits and pieces of information on subversives in the government and elsewhere. At first, these patriotic souls were congressional staffers and newspapermen, and they could only offer thin and stale gruel, like the three-year-old list of one hundred eight State Department employees. Later on, as Joe became more powerful, better-placed "patriots" in the FBI and in the intelligence branches of various agencies, came along to offer the kind of classified information that could really ruin lives.

CHAPTER IV

For Whom
the Bell Tolls

McCarthy eagerly plunged into the 1950 Senate election campaign. He
went wherever the Republican committee could schedule him, but he
paid particular attention to two of his tormentors: Democratic Majority
Leader Scott Lucas, who was being challenged in Illinois by former
Congressman Everett Dirksen, and Millard Tydings, who faced a con-
test for re-election in Maryland.

Lucas's rival, Dirksen, had dropped out of the House two years
earlier to concentrate on the Senate race, and he had the enthusiastic
support of both the Chicago *Tribune* and the large circulation Hearst
daily in Chicago. McCarthy had made a number of forays into Illinois
on Dirksen's behalf. Lucas's defeat was so narrow that McCarthy
claimed—and many agreed—that his intervention had made the difference.

It was a feather in McCarthy's cap that he readily accepted; it further
endeared him to the Chicago *Tribune* and to the Hearst syndicate; and
Dirksen became a faithful ally.

But his greatest 1950 interest was in Maryland, where Millard Tydings was seeking his fifth Senate term.

McCarthy found and groomed an unknown but respectable Baltimore lawyer named John Marshall Butler to be Tydings's Republican opponent. He solicited large sums of money from Texas oil barons to grease the Butler coffers and organized Butler's advertising campaign out of his own office. Employees on his Senate payroll worked both openly and furtively in Maryland.

McCarthy's final and most destructive stroke was to paste together two photographs, one of Tydings, the other of Earl Browder, the former Communist leader. Under this "composite picture" the caption read:

> Communist Earl Browder, shown at left in this composite picture, was a star witness at the Tydings committee hearings, and was cajoled into saying Owen Lattimore and others accused of disloyalty were not Communists. Tydings (right) answered "Oh, thank you, sir." Browder testified in the best interests of those accused, naturally.

Four hundred thousand of these pictures, each with a four-page accompanying narrative, were sent by McCarthy's staff to Maryland voters, reaching them just a few days before the election. The narrative described Tydings's recent activities as subcommittee chairman, with devastating lies and half-truths.

Tydings was defeated in a stunning upset, and McCarthy had his revenge. So, no less that two Senate scalps seemed clearly on McCarthy's belt, and he claimed various others for good measure.[1] If he had campaigned in a state which defeated a sitting Democrat, he claimed the credit.

With the coming of the new Congress, the Eighty-second, in January of 1951, a special investigation into Tydings's defeat was undertaken, mostly because of the national publicity the dirty campaign had received.

The Special Investigations Subcommittee reported that the entire effort had been a "despicable back street campaign." It attributed both the four-page tabloid and the composite picture of Tydings and Browder to McCarthy.

1. McCarthy's impact on the elections has been exaggerated. But he was widely perceived to have been a decisive force, and as McCarthy's biographer, Thomas C. Reeves, writes, "Perceptions of reality are of more importance than reality itself."

In an obvious reference to McCarthy, the subcommittee also said, ". . . the question of unseating a Senator for acts committed in a Senatorial election should not be limited to the candidates in such elections. Any sitting Senator, regardless of whether he is a candidate in the election himself, should be subject to expulsion by action of the Senate, if it finds such Senator engaged in practices and behavior that make him, in the opinion of the Senate, unfit to hold the office of Senator."

This slap on the hand was all very well, but it neither returned Tydings his seat, removed the winner who had benefited by the improper campaign, nor did it in the slightest manner penalize McCarthy, who had masterminded the "despicable back street campaign."

On January 6, 1951, the New York *Times* featured an article headed: "MCCARTHY'S INFLUENCE IS GREATER IN THE 82D (Congress)." It carried a subhead saying, "REPUBLICANS BOW TO POLITICAL SUCCESS AS THE SENATOR PLANS NEW CAMPAIGN." The article stated:

> The man who pursued the highest member of the American Cabinet, Secretary of State Dean Acheson, now finds that the Republican membership of Congress officially has demanded Mr. Acheson's head.
>
> The man who in the late campaign pursued across country the two most formidable Democratic fighters in the Senate—Scott W. Lucas of Illinois and Millard E. Tydings of Maryland—now surveys a scene in which both are retired to private life.
>
> The lessons of these matters have not been lost, in this first week of the new Congress, on the Republicans. Nor have the Democrats ignored Mr. McCarthy, as so long they have tried to. . . .

The article told of the Democrats' fear that "what happened to Senator Tydings, with all his standing in the Senate, could happen to any other man . . ." It quoted a "powerful Senator" who said, "For whom does the bell toll? It tolls for thee."

Anyone who read the newspapers could sense McCarthy's growing power in the fall of 1950. But from my observation point as a mid-level government official, I still regarded McCarthy as something of a flash in the pan, and, if anything, somebody else's problem, not mine. I continued to think that Red-baiting was absurd and highly overemphasized, and I thought that sooner or later people would understand

Millard E. Tydings, Democratic senator from Maryland (1927–1951), was the premier Maryland combat hero of World War I. He served three terms in the House of Representatives and then entered the Senate at the age of thirty-six. His 1950 election defeat was due to the "despicable back street campaign" orchestrated by McCarthy. The campaign was marked by the mailing from McCarthy's camp of 400,000 copies of a composite (pasted together) photo suggesting that

Tydings and the leading American Communist were standing together on a speaker's platform. He is shown here with a recording of a McCarthy speech which he tried unsuccessfully to play on the Senate floor on the occasion of his July 1950 speech in which he accused McCarthy of being a "fraud and a hoax" and of "white-washing with lies and filth." COURTESY WIDE WORLD PHOTOS.

this and that McCarthyism would collapse like a gas balloon. It also seemed somewhat remote as far as I was concerned—something for liberal newspapers and Ivy League diplomats to worry about, but not something which a conventional government worker with moderate Republican credentials should spend his time fretting over.

Then, in the autumn of 1950, I had a firsthand experience of the way McCarthy worked. It should have served as a warning to me.

In 1949, when the Democrats took over the Senate, I lost my Senate job and moved over to the executive branch, to the Pentagon, as legislative counsel of the Defense Department. Some of my duties involved helping to prepare Pentagon officials for testimony before congressional committees. One of those whom I helped prepare for Senate confirmation hearings was Anna M. Rosenberg.

Mrs. Rosenberg was a Hungarian immigrant, and a product of New York's public schools. She had impressed General Marshall during World War II by her work in labor affairs, and when Marshall became secretary of defense, he wanted to make her an assistant secretary.

At first, things went smoothly, but then rumors began to reach the Senate. A man said that he had seen her at the John Reed Club, a Communist meeting place, in New York in the early 1930s. The Armed Services Committee decided to take a closer look. At a secret hearing one evening, Senator Richard B. Russell told her that she had been accused, under oath, by a man named Ralph DeSola. Mrs. Rosenberg was magnificent in reply:

> He is a liar,[2] and I would like to lay my hands on that man, Senator. It is inhuman what has been done to me in the past few days, and I am grateful to you people for the time you have spent; but I listened to the radio last night, and my family listened and heard that I am charged with disloyalty.
>
> Now, if this man is crazy or a Communist, I want to face him, Senator. I have never been a member of the John Reed Club; I have never been a Communist; I have never sympathized with Communists; I have spent my life trying to do something to help my country. I was ashamed to put these things on today, to have charges like that made against me. Forgive me, I know you have been here all day, but this has been a terrible ordeal for me.
>
> I tried to think: Where do I know this man? How do I know him from some place? How can a human being do this to someone? What can he have against me? I don't know him. . . .
>
> SENATOR RUSSELL. No member of this committee has charged you with disloyalty, Mrs. Rosenberg.
>
> MRS. ROSENBERG. I know, Senator; please forgive me. I suppose the newspapers have, and it is hard.

Mrs. Rosenberg got her wish to confront DeSola. As we sat in the anteroom, she said to me mournfully, "Everything is wrong with me for this job. I'm foreign born, I've got no education, and I'm a woman. The only thing I've not got is black skin."

But when she faced DeSola, she was absolutely unflinching. He identified her from the end of a twenty-five-foot committee table. She

2. She had actually said that DeSola was "a god damn liar," but the committee, in one of those bursts of nineteenth-century chivalry which the Senate sometimes displayed, voted unanimously to delete "god damn" from the official record before it was made public.

asked him to come closer. They moved to where they were face to face. After a short exchange she said icily, "I have no questions to ask. . . . I have never seen this man in my life." Her fierce eyes dared him to identify her again. He dropped his gaze to the floor and didn't look at her again.

Next, the committee quizzed a notorious New York Jew baiter, Benjamin Freedman, who was there reluctantly, under subpoena. He revealed that he had received a letter, hand delivered to him in New York by two men. One of them was Don Surine of McCarthy's staff; the other was Edward Nellor, an employee of the right-wing political commentator, Fulton Lewis, Jr., who had connections with the Chicago *Tribune*. Freedman was forced to produce the letter. It was from Gerald L. K. Smith, the most famous Midwestern Jew baiter of the late 1930s. It said:

> Dear Mr. Freedman:
>
> Congratulations on the terrific job you are doing in keeping the Zionist Jew, Anna M. Rosenberg, from becoming the director of the Pentagon. This is to introduce two gentlemen who are helping in this fight. One is the bearer of this note. I understand that he is Mr. Nellor, the chief aide to Mr. Fulton Lewis. Mr. Lewis and Mr. Nellor should be treated very kindly. You should give any information that will help them, because Mr. Lewis is doing a magnificent job in the Rosenberg matter.
>
> Please destroy this upon reading it.
>
> Sincerely yours,
>
> Gerald L. K.

At the hearing, Freedman was dapperly dressed, affecting a pince-nez which kept falling off his nose. He wore a vested suit, and across his round belly between his two upper vest pockets hung a heavy gold chain. Beads of sweat dribbled off his nose as the committee grilled him.

From his testimony it emerged that much of the attack against Mrs. Rosenberg had been orchestrated by McCarthy and his friends. Many of her accusers had been found by McCarthy, and checked in at McCarthy's office before appearing before the committee. As the full story unfolded, the charges against her collapsed. The committee was outraged, and by a unanimous vote, sent her nomination back to the Senate floor.

When we had all returned to Mrs. Rosenberg's office from the Cap-

Anna M. Rosenberg being sworn in as assistant secretary of defense immediately following her Senate confirmation, which was temporarily delayed
by a McCarthy-orchestrated attack on her loyalty. Holding the Bible is Secretary of Defense George C. Marshall, whose "steadfast support" during
McCarthy's attack she warmly remembers after thirty years. Watching is
Robert A. Lovett (right), Marshall's deputy secretary, who succeeded him
as defense secretary in 1951 upon Marshall's retirement. Administering the
oath is Felix Larkin, defense's general counsel, who left the department a
few months later to join W. R. Grace Company, where he ultimately
became chairman of the board. COURTESY THE NATIONAL ARCHIVES.

itol after she faced Ralph DeSola, she burst into tears and buried her
face on the chest of Felix Larkin, the Defense Department general
counsel. He put his arm around her and said, "Now Anna, it's all
right, it's all right."

Some of the Senate's most illustrious and powerful figures, both
liberal and conservative, including Russell of Georgia, Harry Byrd of
Virginia, Lyndon Johnson of Texas, Leverett Saltonstall of Massachusetts, and Wayne Morse of Oregon, had seen the patent anti-Semitism

of the McCarthy attack, yet none of them had said a word about it, not in the committee, not on the Senate floor.

It could have been because of the peculiar tradition of Senate courtesy—that one senator should not criticize another. But I didn't think so. Tydings and Lucas, who both had fallen less than six weeks earlier, were too fresh in their minds. It occurred to me that they were scared.

In McCarthy's tactics the Republican leader, Senator Robert Taft of Ohio began to see a weapon. He announced that the "Pro-Communist policies of the State Department fully justify Joe McCarthy in his demand for an investigation." To McCarthy he said, "If one case doesn't work, try another."

McCarthy began to stalk bigger game. On June 14, 1951, in his longest and most famous speech (written for him by right-wing academics outside the Senate), McCarthy charged General George C. Marshall, the wartime Army Chief of Staff, who had later been Mr. Truman's secretary of state and who was now serving as secretary of defense, with "a conspiracy so immense and an infamy so black as to dwarf any previous such venture in the history of man."

McCarthy was a hit at the 1952 Republican Convention. When he appeared on the convention platform the band struck up the Marine's hymn and the delegates cheered lustily, waving placards to the memory of his victims: HISS (whose fate was none of his doing), ACHESON, LATTIMORE. Joe was in top form. "We are at war tonight," he said, and he attacked the enemy: "The Red Dean's State Department" and other "slimy traitors."

In September, in a nationwide television address paid for by McCarthy's oil men, McCarthy not only implied that Adlai Stevenson, the 1952 Democratic presidential candidate, wanted Italy to go Communist, but bluntly stated of Stevenson ". . . we are finding proof not of guilt by association but guilt by collaboration . . ." and smirkingly referred to him as "Alger, er, I mean Adlai." He snickered and waited for the applause. McCarthy clearly relished the role of bully, with Stevenson as his ninety-pound weakling opponent. "If somebody would smuggle me aboard the Democratic campaign special with a baseball bat in my hand, I'd teach a little patriotism to little Add-lie."

It was at about this time that people began calling McCarthy the second most powerful man in the United States. Some didn't bother to throw in the qualifier. McCarthyism had become almost a mythic force; it seemed to reach everywhere.

In New York, a rabbi blamed college panty raids on McCarthyism. Since dissent had become dangerous, the rabbi explained, college kids had to find their outlets elsewhere. Drama critic Brooks Atkinson blamed a bad Broadway season on McCarthyism; he claimed that all the good playwrights had been frightened into silence or else writing trivia. Left-leaning artists were indeed blacklisted by Hollywood, and librarians and university professors were required to take loyalty oaths. A state commissioner of education announced at a press conference that he was rereading the tales of Robin Hood, looking for subversive ideas. The chief justice of the United States grumbled privately that if the Bill of Rights were put to a vote, it would lose.

Nor was McCarthy's impact confined to the United States. "Hitler had less support in Germany when he took over than McCarthy has today," wrote *Dagladet,* Norway's largest daily in March 1953. To many Germans, McCarthy became a vindication of their own sense of guilt about Hitler. The *Times* of London editorialized against McCarthy, and Winston Churchill managed to work in an anti-McCarthy paragraph in his coronation speech for Queen Elizabeth. By autumn of 1953, the Washington *Star* was reporting back from Europe that "McCarthyism is more discussed . . . here . . . than . . . (the) Soviet threat or Eisenhower." The New York *Herald Tribune* reported from Paris that McCarthyism cast doubts on America's capacity for leadership, and from Rome that Italians were bewildered to see America tolerate McCarthy's fanaticism.

A good part of the U.S. government was paralyzed by McCarthy. Dean Acheson had been forced to spend most of 1950 telling various Elks and Rotarians that he wasn't a Communist, rather than conducting foreign policy. The new secretary of state, John Foster Dulles, had to clear all foreign service appointments with a McCarthy supporter, State Department Personnel and Security Officer R. W. Scott McLeod. The new administration did get one faintly controversial appointee past McCarthy—Assistant Secretary of State Charles Bohlen. But the victory was Pyrrhic. Senator Taft sent word back to the White House: "No more Bohlens."

Eisenhower personally disliked McCarthy, but he avoided crossing him. During the campaign, Ike considered one small gesture of defiance: inserting a few paragraphs in a speech defending General Marshall, to be delivered in McCarthy's home state of Wisconsin. But campaign aides persuaded him to take it out.

CHAPTER V

The Army
Becomes the Target

After the Republican victory in November, 1952, McCarthy found himself in an uncomfortable position. He was no longer an outsider, railing against the Establishment. He was a member of the ruling party now—an insider with an obligation to protect the new order.

McCarthy succeeded by seniority to the post of chairman of the Government Operations Committee. The Republican leadership naively hoped that this committee chairmanship would keep him busy and out of mischief. Said Taft, "We've got McCarthy where he can't do any harm."

Vice-President Nixon reassured the White House that "Joe is going to be good." Retorted Joe, "Whoever said that is a liar."

McCarthy proceeded to appoint himself chairman of his committee's Permanent Subcommittee on Investigations, which he quickly turned into a launching pad for more and more outrageous travesties. Within a few months, McCarthy had so infuriated the Democratic members of the committee that they just quit. And since the Republicans almost never attended the subcommittee's hearings, McCarthy quickly became a committee of one.

By now, McCarthy had become very nearly a government unto himself. "Wasn't that a classified document you were reading?" a reporter once asked him. "It *was*," McCarthy replied. "I declassified it." When he felt like it, McCarthy conducted foreign policy, even though he had no more right to do so than to declassify government secrets. Grandiloquently, McCarthy announced that he had persuaded Greek shipping interests not to make deliveries to Communist ports. "It's like a naval blockade," he explained.

No one stood in McCarthy's way. Once, when McCarthy didn't like what the chairman of the Senate Appropriations Committee was doing, McCarthy simply took his gavel and seized control of the meeting. No one protested. When McCarthy demanded an appropriation of $214,000 for the increasingly bizarre activities of his subcommittee, only one senator—Fulbright of Arkansas—voted against him. McCarthy took it as a tremendous vote of confidence, and thereafter referred to Fulbright as "half-bright." "The truth is," wrote Richard Rovere, of *The New Yorker,* "that everyone in the Senate, or just about everyone, was scared stiff of him."

McCarthy's little empire had no plan, no particular direction. Not exactly a deep thinker, McCarthy preferred to make things up as he went along. Improvisations suited his style: He was fast on his feet, and it left the evenings open for poker and other amusements.

Nonetheless, it now became clear that since he had a congressional committee at his disposal, McCarthy needed a good first lieutenant.

He found his man Friday in Roy Marcus Cohn.

Cohn was not a rabid know-nothing or a suspicious hick like the young Joe McCarthy. He came from a good Jewish Democratic family in New York City. His father was a New York State appeals judge. Both of his parents idolized him, and it was an affection he returned in kind. Even long after both of their deaths he continues to refer to them in his annual biographical sketch in *Who's Who* with a warm and affectionate remembrance.

Cohn was very bright, possessed of a photographic memory, and very precocious. He had a soft mouth and deceptively heavy eyelids, but he was a hard young man who missed nothing. He had graduated from Columbia and Columbia Law by the time he was twenty, and on the day he passed the New York Bar, he was sworn in as an assistant U.S. attorney.

Though he was unmarried and had been eligible for the draft since the last year of World War II, he had served neither in that war nor in the Korean conflict. Toward the end of World War II he was given consecutive West Point appointments from the same congressman. The appointments protected him from the draft in the last part of the war since the second appointment was given to him immediately after he failed the running test for the first appointment. In 1950, when the draft was again instituted during the Korean War, he had become a member of the New York State National Guard which gave him continuing deferment.

As an assistant U.S. attorney, he helped to prosecute the Rosenbergs and various other alleged subversives. By night he became a member of café society, a regular at the Stork Club (though he never drank alcohol), and an intimate of gossip columnist Walter Winchell and of George Sokolsky, the anti-Communist Hearst columnist. Winchell mentioned him in his columns as "the rising young legal eagle." Sokolsky introduced him to Joe McCarthy.[1]

After a brief interlude at the Justice Department, Cohn became chief counsel of McCarthy's Permanent Investigations Subcommittee. He was twenty-six years old.

Very early in his tenure Cohn recommended hiring G. David Schine. His title was special consultant, and his pay was none.

Schine needed no pay. His parents owned a hotel chain that included the Ambassador in Los Angeles, the Ritz Carlton in Atlantic City, and the Roney Plaza in Miami Beach. He had been educated at exclusive schools—Andover and Harvard, where he had a valet and a big black convertible with a two-way radio phone. The Harvard *Crimson* of May 7, 1954 (p. 4), described his way of arriving at parties:

> This consisted of phoning from his car and saying, "This is G. David Schine. I'm now driving through Copley Square. Could you direct me a little further," and then later, "This is G. David Schine. I'm now at Kenmore Square. Could you give me more directions please."

With his wavy blond hair and classic good looks, Schine could have been a matinee idol. He held an executive position in the Schine organization and had published a thin, six-page pamphlet called *The Defi-*

1. On a Sunday-morning walk during the Watergate trials in 1974, Judge John Sirica told me that in 1950, while he was still a private practitioner, Joe McCarthy had offered him the chief counsel post before offering it to Cohn. He said he did not take the assignment because he thought McCarthy was uncontrollable.

nition of Communism, a copy of which Schine's company put next to the Gideon Bible in every Schine hotel.

Cohn and Schine made a famous team. For starters, they began an investigation of the Voice of America (VOA). With the help of various disgruntled VOA employees who acted as tipsters, they unearthed subversion: unmarried couples living together; Free Thinkers on the religion desk; an engineer who had picked the "wrong" place to set up radio transmitters. The administration was forced to disown the VOA, and most of the agency's leadership resigned.

In April Cohn and Schine embarked on an eighteen-day fact-finding mission through Europe, where they were followed by a large contingent of newspaper reporters. They visited Radio Free Europe for thirty minutes and held a press conference to report on their findings; in Paris they announced that they were seeking "inefficiency" in government; in Bonn they said they were seeking "subversives"; in Vienna, they inspected the U.S. Information Agency's bookshelves looking for subversive books. Back in Washington, McCarthy was asked just what their mission was, and replied that they were seeking facts about advertising funds used by the Truman administration to publicize itself. Hearing this in Rome, Cohn said, "Anything our chairman says goes." One night in Vienna, Schine was observed chasing Cohn around a hotel lobby, hitting him over the head with a newspaper. The European press called them the "Keystone Kops," and sometimes the "Katzenjammer Kids."[2]

McCarthy had more serious things to worry about in the spring of 1953 than what Cohn and Schine were up to. Ever since the Wheeling speech, he had attacked "twenty years of treason." By that, he had meant the Democratic rule, 1933–52. But now the Republicans were in power. Did that mean it was time to lay off the administration?

It is doubtful that McCarthy pondered too long over this one. He was not a reflective man. He began talking about "twenty-one years of treason," and looking for a new target.

In the late summer of 1953, he found one: the United States Army.

---

2. Cohn later acknowledged that the trip was a public relations disaster. But he steadfastly maintained that he and Schine were just trying to rid embassy bookshelves of pro-Communist propaganda.

[II]

AUTUMN 1953

CHAPTER VI

The Purloined Letter

On a warm afternoon that September, I was staring out the window of my office, wondering what to do. The administration had changed in January, and a new group had come in at the Defense Department. Since there wasn't a large volume of work parceled out to me, my afternoons were getting slower and slower.

The phone rang. It was an invitation to meet with the new secretary of the army, Robert T. Stevens. He wanted to offer me a job as counselor of the army.

The next day I was offered another job, as general counsel of the U.S. Information Agency (USIA). The USIA had been a target of frequent attacks by Joe McCarthy. I wanted to stay as far away from that nonsense as possible.

I called on a friend of mine, William P. Rogers, the deputy attorney general, who later was to become attorney general and then secretary of state, and asked his advice. "Stevens is such a hell of a nice guy," said Rogers. "Take the Army job."

I was forty-one years old, with a lovely wife, a two-month-old baby girl, a nice apartment, and a three-year-old Ford convertible. My career looked promising. I took the Army job.

Few government officials were interested in standing up to Joe McCarthy in the summer of 1953, and Bob Stevens was not one of them.

Robert Ten Broek Stevens graduated from Andover and Yale. He was pink and chubby cheeked, with his gray hair slicked back, and he always wore double-breasted gray-flannel suits. Before becoming Army secretary he had run his family textile business, one of the largest in the world. At the age of twenty-nine, on the death of his father, he took over the J. P. Stevens Company and managed it successfully for the next twenty-five years. During those years, Stevens built up a deep suspicion of organized labor, and even more of communism. He was a great supporter of the Army, in which he had served with distinction as a procurement official during World War II. He was a preconvention supporter of Dwight Eisenhower, and this support was rewarded when he was appointed to the top civilian post in the Army by the new Republican administration.

During Stevens's confirmation hearings, the question of conflict-of-interest was raised, since J. P. Stevens sold uniforms to the Army. At a huge personal sacrifice, Stevens sold all his stock in the company. He was to pay an even greater price in the months to come.

Stevens was sworn in on February 3, 1953. The Army was in the midst of a war then, one that had already cost fifty thousand lives. Yet one of Stevens's first acts was not concerned with the real Communists his troops were fighting in Korea, but rather with imagined Communists among his own troops. On February 4, the secretary issued a directive demanding a briefing on the Army's Loyalty and Security Program. "The presentation should set forth what steps are taken to prevent disloyal and subversive persons from infiltrating the Army," wrote Stevens, "and what steps have been taken to discover and remove such persons who may have found their way into the Army Establishment." Three weeks later, Stevens called on J. Edgar Hoover to solicit his advice on how best to combat subversion in the Army.

In mid-August, while Stevens was vacationing on his ranch in Montana, the Army got yet another volunteer in the search for subversives: Joe McCarthy. In New York, Tail Gunner Joe announced that he was very concerned about lack of security and possible subversion at Fort Monmouth, the Army Signal Corps' research base in New Jersey.

As soon as Stevens heard about McCarthy's interest, he rushed to the nearest telegraph office and wired McCarthy. He was just as opposed to subversives and Communists in the Army as was McCarthy, he signaled. As soon as the secretary got back to Washington, he would ''call your office to offer my services in trying to assist you to correct anything that may be wrong.''

It may seem peculiar that the secretary of the army offered his services to help a senator administer the secretary's own department. But the senator was Joe McCarthy and the year was 1953. It was not at all unusual for Cabinet heads to stop and ask, ''What will McCarthy do?''

Stevens returned from Montana, and on August 30 went to McCarthy's wedding, as did Vice-President Nixon, several Cabinet officers, three top White House aides, and scores of senators and congressmen. In all, about a thousand people attended. The bride, a former McCarthy legislative aide, Jean Kerr, wore a magnificent white gown. Afterward, the bride and groom left for the Caribbean on a month's honeymoon.

But the honeymoon was brief. On September 10, McCarthy's subcommittee staff announced that it had unearthed some ''very serious'' information about espionage at Fort Monmouth, and that the committee's chief counsel, Roy Cohn, was even then racing down to the Caribbean to fill McCarthy in on the details. McCarthy gravely announced that he was cutting his wedding trip short and coming directly to New York to take personal charge of the investigation.

The ''very serious'' information was contained in a two-and-a-quarter-page document headed ''Aaron Hyman Coleman, Espionage (R).'' The R stood for Russia. The document purported to be a letter from FBI Director J. Edgar Hoover to General Alexander Bolling, chief of Army Intelligence. It listed Coleman and thirty-four other Fort Monmouth employees—scientists, engineers, technicians—who were suspected of subversive activities by the FBI. The letter was to become famous as the ''Purloined Letter.'' But for the moment, its existence was known only to McCarthy and his staff and to the ''young patriot'' who had slipped it to them.

The letter was later proved to be phony. A member of McCarthy's ''Loyal American Underground''—a civilian or military officer assigned to Army intelligence work—had taken a fifteen-page letter from Hoover to Bolling and condensed it into two and a quarter pages, including anything that seemed juicy from the original, but deleting some essentials. The original letter did not accuse any of the thirty-five of espionage or subversion. It merely recited what the FBI field

Senator Joe McCarthy, forty-three, and his bride, the former Jean Kerr of Washington, twenty-nine, after their wedding on August 30, 1953, in Washington's St. Matthew's Cathedral. A former beauty-contest winner at George Washington University, Miss Kerr had been on McCarthy's staff as a trusted research assistant for about four years prior to their marriage. COURTESY PHOTOWORLD (F.P.G.).

Aaron H. Coleman is seated before the microphone in the Senate Caucas Room on December 8, 1953. McCarthy had moved the hearing from New York to Washington because the newspaper strike in New York would have muffled his publicity. The Washington hearing was televised. It was on this occasion that I approached Coleman's attorney in an unsuccessful attempt to let Coleman know that McCarthy had no case against him. COURTESY WIDE WORLD PHOTOS.

investigation had gathered—raw, unsubstantiated, and mostly trivial allegations of left-leanings by the employees. The letter was actually old stuff, dated 1951. The Army had already checked out the allegations and found no reason to dismiss any of the employees.

For McCarthy, however, this "Purloined Letter" was a gift from heaven. It listed thirty-five live bodies—mostly people of Russian-Jewish descent, who somehow had been listed as suspect by the FBI. What's more, the bodies worked at Fort Monmouth—where the Atom Spy himself, Julius Rosenberg, had once worked. Some of the thirty-five had even *known* Rosenberg.

Before Rosenberg's execution that summer, the FBI had offered to get his sentence commuted if he talked. But Rosenberg never did. So the suspicion remained—who else was in that spy ring? Was it still feeding secrets to the Soviets? McCarthy couldn't wait to answer.

In mid-September, McCarthy helped himself to an appetizer before the main course. He summoned the chief of Army Intelligence (G–2), General Richard Partridge, and began asking him about subversive books found hiding in G-2 bookshelves. One study of Siberian folkways listed Corliss Lamont in its bibliography. Lamont was known to have Communist leanings, said McCarthy. And by what authority could the book's author claim that the Siberian masses were unlikely to be anti-Communist?

General Partridge, who had never seen the book before, could not respond.

Bob Stevens was at this hearing, watching one of his general officers getting browbeaten. Within a few days, General Partridge was no longer head of Army Intelligence. He was reassigned to an obscure post in Europe.

Stevens wanted his generals to get along with McCarthy. On October 2, Cohn and the committee's chief of staff, Frank Carr, called on the Army secretary. They weren't getting all the cooperation they wanted from Fort Monmouth, they complained. So Stevens got on the phone to the post commander, Major General Kirke Lawton. With Cohn and Carr standing in the room, Stevens instructed General Lawton: "Cooperate! See to it that they interview anyone they wish to."

CHAPTER VII

The Fort
Monmouth Lepers

My first assignment as counselor of the army was Joe McCarthy. He was to be my last assignment as well.

In early October, a day or two after I came on duty, Stevens called me in and told me that he wanted me to be the Army's liaison with McCarthy and his committee. He made it clear that the relationship was to be a friendly one, and asked me to meet with Cohn and Carr. "They're nice guys," he said.

My wife Margaret was not enthusiastic when I got home that night and told her about my newest mission. She was a Roosevelt Democrat, and she had long been revolted by McCarthy. But I wasn't particularly worried. I disapproved of McCarthy, but I had dealt with all sorts of members of Congress during my six years at the Senate and in the Pentagon. I figured I could live with Cohn and Carr or with Cohn and Schine, or even with McCarthy.

I had dealt directly with McCarthy a few months earlier and the incident gave me the illusion that he could be reasoned with.

Among the people Joe McCarthy wanted to "get," was columnist Drew Pearson. Pearson was the prime muckraker columnist of the day, and prided himself on being so known. Pearson liked to expose McCarthy's mud-slinging, and did so regularly. McCarthy was so furious with him that he jumped him in the men's room of Washington's posh Sulgrave Club one night, kneeing him in the groin and punching him from behind. Richard Nixon had to pull McCarthy off the diminutive Pearson, who was about thirty pounds lighter than McCarthy and eleven years older. McCarthy then intimidated Pearson's radio sponsor, Adam Hats, into withdrawing the five-thousand-dollar weekly fee paid for Pearson's broadcasts.

In the spring of 1953, McCarthy thought of a more subtle way to get Pearson. A Pentagon employee had been caught leaking secret data to Pearson and had been fired. McCarthy wanted the Defense Department to take action against Pearson as well, and to charge him with passing the secrets he had received on to the Soviets.

Roger Kent, the outgoing Defense Department general counsel in the Truman administration, was convinced that Pearson had not printed any classified information. He wanted to tell McCarthy to go to hell. But Struve Hensel, the incoming general counsel in the Republican administration, counseled conciliation. He told Kent to go see McCarthy, and said he was sure that he could do business with him.

I went along—Roger did not want to see him alone. Kent had a colorful mastery of the English language, particularly its profanity, and he spluttered as we left for McCarthy's office. "Do business with that bastard? It isn't possible," he said. "Goddamn it to hell, thank God I'm on my way back to San Francisco. You can have your lousy, dumb-assed Republicans," he grumbled all the way from the Pentagon.

We found McCarthy in his office reeking of whiskey, in his shirt-sleeves, necktie loosened at the collar, shirt obviously in its second day of wear. A recent and uncertain shave had cut his face in various places and his fingernails were dirty.

We patiently explained to him that the department could not and would not join in any charges that Pearson was passing secrets to the Communists merely because a foolish employee of the department had read classified data to him.

Through a thick tongue, McCarthy said that he thought that the three of us were "good lawl Amurricuns" and that the department should help him against that "sumbitch" Pearson. The meeting was somewhat chilly, but we just kept saying no. McCarthy gave up.

As we talked, I looked around his office. It was barren of books or pictures. On the wall hung only one item. It was a quote from Abraham Lincoln—

> If I were to read, much less answer, all the attacks made on me, this shop might as well be closed for any other business. I do the very best I know how—the very best I can, and I mean to keep doing so until the very end. If the end brings me out all right, what is said against me won't amount to anything. If the end brings me out wrong, ten angels swearing I was right would make no difference.

On seeing it I thought, Joe McCarthy and Abe Lincoln. "I do the very best I know how."

After leaving I asked Kent if he had noticed the Lincoln quote on the wall. "Yes, I saw it," he replied. "The slimy son of a bitch."

I found McCarthy's two senior staff men, Chief Counsel Roy Cohn, and Chief of Staff Frank Carr to be far more appealing. Stevens was right. They seemed to be nice guys.

I had lunch with them in the Senate cafeteria, and liked them both. Cohn was a bright fellow, personable and precocious. Carr was an amiable man, a former FBI agent who had spent the past few years on the bureau's subversive desk in New York. Cohn had been in the New York U.S. attorney's office, and the two had become friends. It was clear at once that Carr, though older, deferred to Cohn in all matters. A balloon-shaped figure, Carr would always have a big piece of pie or a chocolate dessert with lunch. Cohn, who was always on a diet to control his bulging hips, would take a fork and idly serve himself some of Carr's desserts.

I ate a lot of lunches with Cohn and Carr that autumn. McCarthy had begun his hearings on subversives at Fort Monmouth in October, and every week I would go to New York to see McCarthy try to ferret Communists out of the Signal Corps.

At one lunch, Cohn introduced me to Jewish food at a kosher restaurant named Rattners and corrected my pronounciation of gefilte fish. One evening I went with him to his favorite haunt, the Stork Club; on another, to a fight at Madison Square Garden. I usually stayed at the Commodore Hotel at the government rate of ten dollars per night.

It was all perfectly civilized. But what went on at McCarthy's hearings was not. Technically speaking, McCarthy's Fort Monmouth hearings were "Executive Sessions" of the Senate Permanent Subcommittee on Investigations. "Executive session" was a term loosely used by McCarthy. It didn't really mean a closed session, since McCarthy allowed in various friends, hangers-on, and favored newspaper reporters. Nor did it mean secret, because afterward McCarthy would tell the reporters waiting outside whatever he pleased. Basically, "executive" meant that Joe could do anything he wanted.

On a gray muggy day in mid-October, I went to hear McCarthy quiz a Fort Monmouth scientist, known hereafter as "Z,"[1] at the U.S. Courthouse at Foley Square in New York City. It was my first visit to a McCarthy executive session. The hearing room was actually a windowless storage room in the bowels of the courthouse, unventilated and oppressively hot on this humid morning.

This particular executive session was attended not only by committee staff, but by Governor Walter Kohler of Wisconsin and his wife, who wore a gaily decorated hat, and Willard Edwards, who covered McCarthy for the Chicago *Tribune*.

The Kohlers, who were at the Waldorf on a holiday trip, had been invited to "see Joe handle a Commie," Willard Edwards had been allowed in so he could tell his readers what went on, preferably with two-inch headlines; I was there so as to keep a friendly eye on McCarthy. I was granted the privilege because the Army was "cooperating" with him.

"Z," the "witness" at the hearing, had not yet been charged with being unsuitable for further employment. He was one of about fifty Fort Monmouth employees under scrutiny by the loyalty-security watchdogs for some actual or alleged shadow in their past. Their names had somehow surfaced for background review, either by being mentioned in the purloined letter or perhaps in some similar letter; and McCarthy had their names. Their "offenses" were varied, such as a sister who had once attended a meeting of the Young Communist League, or a college roommate who turned out to be a homosexual or an expired subscription to the *Daily Worker*. Almost anything would do. In a paranoid age, these unfortunates were known around Fort Monmouth as "the leper colony." Friends would cross the street rather

1. The severity of the trauma this witness endured twenty-nine years ago apparently remains with him to the present. He has asked that he not be identified by name.

than greet them; neighbors would draw their blinds rather than look at them.

"Z's" crime was that he once had a slight acquaintance with Julius Rosenberg. That was a high crime indeed, for Rosenberg had been the spy who sold the secret of the atom bomb to Russia. All those who knew Rosenberg were looked on with distrust.

McCarthy's staffers had questioned "Z" about Rosenberg once before, on October 12. Yes, he had known Rosenberg slightly as a student at the City College of New York in the mid-1930s and had seen him again seven or eight years ago at Fort Monmouth when Rosenberg had moved into his rooming house after "Z" had moved out. "Z" also was asked about his fellow car pool riders at Fort Monmouth. He could not remember all of them, but one he did recall was named Joe Levitsky. It was not gripping stuff so McCarthy's staffers finally sent "Z" home.

The next day, McCarthy questioned Joe Levitsky. He refused to answer most of the questions, invoking his Fifth Amendment privilege against self-incrimination. That made him a "Fifth Amendment Communist" in McCarthy's eyes—dedicated to the violent overthrow of the government and obviously also a member of what McCarthy claimed was the still-active Rosenberg spy ring.

Levitsky's "exposure" renewed McCarthy's interest in his fellow car pool rider—"Z." He summoned "Z" to reappear the next morning.

"Z's" mother had died the day before. An orthodox Jew, he was mourning her by sitting *shivah,* which meant that he could not leave his house for seven days. But one did not lightly say no to Joe McCarthy in those days. "Z" came.

The hearing started late that morning. "Z" sat down at a table in a plain wooden chair in the middle of the room. McCarthy stood up to interrogate him. The room was hot and clammy; "Z's" clothes stuck to him.

McCarthy began asking questions in a monotone, his mouth slightly parted, his lips barely moving. Sometimes he would smile mirthlessly, showing his slightly parted teeth. His eyes always remained narrow slits, half-closed against the dim light of the windowless room.

McCarthy was a big man, broad shouldered, and burly, though his muscles had long since run to fat. He had a heavy five o'clock shadow, and the backs of his hands were matted with hair. He moved in close to the frail "Z," whose flat, balding, head now glistened with sweat.

McCarthy asked: "Did you know that Levitsky was a Communist?"

"No."

"Did you once attend a dinner party at which Levitsky was present?"

"No."

McCarthy exploded. In a thundering voice of accusation, he told "Z" that the committee was in possession of sworn testimony directly contradictory to his. The record was going to the Justice Department, and "Z" was on his way to jail for perjury, maybe even for conspiracy against the U.S. government.

For about twenty minutes, both McCarthy and his staff bombarded "Z" with a staccato fire of questions and threats. "Z" was so frightened that he was shaking and perspiring, alternately wiping his head and his hands with his handkerchief. His eyeglasses steamed over. When McCarthy suggested that he had better think it over during the noon hour, he looked like a man dying of pneumonia, as he repeatedly raised his arms and dropped them on the table as if in a futile effort to throw off the unseen force that was strangling him. He could not rise from his chair.

Powerless, I watched, transfixed with helpless fascination. Finally, one of McCarthy's investigators and I took him by either arm and guided him out the door and into a waiting room. We passed a circle of newsmen who eyed him excitedly. They could see that "Z" was on the verge of collapse. They smelled a story.

McCarthy then invited the press into the room and began describing the triumph of the morning. He said that a doctor and nurse had been summoned to treat "Z." (Actually, "Z" had only asked for a drink of water, but McCarthy wanted the newsmen to see the medical missionaries entering the waiting room.) Before long, James Juliana—the investigator who had helped "Z" from his chair—returned and began whispering in McCarthy's ear. "Z" wanted to change his story, reported Juliana. He now wished to say that nine years earlier Levitsky had told him that he was a Communist, and that they had once gone to the same dinner party. "Z" had not revealed the information before because he did not want to get involved or harm Levitsky.

McCarthy smiled and announced to the press that "Z" had just broken down. He now wanted to "tell all." McCarthy did not reveal his name. He referred to him as the "mystery witness."

The next morning I picked up the New York *Times*. Completely taken in, it carried a thirty-nine-column-inch story with the headline:

RADAR WITNESS BREAKS DOWN
WILL TELL ALL ABOUT SPY RING

An "important" employee at the Army's Fort Monmouth, N.J., laboratories, a close friend of Julius Rosenberg, executed atom spy, broke down and agreed to tell all he knew about espionage rings. . . .

McCarthy told newsmen that the witness admitted having been a close personal friend of Rosenberg. . . . They shared an apartment at one time. . . .

Announcing that the witness would be placed in protective custody, Senator McCarthy said, "The witness has indicated a great fear of the spy ring which is operating within Government agencies, including the Signal Corps. . . ."

The term "protective custody" made world headlines. I knew that the only protective custody into which "Z" had been placed was the New York subway system, which accepted his dime into the turnstile as he went to catch a train home to mourn his dead mother. I knew also that the only fear he had was of Joe McCarthy.

CHAPTER VIII

Private Schine

When I returned to Washington from these two-or three-day trips to New York, Margaret would give me a snack or a cup of tea and then ask me to tell her what had happened that day; what the papers said, did not interest her. She would listen silently, her disgust usually surpassing mine. But when I was up there, when I was in that hearing room, I watched silently.

I was the Army's lawyer, sent by the secretary to keep an eye on what McCarthy was doing, not to challenge him. None of us in the Army secretary's complex knew then for sure, exactly what kind of "proof" McCarthy had on his victims. We knew nothing of the "Purloined Letter." I could not altogether dismiss the possibility of some spies at Fort Monmouth because Rosenberg had gone to the electric chair only a few months earlier without talking. But I knew just from sitting there in the hearings and glancing at the newspapers the next day, that what I was seeing, and what the public was reading, were very different things.

Nothing in my past experience as a civil servant had prepared me for what I saw going on in that room, and in subsequent hearings. I was appalled by what McCarthy was doing, but I felt powerless to stop it.

From time to time I tried to figure out how I might persuade Stevens to resist McCarthy, but I always gave it up as hopeless. Stevens would lose his temper whenever his established policy was questioned. Further, more than half of the highest officials in the government—Cabinet members, senators, congressmen, and some of the White House staff—were definitely pro-McCarthy. In the Pentagon, very few people outside the Army counselor's office seemed to share my increasing concerns about McCarthy's tactics.

About a month after I was appointed, John Kane, Stevens's information officer, quit in disgust over the appeasement policy. His resignation letter explaining why, had been noted in a three-inch story one day in the Washington papers; the issue was thereafter ignored.

But I valued the honor of the Army, and it distressed me greatly to see McCarthy smear it. The cost to the Fort Monmouth "lepers" was worse. But no one stood up to McCarthy—not the White House, not the attorney general, not the Department of Defense, not the secretary of the army. And not I.

I had another problem on my mind that autumn. In comparison to the lives being wrecked in McCarthy's inquisition room, it was utterly trivial. But in the twisted world McCarthy created around him, it somehow began to loom large.

In the summer of 1953, Schine got a letter from his draft board. Like half a million young men that year, he had been called to arms.

Cohn thought Schine should get a direct commission. So McCarthy called Major General Miles Reber, the Army's chief of liaison on Capitol Hill, to arrange things. Indeed, Reber later recalled that when he interviewed Schine, the young man was ready to raise his right hand and be sworn in as an officer right there. Reber gently explained that there was a bit more to it. Schine was put out: "He apparently felt that the business of filling out forms and going through with the processing was an unnecessary, routine step," recalled Reber.

This effort having failed, Cohn then went to see the secretary of the army. On October 2—the same day he complained about the lack of cooperation at Fort Monmouth—Cohn demanded that, if drafted, Schine at least be stationed in New York so he could "complete his committee work." Stevens was all smiles, and said that after Schine completed basic training, he'd discuss the future.

A few days later, during my first week on the job, Stevens told me of this concession. I was dumbfounded. My prior employment at the Defense Department during the Korean War had burned into my brain that an impartial administration of the draft was absolutely crucial to its acceptance by the American people. Men were drafted for two years, and any meddling which permitted favored people to get special assignments after 16 weeks of basic, or at any time, was terribly damaging to the integrity of the system. I couldn't believe that someone who had been the Army secretary for nine months would not understand this, and I was sure that this first "carrot on the stick" concession by Stevens would tantalize McCarthy's group into trying to push the Army further and further. But the secretary had made the commitment, and I would have to live with it.

Two weeks later, Stevens accepted an invitation to dine with Schine's family at their Waldorf suite in New York. The next morning Schine picked up Stevens in his chauffeur-driven limousine, and gave him a ride downtown to watch one of McCarthy's hearings. Stevens later said that en route, Schine, then twenty-six, had told him that he was doing a good job "ferreting out Communists" and that Stevens should "go far in this line of work." Schine proposed that, if drafted, he could help Stevens in this work by being assigned to the secretary's office as an aide. Better yet, as a civilian aide, and deferred from military service. Stevens politely demurred.

I met Schine on one of my first trips to New York, in mid-October. He was tall and handsome; he wore an expensive, nail-head, sharkskin suit. He was anxious to please and be part of all the exciting things the McCarthy committee was doing.

Schine was a little too pushy even for McCarthy's taste. At lunch the day after I met Schine, I sat next to McCarthy's wife, Jean, as she looked at some snapshots from their wedding. Shaking her head, she showed some of them to me; in each, Schine could be seen craning his neck to get his face into the picture with the McCarthys. Wordlessly, she passed the pictures to McCarthy. He too shook his head.

That evening, I wandered out onto the grass of Foley Square after watching McCarthy demolish another hapless soul from Fort Monmouth. It was a warm evening in October, and my new shoes hurt. So I took them off. I was standing there in my stocking feet in the grass when Phil Potter, a reporter for the Baltimore *Sun,* came up to me. "Do you know about Schine?" he asked.

I said nothing. I knew about Schine, but I didn't know what the newspapers knew. "He's about to be drafted," said Potter, "and he's got to report soon. Every newspaperman knows about it. Schine has been trying to get a commission."

Over the past few days, Roy Cohn had begun to pester me about Schine, asking if I could get him assigned to New York. I had put him off, promising nothing. I knew how Stevens was also being pressed. When Potter spoke to me, I knew there might be trouble.

Schine was due to report in November, but he remained active with the committee through October. At an evening hearing at Foley Square, Cohn and Schine brought two attractive girls to the hearing. Their dates sat beside me in the room, and dumbly watched the terrorizing of another Fort Monmouth employee.

During a recess, a photographer from the Newark *News* managed to snap a picture of the girls, but Cohn ran him down and made him promise not to print the picture.

These particular guests may have been a bit much, but guests per se, were not unusual at McCarthy's "executive sessions." Governor Kohler of Wisconsin and his wife had attended the terrorizing of "Z." Mr. and Mrs. Richard Berlin (he was the president of the Hearst chain) took in several hearings. Mrs. McCarthy was a regular spectator; sometimes she brought her mother, and once her mother brought an old friend from Connecticut. The "secret" hearings were, after all, quite a show.

On this particular day, Cohn and Schine and their dates wanted to go off together in the Schine limousine, so McCarthy and his wife took the subway uptown. I rode with them. McCarthy was irritated that Schine was always trying to worm his way into pictures with him. He felt that Schine was interested in nothing but the photographers, and that he was becoming a complete pest. He hoped Schine would get drafted, soon, and that when he was drafted, the Army would send him as far away as possible. "Send him wherever you can, as far away as possible," emphasized McCarthy, as I swung on a strap next to his seat. "Korea is too close."

I asked him if I could relay his sentiments to Secretary Stevens. I could, he said. "But don't tell Roy."

CHAPTER IX

Fifth Amendment Communists

McCarthy had a "genius for publicity, for obtaining maximum mileage from the flimsiest piece of news," wrote Daniel Boorstin. "He was master of the 'pseudo event,' news which is not news." He could play newspaper deadlines like a trumpet. In the late morning—just in time to catch the noon deadline for the afternoon paper—he would let it be known that he had a "big announcement" coming up. He would hint, for instance, that he had "new evidence" of espionage at Fort Monmouth. Wanting to get the jump on the morning papers, the afternoon papers would print this non-news. Television was still in its infancy, and the afternoon paper, now a dying breed, was the chief evening news source.

Then at about 3:30 or 4:00 P.M., McCarthy would accuse someone of being a Communist or a subversive. The morning papers would have just enough time to meet their early evening deadlines—but not enough time to check out the charge. Strictly speaking, the "news" was that McCarthy, a U.S. senator, was making this charge, not that the charge was true. But mud sticks, and the rebuttals and clarifications came later, if at all. In most papers, denials drew less prominence than the original charge.

McCarthy benefited from the fact that many newspapermen, like himself, were too lazy to check the facts. He was helped even more by a few reporters who had reason to know that McCarthy was distorting the truth and chose to ignore it.

Colonel Robert McCormack, the owner of the Chicago *Tribune,* wanted McCarthy to be just as powerful and famous as the press could make him. An arch right-winger, Red hunter, and charter member of the China lobby, McCormack had helped discover and create McCarthy. The McCormack family papers—the Chicago *Tribune,* the Washington *Times Herald,* and the New York *Daily News,* all of which carried similar stories—gave McCarthy a large and strident mouthpiece.

That syndicate wasn't McCarthy's only champion, or the largest. The Hearst papers were also fervently pro-McCarthy, and Hearst columnist George Sokolsky had the same inside track McCarthy gave the *Tribune.* Sokolsky became a fixture in the McCarthy camp, advising him and acting as a go-between with government agencies.

The Hearst chain in the early 1950s was an empire. Hearst owned the leading paper or the top competition in about eighteen major newspaper markets, from San Francisco, to Chicago, to New York. Its yellow journalism and screaming headlines reached more people than any other single news source.

Some reporters and major newspapers did see McCarthy for what he was and told their readers. The Washington *Post* and the New York *Times* attacked him, and reporters like Murry Marder of the *Post,* Phil Potter of the Baltimore *Sun,* James Reston of the New York *Times,* and Homer Bigart of the New York *Herald Tribune,* took the trouble to expose some of his fabrications. The Milwaukee *Journal,* in McCarthy's home state, took pains to check McCarthy's "facts." Late in McCarthy's career Edward R. Murrow of CBS, a highly respected radio-TV journalist, laid bare McCarthyism on a famous *See It Now,* and even right-wing Henry Luce's *Time,* looked askance at McCarthy's gutter campaigns. It was a cartoonist, Herbert Block (Herblock) of the Washington *Post,* who, in March 1950, coined the famous eponym "McCarthyism."

McCarthy countered with a cheap paperback called *McCarthyism: The Fight for America.* His tactics were as usual. He called the *Post* the "Washington edition of the *Daily Worker,*" the Communist party paper, and accused other papers, like the St. Louis *Post-Dispatch,* the *Christian Science Monitor,* and the Portland *Oregonian,* of being Communist "tools." He would threaten libel suits and intimidate advertisers.

He accused the rewrite desks of the three major wire services of doctoring the news, and *Time* of obstructing the fight against communism, a rather incredible charge considering the fact that Luce thought he was *leading* the fight. At a grocer's meeting in Milwaukee, McCarthy warned: "Keep in mind that when you send your checks over to the (Milwaukee) *Journal,* you are contributing to bringing the Communist party line into the homes of Wisconsin." McCarthy even announced that he had asked the Postmaster General to give him the costs of the "subsidized distribution" of the Washington *Post,* the *Wall Street Journal,* and the Communist *Daily Worker.* When the brothers Joseph and Stewart Alsop wrote an article critical of McCarthy in the *Saturday Evening Post,* McCarthy wrote the *Post* that the article was ". . . almost 100 percent in line with the official instructions issued Communists . . . by . . . (the) national secretary of the Communist Party."

His most brutal punishment he reserved for the editor of the New York *Post* James Wechsler. He summoned Wechsler to his committee to testify about his past. After the experience, Wechsler wrote:

> It is not quite possible to communicate the quiet horror of an examination by McCarthy . . . I bear no wounds. . . . but I do not commend the experience to anyone. . . . No moment can be more hideous than that in which your own estimate of yourself is alleged to be a case of mistaken identity . . . and worst of all when you know that the men who are making the charge do not believe what they are saying . . .

That sort of reporting could bring to the public, firsthand, the horror of McCarthy's witch-hunts. Unfortunately, far more reporting was devoted to simply repeating his charges.

Even such a responsible papers as the New York *Times,* was used by McCarthy. His charges were news; they could not just be ignored. The *Times* printed the headline after the "Z" hearings: RADAR WITNESS BREAKS DOWN: WILL TELL ALL ABOUT SPY RING. The reputable papers recognized this institutional weakness and tried to balance it on the editorial page. The press served, wrote the Washington *Post,* "in a sense as irresponsible executioners of his decrees, inflicting punishment by publicity upon the innocent." But there was no real antidote. Defensively, the New York *Times* could only declare, "The remedy lies with the reader."

In mid-October, McCarthy decided to give the Chicago *Tribune* a scoop. The story appeared on October 15 on page 1 of both the Chicago *Tribune* and the Washington *Times Herald:*

INSIDE SPY RING STORY TOLD:
TRIBUNE BARES RED THEFT OF RADAR SECRETS—
PAPERS MICROFILMED, SENT TO EAST GERMANY—
SIGNAL CORPS LAX IN SECURITY AT LABORATORY—

A refugee scientist from the Russian zone in Germany has supplied evidence that America's radar defense secrets flowed in a steady stream to Russia.

This electronics expert, who is being closely guarded for fear of attempted Russian reprisals, escaped his communist masters in an East German laboratory early in June, 1952.

He crossed into the American zone and gave copious data to military intelligence which disclosed organized espionage in the secret radar research center of the army signal corps at Fort Monmouth, N.J.

—Withheld to Aid Probe—

The dramatic details of this revelation, of the subsequent frantic search for traitors at Fort Monmouth, and of the appalling lax security conditions prevailing there can now be made public by The Chicago Tribune. The story has previously been withheld lest premature publicity interfere with the investigation.

Senator Dirksen (R. Ill.) last night stated in Chicago that a number of secret documents missing from the secret files of the signal corps had been located in East Germany. Chairman McCarthy (R. Wis.) of the senate permanent investigations subcommittee confirmed this announcement today, describing the evidence as "completely convincing."[1]

The story was entirely hot air. In 1951, a nineteen-year-old East German citizen had defected, offering to tell all he knew of East German electronics development. It turned out that he knew almost nothing; he was not a "scientist" but a high school graduate with limited trade school training. He also boasted to U.S. authorities that he could give them significant information about stolen U.S. classified electronic documents that had reached East German hands. This, too, was

1. Copyrighted, 1953, Chicago *Tribune*. Used with permission.

untrue. After hours of interrogation, he admitted that he knew nothing about stolen documents. Nor was he being "closely guarded for fear of attempted Russian reprisals," as the *Tribune* had stated. He was, instead, working as a stock clerk in the U.S. Army Post Exchange at Weisbaden, West Germany.

I told all this to McCarthy within two days after the story first appeared. But it didn't even slow him down. He had been fed information by one of his "patriots," and he was going to make hay out of it, whether or not it was true. He raged that the "scientist's" report on stolen documents had never reached Fort Monmouth, where McCarthy decided that it should have gone, even though there was no reason to send it there. He vowed to find the person who had kept the vital information from the Commanding General at Fort Monmouth, information that was essential to cracking the Fort Monmouth "spy ring."

To milk more headlines from the story, he decided to send the committee investigator, James Juliana, to Germany to talk to the "scientist" about the security breach. On three hours' notice, Juliana rushed to the New York airport from Fort Monmouth and flew to Germany. Juliana didn't want to go so quickly; he sidled up to me two or three times during the day and urged me to intercede with Cohn, so he could go back to Washington, get some clean clothes, and see his family. But it was too urgent; McCarthy needed to get Juliana to Germany to see the scientist before the Army could spirit him away.

Instead of spiriting the so-called scientist away, the Army met Juliana's plane, took him to headquarters, and supplied him with interpreters, transportation, an interview room, tape recorders, and the "scientist" himself, who stopped working at the PX long enough to answer Juliana's questions.

He didn't tell Juliana anything, because he didn't know anything. Nonetheless, Juliana arrived back in New York a week later where he and his valuable tape were rushed by motorcycle escort to McCarthy. McCarthy managed to squeeze out a few more headlines. On October 22, the Washington *Star* quoted Juliana as saying: "I have interviewed this scientist and I have obtained from him and now have in my possession highly classified documents which strongly substantiate the information already reported in the newspapers" that classified documents had reached the East Germans.

The Washington *Times Herald* editorialized on October 24:

THE RADAR SPY RING

Senator McCarthy's investigation of espionage at Fort Monmouth is far from finished but enough has been disclosed to show that bureaucracy may still be covering up for the Communists. Call it disloyalty or call it stupidity, something is rotten when two newspapers and a congressional committee must act to break up a spy ring at the secret research center where electronic war devices are developed and the nation's radar defenses are planned by the signal corps.

As our readers know, the newspapers were the Times-Herald and the Chicago Tribune. It was our distinguished reporter, Willard Edwards, who learned of the damning report made by a refugee scientist from the Russian spy zone of Germany and turned it over to the McCarthy subcommittee. It was Mr. Edwards who on Oct. 6 broke the first story of the scandal—the suspension for security reasons of five employees at the radar factory.

The refugee scientist's report, which stated that the Russians "could get anything they wanted" at Fort Monmouth, was made to an Air Force intelligence officer 16 months ago. The report arrived in Washington in July, 1952, labeled secret. Apparently the information stirred excitement in the intelligence branches of all of the armed forces, but nobody informed the one man who was most concerned—the commanding general at Fort Monmouth, Maj. Gen. Kirke B. Lawton. He said he first learned of the report last Wednesday, the day we published the details of the scientist's revelations. We can recall only one worse example of official negligence—if that is the word for it—the failure to notify the commanders at Pearl Harbor that war was imminent.

The McCarthy Committee, it may be hoped, will find out not only who has been responsible for the appalling lack of security precautions at Fort Monmouth, but who in the Pentagon bottled up the story of espionage for so many months.

Ordinary people were helpless against this sort of collusion. They had no way to fight back or to learn the truth. Only trusted newspapermen were allowed in McCarthy's "Executive Sessions," and McCarthy never made public the transcripts of the sessions. He pretended that the reason for this was to protect the privacy of those interrogated. But since he would promptly tell the press a twisted version of what the witness had said, privacy could hardly have been the objective. Moreover, when the witnesses asked to see the transcripts so they could go to the press and set the record straight, McCarthy refused. The witness could deny McCarthy's version, but he could offer no proof.

McCarthy didn't even care if there was a transcript. At one hearing, when the court stenographer failed to appear, he simply told one of his investigators to sit at a table and pretend to be taking notes. The witness was brought in and browbeaten while McCarthy's man furiously pretended to record it all. From time to time, he would make a show of interrupting the proceeding to ask McCarthy or the witness to slow down or repeat something.

I was annoyed by this performance and asked McCarthy, "Why did you do that?"

"We didn't want to disappoint the witness," shrugged McCarthy. "He had to come in from out of town."

McCarthy made the most of his senatorial perogative. He made an art form of the "congressional investigation," developing techniques that were to be used by congressional committees long after McCarthyism faded, for causes good and bad.

First, there was the subpoena power. McCarthy could compel testimony, under oath, from almost anyone. He usually did it on short notice, giving his victims just a few hours to prepare themselves for the slaughter. Theoretically, it was the committee, not McCarthy, that issued subpoenas. But McCarthy ignored the Senate rule that required a vote of the other members every time he wanted to haul someone in. He signed scores of blank subpoenas which his staff members carried in their inside pockets, and issued as regularly as traffic tickets.

And then there was the one-man subcommittee employed by McCarthy. Senate custom and the more strict rules of the House of Representatives did not permit committee or subcommittee meetings with a quorum of less than three persons present. Nor would either House permit a subcommittee to operate through an entire five-month congressional recess without proper authorization. Furthermore, in the Senate, the investigation of subversive activities was under the exclusive jurisdiction of the Judiciary Committee's Subcommittee on Internal Security. Neither the Government Operations Committee or its Permanent Subcommittee on Investigations had any jurisdiction in this area, a fact that both McCarthy and the entire Senate ignored.

Then there was a senator's privilege against libel. As long as McCarthy's statements were made on the Senate floor or at a committee hearing, he was virtually immune from libel suits. Thus, he could say almost anything he pleased, and he did. The newspapers could print it, safe in the knowledge that they were accurately printing the pronouncements of a U.S. Senate subcommittee chairman.

The most powerful and destructive weapon McCarthy had came right out of the U.S. Constitution. With his extraordinary capacity to twist good into bad, McCarthy managed to pervert one of the most basic elements of the Bill of Rights.

The Fifth Amendment to the Constitution guarantees the right against self-incrimination. But when invoked before Joe McCarthy, it somehow became an admission of guilt. Anyone who "took the Fifth" in response to a McCarthy question was immediately branded a "Fifth Amendment Communist." The witness *must* be a Communist, McCarthy implied. Why else wouldn't he just answer my questions?

The reason why is often misunderstood. The Fifth Amendment cannot be used selectively—to answer some questions but not others. If a witness on the stand answers one question beyond basic identification, he waives his right to use the constitutional privilege against subsequent questions.

Take, for example, a person accused of selling marijuana, who might answer one too many questions and thus "waive," or lose, his privilege against self-incrimination:

Q: What is your name?
A: John Doe.
Q: Where do you live?
A: One Constitution Avenue, Washington, D.C.
Q: Did you cut your mother's throat and murder your sister?
A: Of course not. What kind of a crazy question is that?
Q: Did you sell an ounce of marijuana to Bill Smith?
A: Under the Fifth Amendment, I assert my right not to answer.
Q: Too late for that. You've waived your right. Either answer the question or face contempt of court proceedings.

To McCarthy, this all-or-nothing rule was an invitation to destruction. Many of the people he brought in did have something to hide. Usually, it was pretty mild, like attendance at a Communist rally many years before. But in that age of suspicion, no one wanted to admit any earlier contact with communism, no matter how remote or innocuous. So many witnesses would take the Fifth.

As soon as a witness had invoked the privilege, McCarthy would ask all sorts of outrageous questions, like "Are you a Soviet Spy?" or "When did you steal those classified documents?"

If the witness made a denial to any such questions, he waived his constitutional protection. The witness was thus obliged to answer all subsequent questions, regardless of their relevance, even if they might embarrass a neighbor, friend, or relative. Not to answer, after having fallen into the waiver trap, made a witness subject to a charge of criminal contempt.

When a witness takes the Fifth before a grand jury, the prosecutor usually asks just one or two questions and then sends the witness home. But McCarthy was more interested in humiliating witnesses than finding out what they knew. After the witness had invoked the privilege, McCarthy would then ask them forty or fifty questions. Having finished, McCarthy would go out to the waiting reporters and pronounce the witness a "Fifth Amendment Communist," who had "refused to answer 40 questions about his espionage activities."

Occasionally, a witness would slip up and answer one question too many. Once when McCarthy broadly asked whether a witness had engaged in "any illegal activities" at Fort Monmouth, the witness tried to answer by saying, "If the question were asked me whether I ever committed espionage, my answer would be 'no.' " The witness then refused to answer any question that dealt with his political beliefs. McCarthy told him that he had waived his privilege, and ordered him to answer.

McCarthy never did try to get the Justice Department to prosecute the man for contempt. He just wanted to scare him and get a headline.

Most witnesses came before McCarthy defenseless and terrified. Usually they were not accompanied by counsel, and when a few finally did begin to bring lawyers, McCarthy would refuse to let the lawyers object, or even talk to the witness unless the witness himself initiated the conversation.

A couple of witnesses brought their rabbis with them. One rabbi told Cohn that he feared McCarthy's hearings were anti-Semitic, since all the witnesses were Jewish. Cohn and Schine had immediately run off to telephone influential leaders of Jewish organizations to reassure the rabbi. Cohn told me he was lining up the presidents of both the Jewish War Veterans and B'nai B'rith. McCarthy used his folksy approach. He grabbed one uneasy rabbi in a brotherly bear hug and pulled him over to meet "my good right arm, Roy Cohn, who is such a great help to me in this fight I am waging against Communists and espionage." Cohn reassured the rabbi that he wouldn't work for McCarthy if he were anti-Semitic.

Of all the witnesses that I saw hauled before the committee, only one had the will and courage to tell McCarthy to go to hell. He was a huge man, a naturalized citizen from Rumania, with a black mustache, and a deep, heavily-accented voice. He was the business agent for a labor union in upstate New York, most of whose members worked at companies with defense contracts. He had taken the Fifth Amendment, as McCarthy knew ahead of time he would.

McCarthy started off with the usual bullying questions, but the big Rumanian refused to sit there and take it. He just roared right back at McCarthy. "What right have you to do this?" he bellowed over and over again. McCarthy threatened him with criminal charges. "Go ahead!" shouted the witness. "I dare you!"

For once a witness was intimidating McCarthy, not the other way around. McCarthy backed off, and let the witness go home.

CHAPTER X

Espionage "R"

At Fort Monmouth, the post commander, General Lawton, took to heart Secretary Stevens's order to "cooperate" with McCarthy. He began suspending employees suspected of subversion. By the end of October, thirty-three employees had been suspended from their jobs. They were all among the thirty-five mentioned in that Hoover-to-Bolling letter which formed the basis of McCarthy's "Purloined Letter."

The Hoover letter was almost three years old by then, yet no dismissals had resulted. To McCarthy's mind, that meant someone was protecting Communists. General Lawton knew better. He knew that all the allegations had been carefully reviewed, in many cases more than once.

On a Friday afternoon, late in October, Stevens handed me folders containing the dossiers of all the suspended employees. He wanted to know how to dispose of each of them—by Monday.

I was thoroughly shaken. Here were the careers and reputations of more than thirty people on the line, not to mention the welfare of all their families, and I—after less than four weeks on the job—had a weekend to decide their fate.

I began reading folders at once, and kept at it for most of the next sixty hours, except for small snatches of sleep. One, years before, had attended a benefit rally for Russian children; two reported Communists were also at the rally. This suspect also belonged to a CIO local, called, dangerously, the "Egg Local," and considered subversive. Another, a physicist, was accused of belonging to a Brooklyn College Physics Club whose faculty advisor had been fired for failure to testify before a state legislative committee investigating Communists. He was also accused of having been a member of the American Labor party in 1947 and 1949 (as were five hundred thousand other people); his close association with his brother, who was alleged to have Communist leanings, also made him suspect.

Another was charged only because he was married to a woman who was allegedly pro-Communist. Yet another was charged with having an uncle who was a member of the Communist party, a cousin who signed a Communist party candidate's petition fourteen years ealier, and parents who had done the same thing.

About the most "dangerous" person in the bunch was Aaron Coleman. It was his name that graced the title of the "Purloined Letter." I was particularly interested in his case because I had seen McCarthy working him over at one of his "Executive Sessions" a few days earlier, this time in a special room at Fort Monmouth generously supplied by General Lawton as part of Stevens's cooperation order. (Among the guests at this abuse was Fort Monmouth's "Soldier of the Week," who happened to be from Wisconsin and who was brought in to see his home state war hero, McCarthy, in action.)

Coleman had been a schoolmate of Julius Rosenberg's at City College. He knew Rosenberg sufficiently well that once in 1936 or 1937 they had talked about communism. Rosenberg had persuaded Coleman to go to a meeting of the Young Communist League, but Coleman had been disenchanted and never went back. They both later found work at Fort Monmouth, though not at the same time. While being interrogated after his arrest, Rosenberg once mentioned seeing (but not speaking to) Coleman there. During the war, Coleman went into the Marines, and once wrote back from the South Pacific to an Army friend at Fort Monmouth asking him to mail him a radar manual that he had helped to write. He used the regular mails because a formal request for the manual would take a year or two to process. The mail was censored so the letter was intercepted; years later McCarthy turned this incident into an obvious attempt to get radar secrets to the enemy.

After the war, Coleman came back to Fort Monmouth and quickly progressed as a radar scientist. He asked for—and received—permission to take forty-eight declassified documents home. Unfortunately, not all of them had been properly stamped as declassified when he stuck them under his bed. And two of them were still technically "Confidential," which was Army parlance for "don't leave this around loose." A few days later, Coleman was asked during a security check if he had any documents in his room. "Yes, quite a few," he answered. He readily agreed to a search and the documents were found.

A disciplinary board at Fort Monmouth looked into the incident and fined him two week's pay for careless handling of documents. But McCarthy got hold of the "Purloined Letter" and, in the autumn of 1953, destroyed Coleman's reputation completely.

When I had finished reading all the folders, I sat down at my dining room table on Sunday afternoon; I wanted to reinstate all thirty-five of them, but I knew that was out of the question. For hours I sat there, trying to work up the courage to put one more folder on the "reinstate" pile, and then another, and another.

I knew that if the secretary reinstated the whole batch at once, some "patriot" would squeal, and McCarthy would come crashing down demanding blood, probably mine. I wasn't too sure I could get away with too many reinstatements, but in the end, my recommendation was that nearly all of the employees be put back on the payroll, and that full security clearances be returned at once to nine of them. The rest would be without security clearances until security boards had reviewed their cases, but they would still be employed.

Before talking to Stevens, I telephoned General Lawton at Fort Monmouth and asked him if he couldn't reinstate some or all of the suspended employees. "No," he replied. "I have suspended them as I have a right to do. If the secretary wants them reinstated he can do it himself, because I won't." He didn't know that when he said "the secretary," that he meant me.

It was a slow, rather blundering process. Not all escaped without severe scars, but for most, at least a bit of due process resulted, and before long, twenty-five of them were restored to full duty. The other eight had to wait five years before the courts rescued them.

About Coleman, I said to Stevens, "He's either a spy, or just the unluckiest guy alive, and I'm inclined to think he is the latter." Stevens laughed heartily. But I didn't think it would have seemed very humorous to Coleman, who had candidly and earnestly answered every question asked him in three different brutal McCarthy inquisitions, one on national television.

CHAPTER XI

No Spies
at Monmouth

Morale was low at Fort Monmouth by late October. The arbitrary suspensions and McCarthy's "executive sessions" had spread fear and distrust throughout the base, making "lepers" out of the employees under investigation.

To boost morale, Secretary Stevens decided to make a trip to the base and perhaps try to give the Fort Monmouth employees some sense that the Army hadn't just abandoned them to McCarthy's inquisition. Stevens then enlarged the mission and it became a joint Stevens-McCarthy visit. First McCarthy bamboozled Senator H. Alexander Smith, a timid and ambivalent former Princeton professor, into coming. Then Congressman James C. Auchincloss, who represented the Fort Monmouth area, came along as well. I figured they were afraid not to be there—after all, McCarthy was uncovering spies within their constituencies.

This large entourage was about to be shown a research laboratory when a guard asked for their security clearances. None of the politicians or their aides had any. Forced to make a quick judgment so as to avoid an embarrassing situation, Stevens preemptorily ruled that it was safe for elected officials to see the lab.

This left Roy Cohn standing outside, along with some others. I stayed outside also because he seemed quite angry. He asked me to get him a car to go to New York at once, since he felt that the action had humiliated him. My soothing words didn't help; he began pacing up and down and, as I later testified, telling everyone that "This is war! We will really investigate this place now! They let Communists in and keep me out!"

At lunch, I told Stevens about Cohn's behavior. The secretary's response was to stand up there in front of the entire party, plus numerous Fort Monmouth employees, and publicly apologize to Cohn.

Cohn seemed mollified. And by early November, McCarthy himself was beginning to lose interest in the Army. It was quite clear that he wasn't finding any spies, and Cohn several times said to me that McCarthy was "about ready to turn the Fort Monmouth investigation over to the Army."

Hopeful, I suggested to Secretary Stevens that he invite McCarthy over to the Pentagon for lunch, where he could arrange this "transfer," so that McCarthy would seek his headlines elsewhere.

On November 6, McCarthy came to Stevens's office for lunch. It was in the E ring of the Pentagon, where the top brass could look out their windows at vistas of Washington and the Virginia countryside. Stevens's office had a view of the Lincoln Memorial, a big desk, an American flag, and an Army flag posted on either side of his chair. A portrait of Henry L. Stimson, the first secretary of war to occupy the Pentagon, hung on the wall; a portrait of Stevens's predecessor as Army secretary, Frank Pace, hung on another. Stevens had added the framed front page of the Paris edition of the New York *Herald Tribune* of May 23, 1927, the day after Lindbergh's landing in Paris, because he had himself been in Paris that day and still remembered the thrill of the event.

There were five of us at lunch: McCarthy, Cohn, Carr, Stevens, and me. Cohn had also insisted on inviting Schine, but he didn't show up. Stevens began by trying to point out to McCarthy that his investigation was harming the Army, that it was injuring morale at Fort Monmouth. Besides, he said, the Army and FBI were already engaged in a large-scale investigation of subversives at Fort Monmouth, and had been for months.

McCarthy was amenable to calling it quits. His "investigation" had been a bust and he knew it. He told Stevens he would turn the investigation over to the Army, though not because he would acknowledge that he was hurting Army morale or that he had found no spies. He implied that he had bigger fish to fry.

He wanted to begin an investigation of Communist infiltration into defense industries, and he planned to conduct a series of hearings in upstate New York communities, such as Buffalo, Schenectady, and Albany.

The only discordant note in an otherwise amiable lunch was two or three references to the matter of David Schine, questioning when we were going to arrange a New York assignment for him. And McCarthy—for the first time—joined with Cohn in urging us to give Schine a New York assignment. He suggested that Schine be sent to West Point to look for pro-Red leanings in the U.S. Military Academy textbooks.

I wasn't pleased that McCarthy joined in the New York assignment request, but I didn't take him too seriously. Several times he had assured both Stevens and me that he wanted to get rid of Schine, though he didn't want Cohn to know. McCarthy had disdainfully told Stevens over the phone that "Roy thinks Dave ought to be a general and operate from a penthouse in the Waldorf Astoria." I suppose I should have pitied the defense contractors of upstate New York, but I felt considerable relief at the prospect of McCarthy leaving Fort Monmouth alone.

My relief was to be short-lived. The press had exerted great pressure on the Army to make a statement about the "spies" at Fort Monmouth, and Stevens's public relations men urged him to hold a press conference. Since the Army had just suffered a deep congressional slash in its budget, Stevens welcomed the idea. He thought he could steer the questions to his concern about military strength.

Just before the press conference, Stevens asked me what to say about Fort Monmouth. "The press is only going to ask you about one subject: Is there espionage at Fort Monmouth?"

"Well, there isn't any, is there?" he asked.

Not that we know of, I said, and we know everything in McCarthy's transcripts. It was possible that McCarthy would come up with a real live spy, I added, and if he does, "we're dead." But the main concern was that Julius Rosenberg once worked there.

So, Stevens repeated, what should he say?

"If you are going to answer questions on that matter, you just have to stand your ground and say no."

Stevens said that he hoped to talk primarily about "the strength of the Army," which to him was the "important thing." If he was asked about Fort Monmouth, however, he'd say that because of the Rosenbergs, we'd have to assume that there was some spy activity around the base during the war some years ago, but that insofar as we can tell, there is no current espionage.

I warned him that his statement would "make Joe awfully sore," and that he'd probably raise holy hell about it.

Stevens stood firm. "Well, I've got an obligation to the Army that comes ahead of my obligations to the feelings of any one senator. And, since this is the truth anyway, I'll just have to chance it, and we'll pick up the pieces afterward."

The newspaper reporters weren't much interested in hearing Stevens talk about the strength of the Army. The press conference lasted sixty-five minutes, and was devoted mainly to questions about Fort Monmouth. The Army could find no spies, said Stevens.

Roy Cohn telephoned that night from Albany, furious. I tried to calm him down, saying that Stevens had said little that could be disputed, and urged him to hold off to see what the press reaction was in the morning papers.

STEVENS: NO SPIES AT MONMOUTH was the headline on page 1 of the New York *Times*. Cohn called me to say that McCarthy was outraged. I passed the word on to Stevens.

"Who told me to say those things about Fort Monmouth?" he barked.

"I did," I replied.

McCarthy counterattacked immediately: He announced that there would be public hearings on Fort Monmouth. "The evidence will speak for itself," he told the press.

The siege was on again. Stevens decided to sue for peace with another lunch for McCarthy, this time at his club in New York. We flew by Stevens's military plane to Newark, where a limousine was waiting to ferry us on to the Merchants Club, a comfortable little club in lower Manhattan that Stevens was quite proud of. McCarthy, Cohn, and Carr were there, as well as Hearst columnist George Sokolsky, who McCarthy brought along uninvited. McCarthy ordered a double Manhattan, so everyone else did, too, except Cohn, who never drank. Joe ordered the most expensive steak ("after what you did to us," he explained to Stevens), and everyone else ordered the same, with a lot of chuckling all around.

Stevens started it off: "I really don't know why you are upset, Joe; I said very little about Fort Monmouth except that there was no current espionage there. And I didn't mention the McCarthy committee."

McCarthy remarked dryly, "No, you didn't say anything; you only called me a liar before the whole country." (It was about time someone in the administration did, I thought.) And he ordered another double Manhattan.

Then the negotiations began. After several hours of wrangling (during which Joe ate about a loaf of bread, explaining to me that he was a "farm boy" who needed plenty of bread and butter), a compromise was worked out. Stevens would tell the press that when he said that there was "no current espionage" at Fort Monmouth, he was talking about only what the *Army* knew. Not about what Joe's *committee* knew. The committee, he would acknowledge, might know something the Army did not.

This was complete nonsense. The Army had copies of all the transcripts of McCarthy's "Executive Sessions." By then we knew just what McCarthy had, which was nothing. But for the sake of peace, Stevens agreed to equivocate for the press.

He was given the opportunity almost immediately. McCarthy's camp had tipped off the press to our whereabouts, and a large crowd of newsmen was waiting for us after lunch. They had not bothered to wait outside, but instead burst into the parlor of Stevens's club, tracking dirt, laying TV cables, and generally horrifying the club members as they nodded in their leather chairs.

Some newsmen told me afterward that Stevens had "eaten crow." He had, in fact, retreated somewhat, but at least he had not backed off his statement that the Army knew of no current espionage at Fort Monmouth. In any case, the peace offering did not work. McCarthy decided to go ahead with more Fort Monmouth hearings.

After lunch, having eaten a little crow, gained nothing, and seen his club trampled, Stevens walked into another trap. McCarthy was scheduled to fly north, to Boston, but suddenly, at about 4:00 P.M., he put another event on the schedule. We were all going to fly south, to "see Dave."

Dave Schine had finally been drafted and sent to Fort Dix for basic training a few days before. Presumably, he was lonely and needed company. In any case, all of us were flying down to McGuire Air Force Base, which adjoined Fort Dix. The Army would provide the transportation, the secretary's DC-3 which had brought us up from Washington earlier in the day.

First, a car was sent to pick up McCarthy's wife, Jeannie, and her eight pieces of honeymoon luggage (the recently married couple had been living at the Drake Hotel during the New York hearings at the Senate's expense). Then we piled into two cars—the Army secretary's car, and the Schine limousine, which seemed to be on permanent loan to the committee—and headed out to Newark airport to board Stevens's plane.

The two cars left the Merchants Club together. I was riding in Schine's Cadillac following Stevens's car. McCarthy was in the front seat with the driver. After a few blocks, we stopped, the driver moved over, and McCarthy took the wheel. The Cadillac was equipped with a siren on the front fender and a flashing red light (loans from the New York Police Department to the committee, the chauffeur once told me). McCarthy roared ahead, sending other cars swerving off to the side as he swept through the Holland Tunnel, siren howling and red light flashing. He was giggling delightedly all the while. I sunk as low in the rear seat as possible.

At McGuire, we were greeted by the base commander, some public relations men, and Private Schine. The merry group posed in front of the secretary's plane for pictures. When one of Stevens's aides told me "the boss" wanted me to get in the group, I ducked under the wing. "I'm not going to be in that goddam picture," I said.

Afterwards, the McCarthys, Cohn, Carr, and Schine went to the McGuire officers' club for dinner, and then, minus Schine, they all went on to Boston to investigate communism in defense plants. They took Stevens's plane. The secretary of the army borrowed a small plane from the McGuire commander to take us back to Washington.

How in God's name did Stevens let all that happen, I wondered, as we put-putted through the evening sky hoping to get the Army secretary home in time for a dinner engagement with the secretary of the treasury. Several weeks before, Stevens had invited McCarthy and his staff to use the Merchants Club for lunch any time and charge it to him. And now all this!

As we drove up Rock Creek Parkway in Washington, Stevens spoke ruefully of the reporters piling into the Merchants Club, banging the place up and thoroughly disrupting the privacy of its members. He said that he was so ashamed that he was going to write to the club's president and offer to resign, which he did. Later he received a gracious letter that all was forgiven.

CHAPTER XII

I Am Taken
for a Ride

Draftees in their first month of basic training did not get weekend passes. But David Schine was obviously no ordinary soldier.

In early November, Cohn insisted that Schine was essential to the workings of the Investigations Subcommittee. Reluctantly—and mistakenly—Stevens agreed to make Schine available for committee work on weekends, and even on weeknights if "absolutely necessary." I learned about this, with considerable irritation, after he had agreed to it.

Once or twice I cautiously suggested to Stevens that we just ignore McCarthy's blandishments on Schine's behalf. He rejected my advice, insisting that he did not want to hinder the legitimate functions of a congressional committee. Given the importance of an impartially administered draft, his refusal to question McCarthy's claim that Schine was "essential" to the committee was, I thought, pretty silly. Had Schine been essential, there were legitimate avenues to have accomplished a deferment prior to induction. I felt very strongly that once a man had been drafted, everybody should keep hands off. But Stevens spoke with such firmness that I didn't feel it worth the effort to push him. Shortly after I had been hired, I had learned that such questioning his judgment threw him into quick anger.

Stevens had directed the post commander to make a suitable office room available, so Schine could work there with the committee rather than leave the post. But the staff worked better fifteen miles away at the Stacy Trent Hotel in Trenton, where the New York cut sirloin steaks were more appealing than Army chow. Cohn's and Schine's committee staff dined there often as they conducted "committee business."

Schine's commanding officer later testified that he once found Schine sitting in the cab of a truck while his mates were off on a rifle range. Schine explained that he was studying logistics. Later he told the captain he wanted, "to remake the military along more modern lines."

Before long, the post commander, General Cornelius Ryan, was fed up. He was afraid, for one thing, that Schine would fall asleep on the rifle range and shoot someone. He telephoned me on December 8 and told me the situation was completely out of hand. I told him he could cancel the weekday evening passes, but that since the secretary had made a clear commitment as to the weekends, I felt he would have to continue granting that privilege. I heard no objection from Cohn as to the weekday cancellation.

Meanwhile, Cohn was hounding me relentlessly to get Schine assigned to New York. I told him the same thing over and over again. Schine would have to serve just like the other three hundred thousand men being drafted that year. Schine would get no special treatment, beyond what Stevens had already agreed to, and none from me.

Cohn, however, never let up. Again and again he said the same thing to me: "The Army is making Dave eat shit because he works for Joe."

I finally got exasperated with this litany and went directly to McCarthy. I knew that McCarthy considered Schine to be more of a nuisance than an asset to the committee. He had once said that Schine "is a good boy, but there is nothing indispensable about him." On another occasion, he called him "completely useless." And on the eve of Schine's induction, he had told Secretary Stevens, "I think for Roy's sake, if you can let him come back on weekends or something so his girls won't get too lonesome—maybe if they shave off his hair, he won't want to come back."

McCarthy promised that he would write the Army a letter saying that his committee had no further need for Schine and that he hoped

Schine would be treated just like any other soldier. And he said that he would force his staff to lay off.

Relieved, I went back to the Pentagon. But my relief was premature. Cohn called two hours later. He was even more abusive than usual:

"I'll teach you and I'll teach the Army what it means to go over my head," he exclaimed.

"Is that a threat?" I asked.

"No, that's not a threat; that's a promise."

A day later another peace-making lunch ensued. Stevens, McCarthy, and I went to the Carroll Arms, a Capitol Hill restaurant, and discussed the matter of David Schine. Cohn was absent.

McCarthy had changed his tune from the day before. He began pushing for a New York assignment for Schine. Stevens again stated that Schine would have to finish his sixteen weeks of basic training before anything else could even be considered.

Obviously, Cohn had gotten to McCarthy. The senator told us at lunch that Cohn had threatened to resign because of Schine, going so far as to flash before McCarthy a written invitation to become chief counsel to the House Un-American Activities Committee. McCarthy also said that Cohn had been offered a job with the Senate Internal Security Subcommittee (another Red-hunting committee on the Hill). McCarthy, we knew, needed Cohn. He was very able, and he had a direct channel to the Hearst press through his friends Walter Winchell and George Sokolsky.

I told McCarthy that I was getting awfully tired of having to listen incessantly to Cohn's charges that "the Army is making Schine eat shit." Stevens winced. McCarthy chuckled and said not to take Cohn too seriously.

The next day, Cohn was on my back again. Schine learned that his training would include Saturday morning duty, setting Cohn off on a rampage against me. For over an hour, Cohn ranted at me, repeating this "eat shit" line incessantly. The Army had "double-crossed" Cohn, he said, first by not giving Schine a commission, then by not assigning him to New York, then by taking away his free evenings, and finally, by taking away his Saturday mornings. I could only repeat that Schine was no different from the three hundred thousand other young men we drafted every year. . . .[1]

1. In his 1968 book, *McCarthy* (p. 115), Roy Cohn gave this explanation of his calls:

Were my calls in Dave's behalf more frequent and insistent than was usual in these cases? Probably. And the reason is obvious. I had received word that the Army planned to block a

About a week later, on December 17, I was climbing the steps of the U.S. Courthouse in New York's Foley Square when McCarthy came up to me. He had been to dinner the night before with some leading Irish Catholic lights, including Francis Cardinal Spellman and Joseph P. Kennedy. Also among the guests was General Cornelius Ryan—the commandant at Fort Dix. Ryan told the group about Schine's escapades, describing such irregularities in his basic training as his frequent nightly trips to Trenton. The stories must have shocked the dinner party, because McCarthy was embarrassed and irritated. He told me, "I want all this pressure on the Army to stop." This was another about-face for McCarthy, his third in a month. I decided to try to pin him down. "Fine," I said, "but you're going to have to tell it to me in front of Cohn."

That noon, a large group of us went to lunch at Gasner's Restaurant. Patricia Kennedy, sister of the Massachusetts senator, and a woman whom McCarthy had once dated, was there, along with film actor Peter Lawford, whom she later married. They had been guests at the "Executive Session." Walking over to the restaurant, I had remarked to Lawford that McCarthy turned heads on a street like a movie star.

At the end of the lunch Lawford and Miss Kennedy left, and McCarthy's group and I stayed on at the table. I wanted McCarthy to tell Cohn to lay off, right there before me, just as he had told me he would three hours earlier. So I brought the subject up. But when Cohn began to raise hell, McCarthy began to retreat. For two hours the diatribe went on, with Cohn blaming the Army, Stevens, and me for a host of sins, the worst of which was failing to live up to an "agreement" that Schine would be assigned to New York. Cohn consumed large quantities of ice cream while I missed the 1:30, then the 2:30, trains back to Washington.

Finally I told them I'd like to catch a train home. We rode uptown in Cohn's car, with Cohn at the wheel, McCarthy beside him in the front seat, and Carr and I in back. As we drove, Cohn was raining systematic abuse on McCarthy, who periodically turned to me to ask if I couldn't arrange to get Dave assigned to New York.

When we got to Thirty-fourth Street, where we were supposed to

---

commission for Schine, that it had no intention of handling his case in the normal way, but had decided to retaliate against him for being associated with our committee. I liked Dave. He was a friend. I respected his ability and common sense. He was a valuable trained member of the staff and one of its hardest workers. I was angry that a man, one serving without pay, was being subjected to the same politically motivated attacks that were the lot of any investigator who disturbed the status quo, particularly where security was concerned.

turn left to reach the station, a traffic officer prohibited the left turn and we kept on going north, away from the station. When I finally said that I would miss my train if we continued to go in that direction, Cohn had another fit. He stopped the car in the middle lane of traffic on Park Avenue near Forty-sixth Street and said to me: "Get out and get to the station however you can."

As I was climbing out of the car, McCarthy asked again if there wasn't some way to get Schine assigned to New York. How about having him search the West Point library for subversive books? The car pulled away and I was left standing with a suitcase in the middle of three lanes of traffic in midtown New York.

Later Frank Carr told me that if I thought my departure from the automobile had been ignominious, I should have seen the way McCarthy had been dismissed from the car three blocks farther on, at the Waldorf.

CHAPTER XIII

Witch Hunting

While we were squabbling over what to do about one Army private, McCarthy was up to far more serious mischief. He had not found any spies, of course, but he was still making headlines. The only thing that had changed by December was the location of the Fort Monmouth hearings, from New York to Washington since the New York newspapers were on strike.

This obsession with publicity among the congressional Red hunters was not solely confined to McCarthy. In December, a senior staff official of Congressman Harold H. Velde's House Un-American Activities Committee complained bitterly to me that the Army, by supplying McCarthy with facts, was clearly giving McCarthy "headlines which rightfully belong to us."

On December 8, Aaron Coleman was subpoened to appear in Washington, where he was given a merciless going-over. This hearing was public, and televised. Coleman was allowed to have a lawyer, but the latter was not allowed to interject questions, to object, or otherwise to assist his client, unless Coleman requested it; otherwise, he would be accused of trying to prompt the witness.

As I watched, I decided that things had gone far enough. I felt that the time had come to do something to reassure the sufferers, to make them aware that in the Army Secretariat, we knew that the public was being fed a fabric of pure lies.

The question was how to accomplish this without violating the security rules—or the established policy of cooperation and appeasement toward McCarthy. Yet here I was, the one non-McCarthyite who was seeing it all on a daily basis, who was receiving McCarthy's daily executive transcripts, and who understood exactly the outrage being perpetrated by McCarthy, aided by the might of some of America's most influential newspapers. I felt I just had to do something.

Finding a moment during a recess when the cameras were otherwise occupied, and when no one was watching, I walked up to Coleman's lawyer, a man named Richard Green, from Elizabeth, N.J. I spoke to him with studied casualness. Was it possible for him to speak to me confidentially, perhaps during the noon recess, in a place like the waiting room of the Union Station, three blocks away, where the crowds would assure us a degree of anonymity?

I wasn't sure what I'd say. It was very dangerous ground I sought to tread, because if Green subsequently revealed any assurances I gave him, the least that would happen would be a "close-the-door" reaction by McCarthy to the Army's future access to the executive hearings. More likely, I would be fired.

Green solved my dilemma at once by his answer. He said, "You must understand that I have one duty, and one duty only, and that is to my client and his welfare. I cannot talk to you in confidentiality and respect that confidentiality if there is anything I receive from you which may be helpful to my client. I must reveal to him everything I get, and I must use anything I get as he and I see fit."

My approach had been sufficiently casual and offhand that I was able to turn the conversation in an indifferent manner to other things, and we shortly separated.

As the hearing reconvened, the realization closed in. There I was, the one person outside the McCarthy orbit who knew the truth, who was seeing everything McCarthy was doing through McCarthy's own spectacles. But there was not a single thing I could do to help these people.

I returned to my seat as the hearing reconvened. Roy Cohn came and sat beside me. "What about Dave?" he asked. "What about Dave's thing?"

Richard Green had saved me this time, but there would be a next time. I could sense it. I remembered as a boy how scared I had been when my brother found a stick of live dynamite and dropped it in a stone quarry. I must be doing that, I thought, tossing around sticks of dynamite.

While this was Coleman's last appearance before McCarthy, his problems were far from over. What the government's loyalty security system did to him was in some ways as cruel as what McCarthy had done. It was not publicized, but it was devastating.

After the thirty-five employees had been suspended at Fort Monmouth, I had managed to get almost all of them back on the payroll in some status, even if under a cloud, and to get nine reinstated at once with full security clearances. But then the machine of the Loyalty Boards cranked into gear. The remaining twenty-six were formally charged as security risks, and made subject to losing their jobs.

All of these employees had been cleared of the same charges by other review panels at least once before, some twice. The allegations of disloyalty against them dated from that January 1951 Hoover-to-Bolling letter, so the Army had had almost three years to pick over the skeletons and ferret out any true subversives.

But then in April 1953, the rules had changed. President Truman's internal security program had been tough enough—"Reasonable grounds for belief of disloyalty." Disloyalty could mean anything from treason to disclosing official confidences or belonging to an organization considered "subversive" by the attorney general, such as the Anti-Fascist Refugee Committee formed to send food and medicine to America's Russian ally in World War II. Under President Eisenhower, the rules became even more harsh. The burden was put on the employee to prove loyalty, rather than on the government to prove disloyalty. And the list of "disloyal" acts was broadened to include almost any behavior that was not normal, including "infamous" or "immoral conduct," such as cohabitation of an unmarried couple, homosexuality, mental illness, mendacity—"any behavior, activities, or associations which tend to show that the individual is not reliable or trustworthy."

It was under these broad standards that the loyalty of the Fort Monmouth employees was being tested again in the autumn of 1953 and all through 1954. The boards were all specially appointed, had secret hearings with specially appointed attorneys as prosecutors, and their recommendations and decisions were sent forward for final decision or approval to a special appellate panel in the Army secretary's office.

By the end of 1954, eighteen of the twenty-six had been fully vindicated and reinstated with full clearances. But eight, including "Z" and Aaron Coleman, were in for a longer ordeal.

Their Loyalty Board hearings made a mockery of due process. Each was advised that the charges against him came from confidential sources. (These "confidential sources" were such things as the unevaluated Hoover-to-Bolling letter of 1951—a collection of hard-to-prove or disprove insinuations, including neighbors' gossip, and the hostility of jealous employees.) They were told they could not cross-examine their accusers or even know their identity. They could not see any records, certainly not the FBI report. In fact, as they were to learn, there were to be no witnesses against them, only papers they mustn't see. Coleman was asked questions like these:

> "Would you consider the religious beliefs and opinions of your parents to be strong?"
>
> "May I ask what are the religious beliefs of you at the present time or during your married life?"
>
> "Do you and your wife attend services regularly?"
>
> "Do you as an individual believe in God?"

Other Fort Monmouth employees among the unfortunate eight were asked these questions:

> "What party did you vote?"
>
> "What is your philosophy of life?"
>
> "Have you ever thought about the problem of whether or not public utilities, like big power and light companies, should be owned by the government?"
>
> "Do you think the government should control labor unions?"
>
> "Did you ever think of the four freedoms? Do you think our present political system is capable of achieving those four freedoms?"
>
> ". . . did your mother and father vote in the last general election? Do you know how they voted? Did your brother vote?"

On the basis of their answers to such questions, fortified by the allegations they had never seen, all eight were fired.

Coleman's longtime direct superior at Fort Monmouth, Brigadier General Edward Petzing, obviously not moved by the Red Scare kick, said at Coleman's hearing that he had a brilliant intellect and gave himself to his work unstintingly, adding:

There was never an occasion when I had any serious doubt as to his loyalty to the United States, and it is inconceivable to me that one who worked as hard, enthusiastically and efficiently, could be subversive or disloyal. Mr. Coleman had the respect and admiration of his fellow workers . . . to a degree I have seldom seen. It seems highly improbable that he could have maintained this reputation for a period of many years, as he did, unless his character and loyalty were of the highest order.

At the time that the question of Mr. Coleman's being a security risk was raised, I indicated my belief that he was a conscientious and loyal American and I recommend his retention in the laboratories. . . .

But not even that was enough to save Coleman's job.

Coleman, the most injured and the most angered, sought court relief, as did the seven others. All claimed violation of their constitutional rights. Two were reinstated after a lower court pointed out to the government that neither was doing classified work, and thus could hardly be considered a security risk. The other six lost in the lower courts, but won on appeal. On June 18, 1958—over five years after some of them had been first suspended—a three-judge panel of the U.S. Court of Appeals for the District of Columbia, delivered a unanimous opinion. The Court said that a person cannot be blindly disposed of, that he must be told what has been found against him, and that he must have some basic procedural protections.[1] The opinion was written by Judge George Washington, a collateral descendant of the nation's founding father.

Although Coleman, "Z," and the others were reinstated with back pay and employment rights, there was no way they could blot out the humiliation and suffering of their families during those black years.

It is hard now, twenty-eight years later, to appreciate how seriously the government took the words "loyalty" and "security" in 1953. That was the year that Robert Oppenheimer, the Father of the Atom Bomb, was stripped of his security clearance. The reasons? He had not been enthusiastic enough about the next generation weapon, the hydro-

---

1. Loyalty Boards, and the related loyalty-security programs, are things of the past. In 1978 when I was working on an earlier draft of this narrative, I called on John G. Connell, who was then serving as administrative assistant to the secretary of the army, the Army's highest civilian post of a nonpolitical nature. In the McCarthy era, Connell's assignment in the Army secretary's office had been in the nature of executive director of the Army's various loyalty-security programs. Reminiscing about them, he said that he was not sure that the rules were even in existence anymore, but insofar as he could recall, it had been at least fifteen years since a loyalty-security matter of any sort had been brought to the secretary's office.

gen bomb, and in earlier years he had associated with Communist sympathizers.[2]

It became a prime objective of the Eisenhower administration to prove that it was doing more to root out subversives than had the prior Truman administration. In October, the President proudly announced that in the first four months of his new, stricter loyalty program, 1,456 employees had been sacked. Vice-President Nixon later claimed that "thousands of Communist, fellow travelers, and security risks have been thrown out" of government jobs, citing the figure of 6,926. This was sheer bunk.

Of the first batch of 1,456 firings, only 29 involved charges of disloyalty. This was later revised to 422 "subversives," out of a new total of 2,429 dismissals. The rest were tipplers, blabbermouths, women with children born out of wedlock, and homosexuals. It didn't matter that the search for subversives was such a fruitless exercise. *Somebody* had to be blamed. It helped to explain how Russia got the bomb, and why China fell to the Communists, and how, after winning World War II at such a sacrifice, the postwar world was such a frightening and uncertain place.

The witchhunt was conducted from the highest levels of the federal government to the lowliest town council. It reached from public into private life, and spread suspicion and fear through businesses and factories, publishing houses, courthouses, executive suites, Hollywood, academe, churches, and communities. Some, like Nathan Pusey, the president of Harvard, were brave and powerful enough to keep McCarthyism from their own doors, but no one could simply ignore it. And for most, there was no refuge from the hysteria.

At the State Department, it was necessary to find out who had "lost" China. A prime candidate was John Paton Davies, Jr., who had been the political advisor to General Joseph Stilwell, Commander of U.S. forces in China during the war. Davies, an "old China hand," had seen the decadence and corruption of Chiang Kai-shek's regime, and had warned of a Communist takeover. His goal was to have an open-door policy toward the Chinese Communists, to avoid driving them into the arms of the Soviets. Though "soft" on the Chinese Communists in the sense that he forecast their victory over Chiang Kai-shek— Davies was a hard-liner against the Soviets.

2. In late 1981 I talked to one of the four members of the 1953 Atomic Energy Commission (AEC) who had voted to deny Oppenheimer his security clearance. I asked him if it were happening today, would the AEC give Oppenheimer a clearance? "Of course," he replied.

Davies's approach was no different than the diplomacy advocated by Henry Kissinger and adopted by President Richard Nixon twenty-five years later. Yet to Red hunters like the young Vice-President, Richard Nixon, it was tantamount to treason. Eight times Davies was called before Loyalty Boards; eight times he was cleared. Finally, he was dragged before a ninth that found him not "disloyal," but suffering from "a definite lack of judgment, discretion, and reliability." He was booted out of the State Department in November 1954.

One did not have to be a policymaker to be suspect. In 1948, a former State Department functionary named Lawrence Duggan, was mentioned peripherally in testimony before the House Un-American Activities Committee, and later questioned by the FBI. Ten days later, his body was found sixteen floors below his office window. Congressman Karl Mundt announced that HUAC would release the names of the other suspects "as they jump out of windows."

Local communities resorted to blanket proscriptions. In July 1950, Birmingham, Alabama, warned all Communists and their associates, that they were to leave town within forty-eight hours. In August, Macon, Georgia passed a similar ordinance. Others decreed that Communists must register at city hall, the better to keep an eye on them. In New Rochelle, a Republican businessman dutifully signed up; he thought the ordinance had said "commuter," not "Communist."

One did not have to be a Communist to be branded subversive. One only had to have been associated with them, or share their beliefs. In Brooklyn, a judge sentenced five people to up to a year in prison for painting the word "peace" in Prospect Park. The judge explained: "When you see a bird that has the characteristics of a duck and associates with ducks, then it is reasonable to assume that it is a duck."

Distinctions between a "peacenick" and a Societ spy were lost in the search for subversives. This is not to say that there were no Communists about in 1953. There were. During the depression years, the American Communist party, with Moscow's encouragement and support, had recruited many naive students and radicals. Quite possibly there even had been some Communist spies. But a security risk—a loose-lipped drunk, for example—is not necessarily a subversive, and a subversive is not necessarily a spy. A Communist could be all three— or none of the above. Many who called themselves Communists as college students in the 1930s, had no intention of overthrowing the government in 1950. Yet, during the red scare, they were all swept into the same net.

In some ways, private industry was even more paranoid than the government. On many company organization charts, a new category showed up: "Vice-President for Internal Security." No organization, no person, was immune. An old and distinguished publishing house forced the resignation of its editor in chief because he was publishing not only best-sellers, but progressive and even radical literature. Academe shielded few: One University of California Los Angeles English professor was called before HUAC even though the only organizations he belonged to were the American Association of University Professors, the association of former Rhodes Scholars, and Phi Beta Kappa.

In show business, actors and actresses with supposed Communist backgrounds were "blacklisted" from employment. Madeline Lee, whose speciality was making baby noises on radio, was blacklisted because she had given a party five years earlier to raise money for a Communist "front" organization. This Madeline Lee was confused with a Madaline Lee who played Miss Blue on *Amos 'n Andy*. The latter Miss Lee was so overwhelmed with hate mail that an anti-Communist blacklist sheet had to call off the hounds. The first Ms. Lee *resembled* an actress named Camille Ashland, who had a part on the TV show *Danger*. Miss Ashland was besieged by angry phone calls. Finally, there was an actress named Madeline Pierce who, like Madeline Lee, was a baby gurgler. She was blacklisted. Apparently all baby gurglers were suspect.

What is so extraordinary about this, is the willingness of so many people to suspect the worst. There have always been haters in America, the kind of men who like to dance around a burning cross or bait Jews. McCarthy was a perfect outlet for their bile. And he tapped an anti-intellectual, anti-Establishment streak by villifying the "eggheads" and effete Easterners who had sold out to the Commies at Yalta and in China.

But with the help of the newspapers, McCarthy also won over a good many decent, ordinary people who had no particular bias. These were people who were afraid, who simply could not understand why the postwar world had turned so sour. It is perhaps easier for us to live with the threat of nuclear desctruction today, after thirty years of risk. But to an average person in 1952, the idea of Joe Stalin with an atom bomb, was quite terrifying. It would have been bad enough if the Soviets had the power and resources to build the bomb on their own. But to have someone—an American, an American *Jew*—just hand them the secret, well that was almost unbearable. The Rosenbergs proved that spies existed. Few doubted that the Soviets would do everything possible to steal *all* our secrets.

McCarthy's wizardry was in his ability to blur the distinction between a few real spies, like Julius Rosenberg, and a large number of people who had once flirted with communism—or known someone who had. He did it by touching the nerve of fear, a raw nerve that distorts reality. With his incessant lies fanned and made credible by the press, he led millions from worry to mindless paranoia. To them, the striped-pants "pinkos" at the State Department, and Julius Rosenberg, were all part of the same seamless, treacherous conspiracy.

In the rush to ferret out subversion, to expose and to accuse, all notions of individual rights were wiped away. Values basic to the Constitution—tolerance of dissent, freedom of expression, due process protection for minorities—were ignored and forgotten by great masses of people. In McCarthy's home state of Wisconsin, the Madison *Capital Times* drafted a petition made up entirely of quotes from the Declaration of Independence and the Bill of Rights. A reporter was sent out to a street corner to solicit signatures from passersby. At the end of the day, all of the 111 people he had approached had refused to sign it. "Too subversive," some said. (In another Midwestern town, the same test produced 98 of 100 refusals; in New Orleans, 28 of 34 refused to sign, and some called the FBI to investigate.)

From time to time I was able to rescue a victim of this sickness. I hadn't been able to help Aaron Coleman, but I did gain a bit of due process for the Fort Monmouth "lepers." And I would occasionally review the file of some Army officer who was about to be discharged as a subversive.

One day the assistant secretary for personnel asked for my help with the file of an officer about to face a termination hearing. The file was enormous, about three feet thick and containing about four thousand pages. The officer's security clearance had long since been revoked; he was an officer "leper." His name was Lieutenant Colonel Kenneth C. Haycraft. It was a name I recognized, since Kenneth Haycraft had been one of my high school heroes as an All-American end at the University of Minnesota in 1928.

After college he had been active in the Minnesota Farmer-Labor party and had been their candidate for mayor of Minneapolis in 1938. He was a member of the Minnesota National Guard, and when it was called up in 1940, he went on active duty and served four years in the Pacific. He held a top secret security clearance from 1940 to about 1952, when it was revoked because of alleged prewar Communist ties. He was now about to face a Board of Officers who probably would discharge him as unfit for active duty. The Personnel assistant secretary was floundering. What did Haycraft's four thousand-page file say? I suspected that the file had become so massive because every reviewer had based his own recommendation on other reviewers's assumptions, and that through laziness, person after person had filled the file with junk of no consequence.

I asked Joe Sullivan, one of my associates, to dig through those thousands of pages. Find the original allegations, I said. What are they? Who made them? If we could find them, I thought maybe we could verify them.

Sullivan came back eight days later. The original charges were simple. Some political enemies in St. Paul and in Minneapolis said that in 1938 when Haycraft ran for mayor, he was a Communist. There was nothing else.

I telephoned Warren Burger, an assistant attorney general. He had been a leader of the Minnesota Delegation at the 1952 Republican Convention, and I figured he ought to know. The future Chief Justice said he knew about Haycraft, but not enough, and suggested I talk to Harold Stassen.

So I called on Stassen. The former governor of Minnesota then had a White House office and was running the foreign aid program. Yes, he had known Kenneth Haycraft. Yes, he had been a tough political opponent, and a Farmer Laborite. Yes, there was a Communist group in Minnesota which always supported the Farmer-Labor candidates, which just made it easier for Republicans. But Haycraft a Communist? No.

There was such intense political hatred in Minnesota at the time, said Stassen, that many charges like that were made. If we only had that sort of charge against Haycraft, we should examine it carefully, not accepting it without proof. Stassen's observations encouraged us to run down all the allegations. It took a few months, but Haycraft's security clearance was restored. Haycraft was later promoted to colonel, and served out an honorable career until retirement.

CHAPTER XIV

A Matter of Loyalty

My rescue attempts in the fall of 1953 were mostly aimed at individuals. Any systematic reform, like trying to improve the procedures of the Loyalty Boards, was out of the question. I did not know enough about the detailed workings of the Loyalty Boards to challenge them. I was a conforming civil servant; I did not seriously question the administrations's loyalty policy.

I did have glimmerings of the potential for abuse. It bothered me that FBI reports were given such weight. I had seen many of them in the past seven years and thought they were remarkable collections of trivia, with much sheer garbage. Such reports were, after all, only unevaluated data picked up from all sources, some reliable, some not. To Roy Cohn, it seemed, they were indictments. Once when he was raging to me over the telephone that the Army had failed to fire someone on whom we had an FBI report, I said, "So what; they are merely hearsay." I could hear him say to someone in the room, "He says FBI reports are merely hearsay. Remember that." An FBI agent called on me at the Pentagon a day or so later, saying that Mr. Hoover wanted me to explain why I had called FBI reports hearsay. Stevens and I decided that I'd better call on the miffed FBI director to assure him of the Army's admiration for him and his great organization, which I did the next day.

Before I came to the Army, the only person I knew who had been hauled before a Loyalty Board was Najeeb Halaby, who at the time was a top aide to the secretary of defense. (He later became president of Pan American Airways and his daughter became Queen Noor of Jordan.) His offense? In 1939, upon graduation from Yale Law School, he and his classmate Lloyd Cutler, wanted to ride the Trans-Siberian railroad from Moscow to Vladivostok. The State Department refused permission but the young adventurers went anyway. Halaby soon joined the Navy and served as an aircraft carrier pilot in the Pacific war. Subsequently he entered the government, quickly reaching a high position in the Defense Department. In 1949, the patriotic secretary of defense, Louis Johnson, heard of Halaby's defiance of a State Department visa restriction ten years earlier. He ordered Halaby to stand trial to prove his suitability for continued employment in the face of this outrage. The Loyalty Board laughed at the charge (but not so Johnson could hear them) and sent Halaby back to work.

Years later when I learned the fate of Coleman, "Z," and some of the other Monmouth "lepers," I realized that the procedures of the Loyalty Boards were subject to abuse. But at the time, I had no sense of the potential for injustice. Indeed, I spent most of my time *defending* Army Loyalty Boards from McCarthy. In my experience in the Army counselor's office, I found that the men on these boards all tried to do the right thing, and quite regularly cleared people who had been unfairly accused.

This was a red flag to McCarthy. He was determined to drag before his committee those board members who had cleared the alleged subversives so he could expose the whitewash.

In September, before I took the Army job, McCarthy had demanded that Secretary Stevens make available several Loyalty Board members responsible for clearing employees. These Loyalty Board judges must have been "incompetent or in sympathy with communism," declared McCarthy. Stevens caved in and turned over Loyalty Board members for a grilling in one of McCarthy's "executive sessions." In October, McCarthy announced that his staff was preparing to call more Loyalty Board members; in November he announced that he intended to subpoena one member to testify about his own Communist links. On December 10, he announced that the Army boards did a job "foul beyond words" in clearing certain employees. On December 13, he states that some board members were "as bad as being Communists."

The Republican right wing, including the mighty Robert A. Taft, had long thought that it was necessary that *all* these boards be subject to "congressional review." The boards were, after all, the product of Democratic administrations, of Roosevelt, Truman, Acheson, and Marshall, the crowd that had given the country what McCarthy referred to as "twenty years of treason."

I was dead set against letting McCarthy get at the board members. The people who served on them were fairly high-ranking officers and senior civil servants selected by their superiors. The assignment was not a pleasant one, nor popular, but they did it as a duty. If McCarthy was allowed to smear them every time they cleared an accused, there was no hope of objectivity or fairness. Furthermore, presidential orders decreed that their proceedings were to be secret, both to protect them against just such attacks as McCarthy was trying to make, and also to protect the reputations of the accused, most of whom turned out to be innocent. All that would become a farce if McCarthy was allowed to rehash the proceedings in his "executive sessions" and then publicize his own smear version of the event and the people involved. I told Cohn, and McCarthy also, that until President Eisenhower revoked or modified the existing Truman directives, those directives still governed, and I would fight to stop any McCarthy interrogation of board members until I was "shot down in flames."

I went to Stevens with my concerns, and he agreed that the Army should not reveal any names of Loyalty Board members, or permit future congressional interrogation of former panel members. He had one reservation, however. The Army could not take this position alone. It had to be administration policy; getting the support of the administration he left to me.

I quickly got informal concurrences from Struve Hensel, general counsel of the Defense Department, and from Assistant Attorney General A. Lee Rankin. But I thought written assurances would be more dependable so we asked for a written ruling from the attorney general, Herbert Brownell.

My timing was unfortunate. The attorney general had just made a speech making extensive use of supposedly confidential FBI files to publicly blacken the name of the late Harry Dexter White, a Truman Treasury official. In the same speech he also attacked the Truman Loyalty-Security program. In light of Brownell's speech, explained Rankin, the Justice Department was in no position to respond to our request.

But I did get private assurances of support. At a December meeting with the attorney general, Hensel and I were assured that the Justice Department was on our side. Earlier I had redrafted the old Truman orders, in different form but to the same end, and urged Brownell that my document be published as an Eisenhower Executive Order to supersede the old Truman rules. I hoped that if I could refuse McCarthy's demands using an Eisenhower ruling, it would lift some of McCarthy's heat from us. We would no longer be relying on the old rules of "those traitors." This gambit failed, however. Justice didn't want to put anything in writing.

Brownell did say, in effect, we are for you one hundred percent, but don't let McCarthy know that we support you, and don't let him know that you have consulted us. Fine, I thought. We support you, but don't tell anyone.

As winter approached, I could sense a confrontation with McCarthy, and I began to realize that I was going to be there all alone when it came—walking the gangplank by myself.

McCarthy seemed untouchable. Even high government officials who secretly opposed him were too frightened to say so. When John Foster Dulles became secretary of state, in January 1953, his first speech to the employees of the department, then under relentless McCarthy attack, sounded like a diatribe on loyalty by McCarthy himself. As late as January 1954, only one senator, Fulbright of Arkansas, voted against a huge budget for McCarthy's loose cannon, the Investigations Subcommittee. All the others went along, despite McCarthy's obvious misuse of power all through 1953, and even after McCarthy had boasted emptily on the Senate floor about the number of subversives he had collared and was about to turn over to the Justice Department.

In the past, a few people in public life had dared defy him. During the 1952 Democratic presidential primaries, the four leading contenders spoke out. Averill Harriman, former ambassador to Russia, said that McCarthy was "engineering the beginning of a Fascist movement." Senator Estes Kefauver of Tennessee, famous for his Senate investigation of organized crime, called McCarthy "one of the greatest threats to the nation." And Senator Richard Russell of Georgia, a great Southern power in the Senate, criticized "hucksters of hysteria . . . [who] would curb our liberties in the name of fighting Communism."

The nominee, Illinois governor Adlai Stevenson, called McCarthyism the "trademark of a new breed of political demagogue."

One of the most publicized stands had been taken in June 1950 by Republican Senator Margaret Chase Smith of Maine, who made world headlines when she presented her Declaration of Conscience to the Senate. She stated that the nation should stop being tools of totalitarian techniques, and she urged the Republican party not to try to ride to power on the "four horsemen of calumny—Fear, Ignorance, Bigotry, and Smear." Five other Republicans had joined her in her declaration, but after McCarthy's destruction of Tydings and Lucas in the November election, her colleagues became nearly mute. Mrs. Smith remained undaunted by McCarthy, and he wisely left her alone. By 1953, however, she truly stood alone. McCarthy was able to bully virtually everyone else in the government.

The Eisenhower White House was silent on McCarthy all through 1953. Rumor was strong that the President didn't like McCarthy, but his opinion was not widely known. "I just will not—I *refuse*—to get in the gutter with that guy," he was reported to have told his aides. The McCarthys were the only Senate family not invited to the President's 1953 White House reception for the Congress. Nevertheless, the American public knew that before the 1952 election Eisenhower had suffered a bear hug by McCarthy on his campaign train in Wisconsin. And Eisenhower had proclaimed McCarthy "good for Americans."

By the late autumn of 1953, I had seen, from a singular, firsthand view, the destructive force of McCarthyism. Objectively, I always had known he was wrong, but, for a time, I just found it irritating. The antics of McCarthy seemed ridiculous; I felt that their novelty and popularity would soon wear out, like a cheap toy. It was only when I began dealing with him, and seeing his destruction firsthand, day after day, that I began to recognize the devastation he and his "underground" were having on simple and decent people.

On Thanksgiving Day, 1953, I sat at a family dinner, listening to the cheerful conversation around my dining room table. My brother-in-law, a teacher at Duke University, was talking about a friend of his, a man we all knew, and who had a sensitive government job. He half jokingly referred to his friend as a Communist.

"Don't say that!" I exclaimed, banging my hand down on the table. "Don't say things like that!"

The conversation ceased. Startled, my wife Margaret and her family all turned and stared at me, astonished.

I repeated, "You just absolutely must not say a thing like that in this town. You don't know what it's like here. You live four hundred miles away. But here, in this town, just never, never make a remark like that, even in jest. It can absolutely ruin a person in a classified job."

I had embarrassed myself and the whole dinner table by my vehemence. But what I said was true.

CHAPTER XV

"I Don't Play That Way"

McCarthy was the main subject of discussions at most Washington cocktail parties I attended that autumn. And when people found out about my job, the questions would begin: "Have you *seen* him?" Do you *know* him? What's he really like?" Young women in particular were fascinated by him, in a horrified sort of way. I even put out my hand to one young woman and said that I had actually shaken hands with him, that very afternoon. "Ick," she said as she shuddered and drew back.

"How could you stand to be with him?" they'd ask. "Isn't he revolting?" I would say no; he's really very amiable, which was true—when he was offstage.

What I didn't tell them was the uneasy feeling I always had that McCarthy was somehow trying to trap me. He had a very sharp and retentive mind, and could twist one's words into a weapon. Being around him was like sticking your hand into a snake pit to see if anything was there.

After a few such cocktail party experiences, Margaret and I agreed that we'd avoid talking about McCarthy. If cornered, I'd only say something like, "Oh, I've met him once or twice," and try to change the subject.

In some ways, McCarthy was not an easy man to explain. He was lazy, unprepared, and cared nothing about the accuracy of his "facts." Yet he once amazed me at lunch by delivering a very thorough, well-thought-out discourse on the administration's farm policy. He was by no means a stupid man, and if he had applied himself he could have been even more dangerous and powerful than he was.

McCarthy always carried around a briefcase that was supposedly stuffed with "secrets" and evidence of Communist plots. Actually, the briefcase carried nothing more than a bottle of bourbon, either Old Taylor, I. W. Harper, or Old Granddad. I learned this by following him into the men's room during more than one of his "Executive Sessions." He would calmly pull out his bottle, offer me a snort, and slug down about four ounces.

McCarthy was a prodigious drinker who would pour brandy into his breakfast coffee. In the mid-morning and mid-afternoon, he would retire to his private office or a bathroom (stepping into a toilet stall if someone was there) for a quick shot. At lunch he would usually have a cocktail or two, and he would begin drinking in earnest at about five P.M. Cocktails gave way to highballs after dinner, and continued on into the night. He drank about a quart of liquor a day. He showed it, too. Between the time I first saw him in 1946 and the fall of 1953, he put on about fifty fleshy pounds. McCarthy was also afflicted by numerous physical ailments, from a bum leg to a bad stomach to severe sinus headaches.

But he had tremendous energy. He could carouse all night with his drinking buddies, but then after a few hours' sleep on his couch, he'd plunge in again, denouncing traitors, winking, roaring, grinning, and grabbing headlines.

I had considerable social contact with Roy Cohn and Frank Carr that autumn. Despite the abuse he gave me over Schine, I genuinely liked Cohn. Except where Schine was concerned, I saw him as the only restraining influence on McCarthy. Carr was pleasant enough, but I knew that whatever I said to Carr was immediately repeated to Cohn.

One evening in early December, Cohn and I went to a radio studio to hear McCarthy make a nationwide radio address. Ex-President Truman had made a radio broadcast statement critical of McCarthyism. He had said he was not criticizing McCarthy but the "ism," so McCarthy demanded equal time from the networks. Most people doubted he would get it, including me. I asked McCarthy how he expected to pull it off. He replied, "The boys say I have a majority of the FCC (Federal Communications Commission). I think I'll get the time.''

He did, and used it, not to reply to Truman, but to attack the ''whining, simpering appeasement'' of the new administration. This was ten months into the Eisenhower presidency. The administration made no reply.

After the speech, we went to one of Cohn's favorite haunts, the Cub Room of the Stork Club (the tourists waited behind a red velvet rope to get a table in the main dining room; celebrities like Cohn were ushered immediately to the more intimate Cub Room.) We sat at a table with William Randolph Hearst, Jr., and his wife, and Hearst told McCarthy how delighted he was with the speech. Joe ate lavishly and had a few highballs; I had a Coke, as did Cohn. From time to time Cohn would tell Leonard Lyons, a gossip columnist who was at the next table insulting him, to get lost. Hearst picked up the tab, expensive for those days. I asked McCarthy, ''Doesn't it bother you to have Hearst pay for your meals?'' He chuckled: ''If they want to bribe me by buying my meals, it doesn't bother me.''

Roy Cohn paid for a few of my lunches that fall as well. I was amused at what a big shot this twenty-six-year-old was. He seemed to have plenty of resources, and when he went to a place like the Cub Room or a restaurant where he was known, the check would simply never appear.

One morning after I had spent the night at the Drake Hotel, I found that my room had been paid for and charged to Roy Cohn's account. I insisted on paying anyway, and got a receipt. But I was not always so foresighted.

Once, when I suggested we go to the fights at Madison Square Garden, Cohn got the tickets. They were expensive—twenty dollars apiece—but when I tried to pay him at the Garden he said that he had gotten the tickets for nothing and refused to take my money. Not long after that I asked him to reserve theater tickets for me and two of my aunts at a popular Broadway musical show. At the box office, my money was refused; Cohn, it turned out, had prepaid the tickets. I was suspicious of this generosity since I did not want to be in Cohn's debt. I decided to pay him back. When I next saw him I stuffed the money into his breast pocket. I told him I didn't want to be obligated to him. He was highly offended and said, ''I don't play that way.'' But I found out later, and painfully, that he did.

With me, Cohn was usually pleasant except on the subject of Schine.

He later broadened his abuse to include criticisms for "subversives" we had not fired. He would call me at all hours of the night, always from a table at the Cub Room or some other night spot, coupling an attack on the Army for failing to fire an employee on whom we had an FBI report with inquiries as to when Dave was getting assigned to New York. On that subject he was particularly generous with his abuse.

At the time, our four-month-old daughter, Rebecca had colic. Between Roy's late evening complaints about Schine and Rebecca's nocturnal complaints, I didn't get much sleep.

By January there was no respite from Cohn on the subject of Schine. On Friday, January 8, I went to Amherst College in Massachusetts to make a speech to the senior class about Army draft requirements. It was a subject of great interest because about half a million men were being drafted yearly. Following the speech, as I was packing my bag to leave the Lord Jeffrey Inn, the phone rang. It was Frank Carr this time, with a crisis: Dave Schine had been ordered to do KP duty at Fort Dix on Sunday morning.

I refused to intervene, and told Carr not to tell Cohn where he had found me, or how to reach me. He insisted that he had to do so, and so I asked him to give me a few minutes to pack and get out of the room. I then immediately called the front desk and told the man at the switchboard to say, if any call came to me from New York, that I could not be found.

Cohn proved to be more clever than that, however. Within moments he telephoned the hotel from New York via a station-to-station call, which did not identify the call as being long-distance. The operator put him through to my room. I picked up the phone and said, "Hello." Cohn said, "Hello, John." I hung up the phone.

[III]

WINTER 1954

CHAPTER XVI

"Have You a Record
of This?"

The New Year found the Army still on the defensive. With only occasional lulls, McCarthy and his men were attacking on all three fronts. They were still searching for subversives in the ranks and getting headlines, even if they weren't finding any spies; they were still demanding the heads of Loyalty Board members who had cleared alleged Communists; and they were still pressing for special favors for Private G. David Schine.

The resistance from the Army was at best fitful. Officially the policy was still appeasement, though I had tried to convince McCarthy that his investigation of Fort Monmouth was fruitless. From time to time I tried to persuade Stevens to enlist Defense Department support in our negotiations with McCarthy, but he wouldn't hear of it. Once he snapped, "Let me quarterback this thing, will you, John?"

But then in the winter of 1954 McCarthy's attack took a new turn. The Army gradually stiffened, suddenly broke again, and then counterattacked. Fed up, I began to refuse McCarthy's demands. And the administration slowly, reluctantly, and secretly, joined the fray.

David Schine's stint at Fort Dix was due to end January 16. After a two-week leave, he was to be sent to Camp Gordon, Georgia, to be trained as a military police officer. When informed that his tour would last eight weeks, I passed along the information to Cohn, who kept up his incessant refrain and demands that Schine be transferred to New York.

On January 15, I stopped in to see Cohn at the Capitol, and told him that Schine would probably be sent overseas after Camp Gordon, like most draftees. What will happen if Schine goes overseas? I asked.

"Stevens is through as secretary of the army," he answered.

"Oh come on now, Roy," I said. "Can that stuff. Really, what's going to happen if Schine gets an overseas assignment?"

"We'll wreck the Army," he shot back. He warned that McCarthy had "enough stuff on the Army" to have an investigation run indefinitely. He threatened to smear us in the newspapers, and to investigate General Cornelius Ryan, the commander at Fort Dix—just as soon as Schine finished basic training. On and on he went, threatening the Army and denouncing "lousy, double-crossing Stevens."

On January 17, Secretary Stevens left for the Far East on a month-long tour of military bases. Before he left we had learned that Schine's tour in Georgia was to last five months, not eight weeks. Stevens had arranged a special meeting with McCarthy on the fifteenth in order to tell him about Schine's future duty requirements, and I just assumed that McCarthy had relayed the new information to Cohn.

On the eighteenth, Frank Carr called me on another matter and I asked him how Cohn had taken the news. What news? he asked. I told him that Schine's assignment at Camp Gordon was to last five months.

That bit of information may seem innocuous enough, but it was a declaration of war to Roy Cohn. He was in Florida at the time, vacationing at the Schine family hotel in Boca Raton. Within ten minutes he called me demanding to know if the news was true. I asked him if he was going to stay in Florida. "How can I when this has happened?" he angrily replied.

Seven hours later, he was in Washington. And the next morning Carr called to say that McCarthy wanted to quiz six Army Loyalty Board members. If they did not show up voluntarily, he said, McCarthy would subpoena them. I asked Carr what had happened. He replied that Cohn was back now, and that Joe wanted these witnesses.

It was clear that two fronts had merged: The McCarthyites planned to use the Loyalty Boards as a weapon to punish the Army for mistreating Schine. Stevens was gone, so it was up to me to decide what to do.

Carr read me a list of the people McCarthy wanted to quiz that afternoon. I was damned if I would send them to McCarthy's star chamber. An hour before the hearing, Carr called me and asked, "Are they coming?" I said no. I would appear at the 2:00 P.M. hearing but no Loyalty Board members.

"Joe doesn't like to be surprised," he warned. "You better go see him first."

I met McCarthy in the hallway of the Senate Office Building. I told him that the Loyalty Board members would not be made available. To my surprise, he was perfectly amicable about it as we walked together down the long corridor toward the committee room. On entering the room, he told the waiting press that he would give the Loyalty Board judges until Friday to appear. He didn't want to ask them about their decision to spare Communists, he said, but about graft and corruption in the execution of their duties.

I thought, you son of a bitch, you've got me. He had found a loophole. My refusal was based on the sanctity of the judical process. So McCarthy had quickly thought up a new gambit: interrogating government officials for corruption, which was well within the charter of the Senate Permanent Subcommittee on Investigations. He was a master at improvisation and I had just seen the master at work. The few minutes it took for him to walk down the hall with me was all the warning he needed.

Late that afternoon I gathered together all Army employees in the Washington area who had ever served on a Loyalty Board. Standing in the secretary's conference room I instructed them that none of them was to respond to any subpoena from the McCarthy committee. Instead, they were to bring their summons to my office where I would decide what to do. This announcement, needless to say, was received happily.

It was time to get reinforcements. I telephoned the deputy attorney general, William Rogers, and said to him: Either stand up now, or the press will say that the Eisenhower administration had backed down before McCarthy. The Army can't do it alone. I asked to see the attorney general, and he agreed.

Rogers called back in a few minutes and asked me to first go to see Senator John McClellan, who had led the walkout of Democratic members from McCarthy's subcommittee many months earlier. Rogers had already set up the appointment, so I went at once. After McClellan heard the story, he irritably advised me that he would do nothing unless the Army gave him a report in writing. Unfortunately, I had no such document.

A month earlier, one of the younger lawyers in my office had drafted a letter to McCarthy justifying our refusal to turn over Loyalty Board members. My staff of eight lawyers[1] were men of superb abilities who expected as much of me as I did of them. The three most junior were law review editors from the best law schools. They had been plucked from the Korean wartime draft pool by the Judge Advocate General's corps, and though actually Army officers, they wore mufti and passed as civilians. Into this letter of defiance one of them—Melvin Dow—had worked artful and well-reasoned arguments. (Around the office his colleagues referred to the document as "The Fuck-You Letter.")

Until now I had been unable to persuade the Justice Department to approve the letter. But now I had a chance to present these arguments to the attorney general. I asked Mel Dow and Charles Haskins to ride over to the Justice Department with me while we rehearsed answers to all possible questions. They were concerned that I might miss a cue.

At about 4:00 P.M. on January 21, I walked into Attorney General Herbert Brownell's large paneled office on the fifth floor of the Justice Department Building. I was surprised to see not only the attorney general and Rogers, but four top White House advisors. Two of them I knew: the chief of the White House congressional liaison office, Major General Jerry Persons, a longtime friend and former Army chief of legislative liaison, and former senator and then U.N. delegate Henry Cabot Lodge, another longtime acquaintance (we had served in the same outfit in Europe in the last months of the war). Then there were two I had never met: Gerald Morgan, a White House special counsel, and most importantly, Sherman Adams, the former governor of New Hampshire who was the President's Chief of Staff and Eisenhower's closest advisor. Brownell, under whom I had served at the Republican National Committee eight years earlier, motioned me to a chair and told me to tell the story of the Army's fight with McCarthy.

When I had finished, Governor Adams, who appeared to be asleep in his chair, looked up and asked, "Have you a record of this?"

1. The lawyers involved were Lewis Berry, Charles Haskins, Howard Sacks, Peck Hill, Joe Sullivan, Melvin Dow, John Simon, and Norman Dorsen. The latter three, who worked most closely with me, I often thought of and still remember as The Young Giants.

I answered that I did not.

"Don't you think you ought to start one?" he suggested.

Brownell agreed that the Loyalty Board members had to be protected from McCarthy's "review." He added, however, that in this case McCarthy may have cornered us by demanding to interrogate Loyalty Board members about fraud and misconduct. If McCarthy subpoened them, we would probably have to let the officials respond, although we could instruct them to refuse to answer any questions directed at their participation in the Loyalty Program. The group as a whole agreed that it would be better not to collide with McCarthy head-on, but rather to try to talk to the Republican members of his subcommittee. I was extremely encouraged by the fact that the White House was finally paying attention.

We began at once. Gerald Morgan and I went directly from the meeting to see Senator Everett Dirksen, whom I had never met, but who knew Morgan well. He seemed genuinely upset, and made it clear that the Republican members of the committee would try to put a stop to McCarthy's abuse of the Army, particularly the pressures on behalf of Schine and the improper threat of subpoening Loyalty Board members in retaliation. He added that it might take a week or two to fire Roy Cohn, but that this, too, should happen. As he put it, "Cohn was put on the committee by the Hearst press, and Joe doesn't dare lose that support."

The next morning Lew Berry and I talked to the other senators. Our blitz on the committee apparently worked: That afternoon, after the committee had met, McCarthy backed down—at least for the moment. He said that it was not urgent for the committee to hear Loyalty Board members, and that he would wait for Secretary Stevens to return from the Orient to discuss the matter further.

Later in the afternoon, McCarthy's secretary called. McCarthy wanted to see me. I was to appear at his home at 8:30 P.M.

It had been snowing that week; the temperature had dipped near zero and the streets were nearly impassable. The McCarthys lived in the Woodner, a then-fancy apartment building on Sixteenth Street. Earl Warren, the Chief Justice, lived there, too.

I was apprehensive about the meeting. McCarthy could be very amiable, but by now I knew how dangerous he could be and I went with great caution. My wife Margaret didn't want me to go at all. She had never met McCarthy but she was afraid to have me go there alone.

It was not long after Christmas, and the apartment was full of loot from McCarthy's many supporters—liquor, hams, sausages, huge cheeses. All through the evening McCarthy drank highballs and sampled the goodies, pressing me to join him. I declined the liquor; but on behalf of the unknown members of the Army Loyalty Boards, I ate sausage, baloney, salami, and liverwurst; I also ate blue cheese, green cheese, cream cheese, Swiss cheese, and limberger cheese. And when I left for the evening, I was carrying as a gift, a package of assorted cheeses and sausages—Wisconsin's best.

Jeannie, McCarthy's wife, sat in the corner "answering Christmas cards." McCarthy's former secretary, she was a stylish, handsome woman. She had played a major role in McCarthy's sabotage of Millard Tydings in Maryland in 1950, helping to orchestrate the distribution of four hundred thousand doctored photographs showing Tydings together with the former head of the Communist party. I was quite sure that she wasn't answering Christmas cards at all this evening, but rather taking notes on what I said. During the evening, I drank five cups of tea. I kept getting up to go to the bathroom, or to reexamine the tables full of Christmas loot, all the while trying to peek over her shoulder to see what she was writing.

Not long after my arrival, McCarthy got a long-distance phone call from George Sokolsky, the Hearst columnist. The call was apparently about Schine, because McCarthy soon handed the phone to me, and I found myself being interrogated about the "flare-up" between Roy Cohn and me. I felt sure the call had been prearranged. I denied any "flare-up," and repeated the same refrain I always gave Cohn: Schine's treatment would be exactly the same as all other draftees, no better, no worse.

When I hung up, McCarthy started in on Schine, asking why it wasn't possible to give him some obscure assignment in New York and then forget about it. He repeated this wish at least ten times during the course of the evening. He also warned that the Army was walking into large-scale "vendetta" attacks from Cohn, who, he feared, was liable to resign over the whole thing. Even if Cohn did resign, he warned, he would carry out his campaign of vilification against the Army.

I told him that I couldn't see why that should worry him, since he had gotten along without Cohn for years. McCarthy then melodramatically dropped his voice and said, "The walls have ears; maybe my room is tapped.'' Then he said he had to be careful about Cohn's resignation—he didn't want to be accused of being anti-Semitic.

At least three times he described Schine as "useless, no good, just a miserable little Jew," I was convinced he wanted me to either agree with him or utter some slur which his wife could record.

With constant references to Cohn's influence with the right-wing press, McCarthy kept on about Schine. Once or twice he referred to an "original agreement" between Cohn and Stevens that stipulated that Schine would be stationed in New York after basic training. Cohn had also repeatedly invoked this "agreement" while berating me. I told McCarthy, as I had told Cohn, that Stevens had never told me that he had made any such agreement. As I had understood from Stevens, he had declared that Schine must complete his sixteen weeks of basic training before the Army would even consider what happened to him next.

McCarthy seemed exasperated by the Schine affair. He told me that Cohn had accidentally done the Army a great favor by interfering so much in the Schine matter. Now, he said, his position was untenable. The Army could always accuse his committee of using its investigative powers as a lever to get better treatment for Private Schine.

So far as he was concerned, he said, the Army investigation was over. But, he added, he needed a way to save face. He had to show the press that he was still determined to interrogate Loyalty Board members. I could even be present so as to protect the Army, he said. Although he wouldn't ask them about the Loyalty-Security Program, he had allegations that some of them had been bribed to let Communists go. I said that we had to wait for Stevens to return before discussing his request. By then, I suggested, perhaps the press would have lost interest.

By about 11:15, Joe, amiable as usual, was helping me out the door with my armload of Wisconsin cheese.

When I got home, after briefly describing the evening to Margaret, I sat at the dining room table and began writing down everything that we said that evening. At eight the next morning, a Saturday, I drove to the Pentagon and dictated my notes into a recording machine. I remember that snow was swirling about outside and the huge building was almost empty.

CHAPTER XVII

The Pink Dentist

It is both typical and ironic that ultimate confrontation between the Army and Joe McCarthy was over the promotion of a dentist. The unpleasantries began, like so many others that January, with a phone call from Roy Cohn. On January 4, he informed me that the Army had "a captain or a major, a doctor or a dentist, who is on duty at Camp Kilmer, and who is a Communist." McCarthy and his boys didn't yet know the name or rank of this "Communist."

As soon as I hung up, I wrote a memo and had it hand delivered to the chief of army intelligence, Major General Arthur Trudeau. In it I told him the details of Cohn's phone call. Within two hours he came into my office and assured me that the Army knew about the situation, and that the officer was being discharged from the service. I thought he meant at once, within a day or so. I should have asked him, "When?"

During and for a time after the Korean War, all the military services suffered an acute shortage of doctors and dentists. Accordingly, Congress enacted a law to permit their draft into service. Irving Peress, a New Yorker, was one of those drafted under the Doctors and Dentists Draft Act.

Assigned the grade of captain, Peress was promoted to major some months later under the provisions of a congressional grade adjustment law that Joe McCarthy had voted for. In the same adjustment, six hundred sixty-seven other doctors, dentists, and veterinarians were also advanced to grades commensurate with their standing in private practice.

A security check later showed that Peress had written "Federal Constitutional Privilege" on his loyalty questionnaire, instead of checking "yes" or "no" when asked about his membership in certain proscribed "subversive organizations." In effect, he had taken the Fifth.

This would have been enough to deny Peress a commission had it been noticed. When it was discovered many months later, separation steps were commenced at once. On December 30, 1953, five days before Cohn heard ot it, the Army Vice Chief of Staff approved Peress's service termination. He was given the standard option, available to any officer facing involuntary separation, of selecting any departure date up to ninety days thereafter. He chose to wait until March 31, 1954.

On January 23—the morning after my visit to McCarthy's apartment, George Anastos, one of Cohn's subordinates, called General Ralph Zwicker, the commandant at Camp Kilmer. Anastos demanded to know the name of the Communist captain-major-dentist-doctor who was hiding at his base. Zwicker was cautious enough to first call McCarthy's office to make certain that Anastos was authentic. Then he made a mistake. He revealed Peress's name. That was a violation of regulations, and it gave McCarthy just the weapon he was looking for to launch a new attack on the Army.

On Wednesday, January 27, Cohn telephoned me and said that the committee wanted to interrogate Major Peress at the New York Courthouse the following Saturday. "We warned you about this fellow," Cohn said, "and you've done nothing about it, and now we want him." I was surprised to learn that Peress was still in the Army. I wanted to get him out, so that McCarthy wouldn't be able to accuse a uniformed officer of being a "Fifth Amendment Communist." But I couldn't. Peress was entitled to up to ninety days lead time.

Three days later, Peress, still in uniform, appeared before the McCarthy committee. He invoked the Fifth, and McCarthy gave him the usual going-over.

That experience was enough to change Peress's mind about staying in the Army.

On Monday morning, February 1, he returned to Camp Kilmer and asked for separation the following day. His request was granted.

McCarthy had already announced that he wanted Peress in an open session three or four days later. The plan, of course, was to show the eager press that the Army had, in uniform, an officer who was a "Fifth Amendment Communist," a villain the Army had been shielding for many months.

McCarthy's patriotic tipster at Kilmer gave McCarthy the news that Peress had asked out and was scheduled to be dropped the next day. McCarthy was furious. He immediately rushed a letter over to Stevens's office demanding that Peress be held for a court-martial. As usual, he gave a copy of his letter to the press.

Stevens was still in the Orient, not due back for two days, so the letter was brought to me. At first, I just put it on my desk in exasperation. After awhile I got up and walked upstairs to talk to Lieutenant General Walter Weible, the chief of army personnel about whether the Army had the right to court-martial a person merely for exercising his constitutional privilege. We knew the answer—the Army had no such authority. In fact, within the previous year the Army had lost exactly such a case on appeal to the highest military tribunal.

I took the letter back to my office. I knew that I could find an assistant secretary still on duty in the building, and that he would insist that we order Peress held as McCarthy demanded. But I didn't want to hear it.

I walked over to my window and looked out into the winter darkness. McCarthy knew that Peress was no spy. There was no reason for the Army to hold Peress except to appease McCarthy.

I wasn't getting much help from the Justice Department or the White House on McCarthy. I was just getting a lot of abuse from Cohn about Schine, and a lot of unreasonable demands from McCarthy's one-man subcommittee. Stevens was out of the country and when he was here he did nothing but appease. There were no grounds to court-martial a drafted dentist who didn't even have a security clearance.

Still, all I had to do was hold Peress for a few days, not let him out of the Army, and tell McCarthy that we were "reviewing" the situation. I could at least play for time.

Then I found myself deciding not to do what McCarthy demanded and, instead, to let the dentist go. In short, to hell with McCarthy.

As I drove home that night, second thoughts began to surface. McCarthy of course would be furious; there would be trouble ahead. I had left the letter on my desk; I could always call the duty officer and tell him to hold Peress.

Despite my doubts, I just kept thinking: Fuck him; This is as far as I go.

Peress was dropped from the service that day. McCarthy was outraged, and his outrage was widely quoted. I knew that Stevens was going to be very unhappy when he returned from Japan two days later, so I sent one of my associates, Charles Haskins, out to San Francisco to meet his plane and to brief him and brace him.[1] If a reporter surprised Stevens with the news, he was likely to fumble and bluster. This way, I figured, he would have time to calmly disassociate himself from me.

When he arrived at National Airport, he did just that. He told the waiting reporters that if he had been here, he never would have permitted Peress to be separated from the Army.

But I had.

And just as simply as that, I had given McCarthy an opening. If Peress's name had been Smith or Johnson or Kelley, the subject might not have stayed alive very long. A bumper sticker that says Who Promoted Johnson? would not have been very exciting. But the name Peress had such a nice musical ring: "Who promoted Peress?"

When Peress was separated on February 2, he told the New York *Times* that McCarthy's charges against him—that he had engaged in subversive activities—were "sheer nonsense." McCarthy knew this to be true. He knew Peress had only one job—filling teeth, and that he had been ordered overseas, but had asked for a compassionate transfer. He wanted to be near his home in New York because his wife and child were both ill. The Red Cross had investigated the facts and had recommended the transfer, which the Army had then approved.

1. Stevens's obsessive fear of irritating McCarthy surfaced in early January when the Washington *Post* carried a detailed story of Schine's present and probable future duty stations. The story enraged Stevens, who ordered the Army Inspector General to put under oath all possible suspects (including me) who might have talked to the *Post* reporter. He was going to fire the leaker. I planned to refuse to be interrogated and see what Stevens would do. But when I learned that the investigating officer was to be Colonel Darien Duncan, a Sioux Falls High School classmate of mine, I decided not to make a ruckus that could cause Duncan any difficulties. In a few days the culprit was located—a brigadier general in Army personnel. At that point Chief of Staff Ridgway stepped in and told Stevens that he would not permit the secretary to discipline one of his generals for disclosing nonclassified information.

Nevertheless, while interrogating Peress, McCarthy asked him if some Communist in the Army had arranged to cancel his overseas orders so he could pursue Communist work in the New York area. Having already taken the Fifth on his political views, Peress could not selectively deny this absurd charge, so he had to invoke the Fifth again. This gave McCarthy another handle—not only had a "secret master" somewhere in the Army promoted Peress, but the "master" had then kept him in the United States for Communist work—and then arranged an honorable discharge when nothing less than a court-martial would do.

Though McCarthy tried to browbeat him into Fifth Amendment silence, Peress was able to get some remarks on the record. He said, under oath, that he had always been loyal to the United States, that he supported the Constitution, and that he opposed any effort to overthrow the government. Then he ended his statement by quoting the Psalms:

> His mischief shall return upon his own head and his violence shall come down upon his own pate.

McCarthy was too busy celebrating the fourth anniversary of his Wheeling speech to heed the warnings of a Jewish dentist. In a Lincoln's Day speech in Aberdeen, South Dakota, he denounced the Army's handling of Peress:

There was a "secret master" in the Pentagon who had made it possible for Peress to avoid overseas duty—the Red Cross, presumably! There was a Communist conspiracy which permitted Peress's promotion—the grade adjustment law which McCarthy himself had voted for! And there was a Communist conspiracy which let Peress slip out of the Army without the court-martial he so richly deserved—me!

My mail increased during this period. Postcards printed in large red letters asking "WHO PROMOTED PERESS?" began pouring in, all sent from Boston for some reason. One week fifteen hundred such cards arrived. The cards were sometimes simply addressed "Adams, Washington."

When I called Roy Cohn seeking some means to soften McCarthy's attacks, he told me in haughty and injured tones that he was "no longer authorized" to talk to me about such matters. From now on, I would have to deal with Frank Carr, or George Sokolsky, the Hearst columnist who had apparently assumed a quasi-official role in the McCarthy organization. Carr, in turn, recommended talks with Sokolsky.

The Hearst press thus moved in the intermediary between McCarthy and his staff on the one hand, and the Army on the other. There followed a strange interlude of phone calls with Sokolsky. I talked to him three times in the next eleven days about McCarthy's attacks on the Army. Two of the calls he initiated; the other I made at Carr's insistence. He repeatedly suggested that the Army arrange Dave Schine's military obligations to suit the McCarthy group, whereupon he said that he would "move in" and get McCarthy to stop his attacks on the Army. His conversation was punctured with such remarks as the Army should "be practical" and use "common sense" in dealing with this problem. I soon gathered that he thought the Army had a bigger problem with Schine than with Peress. He direly warned that the Army was in for a "two-year fight" with McCarthy—the length of Schine's service—unless we were "reasonable."

Dr. Irving Peress, the Long Island dentist who was drafted in October 1952 and who asserted his constitutional privilege instead of answering certain questions on his security-clearance questionnaire. His "Fifth Amendment" answer was not noticed until the following August, and it took another four months to make a final determination to separate him from the service. He was then on duty at Camp Kilmer, New Jersey, thirty miles from his home. He is shown here in April 1954, two months after his separation, holding one of numerous abusive and threatening letters he received after McCarthy's "Who Promoted Peress" campaign got under way. COURTESY WIDE WORLD PHOTOS.

The message was clear: "Be sensible" about Schine and McCarthy and his staff would "drop all that other stuff they're planning for the Army."

Meanwhile, Sokolsky kept me posted on McCarthy's progress in stirring up the country over the issue of Peress. I asked him if he had heard from McCarthy after a speech in San Francisco. "Yes," replied Sokolsky, "he's riding high. He's got California now." The next week when I talked to him he said, "The Irishman is really going good. He's got Texas now, and he's feeling pretty good!"

McCarthy was due back in Washington soon, and these reports made me sure that he was going to give the Army a hard time. I also knew that his return would bring Cohn back to Washington, and that we'd be back in the business of being investigated again.

Other newspapermen, of course, were less fond of McCarthy than Sokolsky. Phil Potter of the Baltimore *Sun* once said to me outside a McCarthy hearing room, "I despise him so; he revolts me so; it actually makes my skin crawl when he tries to shake hands or put his hand on my shoulder; I absolutely have to force myself to go into this hearing room."

The brothers Joseph and Stewart Alsop, whose political columns were widely read, were special irritants to McCarthy, who took pleasure in referring to them as the Allslops.

One day in mid-February, Joe Alsop came into my office looking for information on McCarthy. He told me that he had been sent by Henry Cabot Lodge, a fellow Brahmin, and the White House insider who had attended the January 22 meeting in the attorney general's office. While I had been in heavy and fairly well-publicized conflict with McCarthy for many weeks, Joe Alsop was the first political commentator to ask me what was going on.

I had no qualms about telling him. I began recounting the whole story, from my first meeting with McCarthy. The story was a long and involved one and I thought that I might as well save some time. I had prepared a forty-page memorandum on my dealings with McCarthy. Sherman Adams had suggested that I keep such a record back in January when I saw him at the attorney general's office.

I reached in my desk drawer, took out the memorandum, and handed it to Alsop. "It would be quicker and much more accurate if you just read this," I said.

The information I gave him was off-the-record. I asked him to respect the confidentiality of the source and not to print a word about the document or its contents. He agreed and began reading, snickering from time to time as he read something that amused him.

As he sat there, enjoying himself, I thought, "Now what in the hell did I do that for?" Why was I in such a rush that I couldn't have taken the time to talk to him about the problem instead of showing him those memos? It was going to be big news if it got out that I had a written record of the McCarthy group's misbehaviors of the past months, and it was going to be difficult to keep that fact out of the news if I went around showing my record to reporters, even on an off-the-record basis.

Admittedly, bits and pieces, and sometimes the entire story, were already known within the government, and I had even told it to one newspaperman. I had asked him to keep it confidential, though, primarily because I feared Stevens's wrath if he saw a story attributed to an Army source about how a congressional committee was mistreating the Army. But this was different; I hadn't just talked to somebody; I had now showed written proof to a reporter. I had given Alsop a target—to get that document busted loose from the administration.

After talking to Alsop, I decided that there's no use being just a little bit pregnant, so I called in three other reporters—Murry Marder of the Washington *Post,* Homer Bigart of the New York *Herald Tribune,* and Phil Potter of the Baltimore *Sun.* I showed them the document under the same conditions I had established with Alsop.

The reporters kept the story under wraps. But they dropped enough hints to alert Congress and the administration to the fact that there was a bomb out there, ready to explode. Phil Potter told Senator Symington about "a document" he had seen in the Pentagon; Symington, who already knew the whole story directly from both Stevens and me, was pretty sure that it must have been a document of mine. He knew that it couldn't have been Stevens's, because Stevens was another Yale man. Joe Alsop hinted to Fred Seaton, the assistant defense secretary, that he had seen a document in the Pentagon, and he added darkly that "there are lots of them floating around."

CHAPTER XVIII

"Even If It Is You, John"

McCarthy knew perfectly well that the answer to "Who promoted Peress?" was not "who," but "what"—the grade adjustment bill that he himself had voted for in Congress. But he still had to make a spectacle of finding "the secret master," the Communist spy who had orchestrated what he labelled as "this terrible conspiracy."

He began by summoning General Ralph Zwicker, the commander of Camp Kilmer, who had revealed Peress's name. I knew that Zwicker had almost nothing to do with promoting Peress, but I wasn't able to persuade Carr to call off the dogs. McCarthy's orders, he explained.

I flew to Camp Kilmer to talk to Zwicker before the hearing, taking along Charles Haskins. We were anxious to make Zwicker understand that neither names nor security information could be revealed. We left the meeting with the impression that Zwicker had already made substantial revelations about Peress to McCarthy's staff, starting with the disclosure of his name. This could make McCarthy's interrogation of Zwicker awkward, since Zwicker might now feel that he could not testify at the hearing concerning any information he may have already informally told McCarthy's people.

In the meantime, Stevens and I had written a three-page letter to

McCarthy explaining every step of Peress's military service, including the reason why he had not been held for court-martial. We wrote this letter because of McCarthy's wildly inaccurate speeches and the wave of telegrams they had provoked.

Anticipating more lies, I took with me to New York a number of copies of Stevens's letter, with the understanding that if McCarthy repeated his false charges to the New York press corps after the interrogation, I would concurrently distribute this letter to the press. It clearly branded as a lie each of McCarthy's allegations about the promotion, transfer, and separation of Major Peress.

I met McCarthy in the corridor of the Courthouse before the hearing. He was as affable as ever. Who wrote this letter? he asked. I said that I had drafted it, and that Stevens had approved it, line by line. McCarthy replied, ''Bob Stevens didn't write that letter.'' He said that the phrase ''political beliefs'' used in the letter was ''Communist jargon.'' Surely some ''Communist sympathizer'' had written that, he insisted.

The hearing began at 10:30, with Peress, now a civilian, on the stand. It was public, and the press and about two hundred spectators were there. I had told General Zwicker to sit in the back, out of sight so that McCarthy would not drag him into an argument. This did not stop McCarthy.

In the midst of questioning Peress, he called out to Zwicker:

> If I may say, General, you will be in difficulty if you refuse to tell us what sensitive work a Communist was being considered for. There is no executive order for the purposes of protecting Communists. I want to tell you right now, you will be asked that question this afternoon.[1]

At the lunch break, McCarthy fed the press more nonsense about the Communist conspiracy to promote Peress. I called Stevens, and then released the letter. McCarthy, needless to say, was furious at me for undercutting him that way. He would have his revenge.

In the afternoon, in an executive session closed to the public, McCarthy started in on Lieutenant Colonel Brown, Zwicker's intelligence officer. McCarthy's questions seemed to be bothering Brown, so I got up from my chair in the jury box and moved to a chair next to his. McCarthy was pushing Brown to release information about the

---

1. Some months later, Senator Sam Ervin was to remark that root canal and tooth nerve work were pretty sensitive.

Peress case, and Brown was balking. In a soft voice, I said to Brown, "Don't be nervous; go ahead; just tell him what the situation is."

Suddenly, McCarthy roared, "Mr. Adams take the witness stand." I refused, telling him that I was there as a representative of the Army, not a witness.

"You are ordered to take the stand and be sworn in!" he bellowed, holding up his right hand.

Sparring for time, I asked for permission to call the Army secretary. I could see Cohn trying to restrain McCarthy. Suddenly, McCarthy marched out of the room. A few moments later, he returned, trailed by his staff, and announced a new committee rule barring Counsel from Executive sessions. That meant me. Voted 7 to 0 by phone, I thought.

McCarthy clearly believed that I had muzzled Brown and Zwicker, frustrating him from spreading on the record whatever information he had already picked up from Zwicker. McCarthy apparently thought that if I were out of the room, Zwicker might talk. I went to a small waiting room in the rear of the courtroom, hoping that he would cool off and let me return. At about 3:30 the door opened and McCarthy appeared carrying his famous briefcase, the one supposedly stuffed with "secrets" and evidence of Communist plots. He pulled out its usual contents, a bottle of bourbon.

McCarthy had come back for his afternoon snort, but when he spotted me there, he took his shot and then started in: He was going to "get to the bottom of who promoted this Communist" and whoever did, was "going to pay for it, and pay plenty."

"Goddamn it, Joe," I said. "You know perfectly well, because I told you; nobody promoted him. The law was changed and he was advanced to the grade which was specified for people with the amount of private practice he had had."

McCarthy ignored this. He insisted that there had been "some kind of a Communist conspiracy" to give Peress an honorable discharge.

There was no conspiracy I told him, "nobody but me; I told you I received your letter, and that I determined we had no ground to court-martial him, so I took no steps for his retention. If you're after somebody, and if somebody is going to have to shed blood before you're satisfied, I'm it."

He looked at me. "If that's the way it's got to be, that's it. Even if it's you, John; if you are part of a conspiracy to promote a Fifth Amendment Communist and give him an honorable discharge, you'll pay for it."

Brigadier General Ralph W. Zwicker, commanding general of Camp Kilmer, New Jersey, at the time of Dr. Peress's discharge. Zwicker, a decorated combat veteran of the European campaigns, was the subject of McCarthy's famous charge in February 1954 that he was "not fit to wear the uniform" because Peress had been discharged from his post. He is shown here entering the hearing room in September 1954 to testify at McCarthy's censure hearing about that abuse and  matters related to it. Speaking to him is Censure Committee counsel Wallace Chadwick of Philadelphia. The woman at the left is Mary McGrory, then a reporter for the Washington *Star*. COURTESY WIDE WORLD PHOTOS.

Standing there, looking at him face-to-face, I realized that he fully intended to ruin me. It was not anger I was seeing, but ruthlessness. I was next—I was to be destroyed, unless something derailed him first.

Fortified by this exchange, and by the Old Grandad, McCarthy returned to the hearing room, now cleared of spectators and press, and lit into General Zwicker. By now Zwicker was sensitive to the personnel security regulations he may have violated by revealing Peress's name, and he was a good deal less forthcoming with McCarthy than McCarthy expected. The senator accused him of "hemming and hawing" at first, and of "doubletalk." Then he really warmed up. He said that Zwicker, a brigadier general in the Army, and a legitimate war hero at the Battle of the Bulge, did not have "the brains of a five year old child." "You should be removed from command," he said. He pronounced Zwicker not fit to wear the uniform.

For half an hour he heaped abuse on the general. It was a savage performance.

This time, however, McCarthy had gone too far.

CHAPTER XIX

"Kick the Brains Out . . ."

At 8:00 A.M. the following morning I was in Stevens's office telling him what happened and how I had been kicked out. He was chuckling with obvious amusement when General Ridgway and his deputy, General Charles Bolte, burst into the room. The two four-star generals were outraged. "Mr. Secretary, Mr. Secretary," Ridgway protested, "This is going too far!" He waved a piece of paper. "Listen to this" 'Disgrace to the Army . . . Not fit to wear the uniform.' "

Stevens abruptly stopped laughing. General Ridgway was the Army Chief of Staff. He had been the ranking commander of U.S. paratroops in Europe in World War II, and later was the commander of all ground troops in Korea. He was a very formidable figure, the most highly respected World War II veteran still on active duty.

Stevens had already told me that it was time for us to go to some of the other members on McCarthy's committee and get support against McCarthy's abuse. Ridgway's indignation strengthened his resolve.

For the rest of the day, we called McCarthy's Republican colleagues—Dirksen, Mundt, and Potter—and two of the Democrats—McClellan and Symington (Jackson was out of town). We told them the whole sordid story, from McCarthy's first efforts to get a commission for Schine six months before, to the abuse of Zwicker. Our immediate objective was to get a cancellation of a McCarthy open hearing set for the following Tuesday at which McCarthy planned to try to disgrace Zwicker in public.

The Democratic members had walked out on the committee the previous summer, in protest against McCarthy's one-man hearings, arbitrary one-man subpoenas, sudden one-man executive sessions, and one-man control of the staff. Now they saw a means to tame McCarthy and to get back on the committee. Even the Republicans seemed amenable to reining in McCarthy. Stevens and I both thought by day's end that we had succeeded, and that the public abuse of Zwicker would not take place.

It was not to be so simple. That same evening, Roy Cohn called me highly critical about the Peress matter, insisting that the Army had the most damning evidence of all on Peress—an FBI report—and that we should have prosecuted Peress long ago. Stevens then called McCarthy to tell him of our discussions with other members of his committee. He told him that he would not let any more Army officers go before McCarthy until they had worked out an understanding "as to the abuse they are going to get." But McCarthy was out of control.

"You are not going to order them to appear before my committee?" he asked. "Just go ahead and try it, Robert. I am going to kick the brains out of anyone who protects Communists. If that is the policy of you (*sic*), you just go ahead and do it. I will guarantee that you will live to regret it."

Word of the Zwicker abuse, Ridgway's reaction, and Stevens's attempt to get support in the Senate quickly spread. The press got wind of it; the headline in the Baltimore *Sun* was, STEVENS PROTESTS ABUSE BY MCCARTHY. In the Senate, some of McCarthy's sycophants and supporters, realizing that McCarthy had gone overboard, tried to destroy the evidence. They tried to suppress all stenographic transcripts and "strike from the record," any recorded proof of the Zwicker incident. Had McCarthy himself acted instantly to suppress the evidence, the documents might have just disappeared, just the way proof of some acts of judicial malfeasance by McCarthy had so miraculously disappeared from two different Wisconsin courts some fifteen years before. But McCarthy appeared not to understand what he had done or the danger to himself.

Others, like Everett Dirksen, understood very well. Dirksen told Stevens that McCarthy's remarks had all been "stricken from the record." Dirksen had underestimated the efficiency of the stenographic company. McCarthy had struck; now it was the Army's turn.

CHAPTER XX

The Chicken Lunch

Department of the Army
PRESS RELEASE
Sunday, February 21, 1954, 4 p.m.

Statement by Secretary of the Army Robert T. Stevens:
  I have directed Brigadier General Ralph W. Zwicker of Camp Kilmer, New Jersey, not to appear before Senator McCarthy on Tuesday in New York.
  I am unwilling for so fine an officer as General Zwicker to run the risk of further abuse. . . . I cannot permit the loyal officers of our Armed Forces to be subjected to such unwarranted treatment. The prestige and morale of our Armed Forces are too important to the security of this nation to have them weakened by unfair attacks on our officers corps. . . .

Stevens was an overnight, international hero. The press release showed that the Eisenhower administration had finally decided to stand up. Stevens received hundreds of congratulatory telegrams within hours. "At last," said one, "the dragon has met St. George."

The Army and the administration had allowed McCarthy to ruin the lives of numerous obscure Jewish scientists at Fort Monmouth without a peep. When McCarthy started going after decorated generals, however, he was challenged.

Stevens was to appear before McCarthy on the appointed day in place of Zwicker. Before announcing the plan, Stevens and I had carefully touched base at every government level. Stevens had talked to the secretary of defense and had then gone personally to the White House, where he saw General Jerry Persons, the president's chief congressional liaison officer. I had advised Assistant Defense Secretary Seaton, who was the department's direct liaison to the President and to the Senate. I had also spelled out the plan to Deputy Attorney General Rogers, Vice-President Nixon's closest ally and friend in the executive branch. We wanted to make sure that the administration wouldn't abandon us later on.

One key figure did not go along. After the press release was made public, Republican Senate leader William Knowland balked. He told Stevens that no senator would agree that he had a right to put a stop to the abuse of Zwicker. And, he warned, McCarthy would just keep on abusing the Army.

McCarthy was not much chastened by Stevens's defiance. On Washington's Birthday, he had waved a transcript of the Zwicker hearing before the Sons of the American Revolution in Philadelphia and said, "As I look it over today, I was too temperate. If I were doing it today, I would be much stronger in my language."

Still, his colleagues in the Senate managed to persuade him to postpone the hearing from Tuesday to Thursday. Meanwhile, McCarthy holed up in Cohn's apartment with his claque—Cohn, Carr, and Willard Edwards of the Chicago *Tribune*—and cursed me for getting him into this hole. I was a Communist, he stated. Carr heard the remark and went into the next room, laughing. He said to Willard Edwards:

"Do you know what Joe is saying now? He says John Adams is a Communist."

"Don't laugh," Edwards is said to have responded. "Maybe he'll prove it."

By Tuesday, February 23, there were so many press interruptions at the Pentagon that Stevens decided to work at home, preparing for his forthcoming clash with McCarthy on Thursday. Ken BeLieu, his military aide, and I were with him.

About 2:30 in the afternoon he received a phone call. He had been summoned to a council of war on the Hill. Stevens put on his hat and beckoned me to go with him.

On the way we stopped at the White House and picked up General Persons and Jack Martin, a political advisor to the President, who had been a longtime aide to Senator Robert A. Taft before the latter's death during the previous fall.

As we went east on Pennsylvania Avenue, we discussed the Schine affair. Persons remarked that in all his years of legislative experience in Washington, this was the worst example of improper pressure that he had ever seen. He gazed out the car window at the Capitol dome, looming ahead, and remarked:

> If the bones of all the crow I have eaten in the last fifteen years were piled together, that Capitol dome wouldn't be high enough to cover them. But I always took the attitude that it wasn't hurting me, that I was doing it for the Army. And so I just ate crow. Jerry Persons as a man didn't count, but what was good for the Army did.

Persons believed in peace at any price. His job, like most legislative liaison specialists, was to avoid confrontation. Sometimes he did it by handing out favors. During the war he had made a specialty of getting cush, noncombat assignments for sons of congressmen. Other times he did it by appeasing.

Persons wanted to avoid a clash now, a confrontation that would pit the administration against the Senate. And he wasn't the only one.

We arrived at the Capitol, and moved through the labyrinth of old corridors to the private "retreat" of Vice-President Nixon. There we found Nixon, Deputy Attorney General William Rogers, Senate Majority Leader Knowland, and Senator Dirksen. Almost at once Persons stated that he wanted to get the Thursday hearing canceled. He felt it would be a spectacle, and nothing more. It would just harm the administration.

Both Nixon and Knowland agreed. They pointed out that they had sat through many such spectacles, and that nobody benefited except the headline writers. Everyone in the group warned Stevens that while he might want to talk about Zwicker at the hearing, the chairman— McCarthy—would not let him talk about anything but the conspiracy to promote Peress.

Finally, Dirksen spoke. He said that McCarthy's abuse of Zwicker had been outrageous, that the Schine affair was unpardonable, and that the members of the McCarthy committee had an obligation to make sure this sort of thing would end. He was McCarthy's best friend in the Senate, he said; McCarthy would listen to him when he wouldn't listen to anyone else. Dirksen would leave the meeting at that very moment and insist that McCarthy must agree that day to four fundamental things: (1) an end to the arbitrary subpoena power McCarthy was exercising; (2) an end to the one-man subcommittee meetings that McCarthy was conducting; (3) an end to what he called the senseless abuse of the Army; and (4) termination of Cohn's employment. He said that only the latter might take awhile because of Cohn's ties to the Hearst press.

It had become clear that we had been called to this meeting in Nixon's office to talk us out of a confrontation between Stevens and McCarthy. Instead, the senators would privately rein in McCarthy, something they had failed to do for the last four years.

As the group left the meeting, Vice-President Nixon said, "Remember, this meeting never occurred."

The first thing Dirksen did when he saw McCarthy was not to deliver an ultimatum. Rather, it was to tell McCarthy that he should ask the administration to fire John Adams. What Dirksen and his cronies had in store for Secretary Stevens, however, was far worse. It would go down in history as the "Chicken Lunch."

Stevens's resolve was softening. Senator Karl Mundt had flown up to Valley Forge with him on Washington's Birthday, a day earlier, warning him that it would not look right for the Army secretary to defy Congress. He was getting the same message from other Republican congressional sources.

He still thought that he should go ahead, however. I did, too. I thought that if he appeared at a public hearing and courteously refused to permit his officers to be further abused, McCarthy's violent attacks on him would simply make Stevens a martyr and more of a national hero that he already was.

On Wednesday—the day before the scheduled confrontation between Stevens and McCarthy—Ken BeLieu, Stevens's senior military aide, confided to me that Stevens had been invited to a "secret" luncheon up on the Hill. BeLieu did not know who would be there. He warned me that Stevens had strictly insisted that no one in the Pentagon was to know of the meeting, not even the secretary of defense. I had grave misgivings, but because of Stevens's consistent and resentful rebuffing of my periodic suggestions that we consult higher echelons on some of these problems, I felt that there was little I could say to stop him. BeLieu warned me not to tell Stevens that I knew, lest BeLieu himself get in trouble with his boss. In a conference in Stevens's office that morning, I did tell Struve Hensel, the Defense Department General Counsel, of my foreboding. He had come back from New York the previous evening at my request to help prepare Stevens for the expected confrontation with McCarthy the next day. Hensel, though visibly irritated, said nothing to Stevens either.

At about 11:30, Stevens arose from his desk, picked up his hat, and started for the door. I followed him there and stopped him. He turned, his face slightly flushed, to see what I wanted.

"Remember," I said, "peace with honor."

He smiled slightly, boyishly, rather embarrassed, and left the room. Hensel stood up and looked at me. He took a breath, expelled it, and said, "Oh, hell!" Then he dryly remarked, "I'll bet when he gets up there he'll find that he's the only one who kept it a secret."

BeLieu walked after Stevens to his car. "I still don't think you should go alone," he said. Stevens said he thought he could handle it, and drove off toward utter humiliation.

The four Republicans on McCarthy's subcommittee—Mundt, Dirksen, Potter, and McCarthy—met Stevens in the Vice-President's private dining room in the Capitol. Outside this "secret" meeting waited a large contingent of newsmen, forewarned to be in on the slaughter. The menu was fried chicken.

Stevens began forcefully enough. "I'm not going to have my officers browbeaten," he told McCarthy. McCarthy, however, attacked right back and never let up. "I'm not going to sit there and see a supercilious bastard sit there and smirk," he sneered. Then he berated Stevens for the Army's action on security, on Peress, and on everything else. One of his strongest charges was how outrageous, how insulting, how unheard-of, how absolutely unprecedented and unforgiveable it was for Stevens to bypass a chairman and to go directly to the other committee members on a matter concerning the committee.

Privately, other senators assured Stevens that there would be no further abuse of Army witnesses. But when it came down to a written agreement on this point, McCarthy would not hear of it.

After lunch, Karl Mundt designated himself composer of a "Memo of Understanding" between the committee and Stevens. He sat down at a typewriter and began typing, hunt-and-peck style. The finished product was a complete capitulation by Stevens, a complete victory for McCarthy:

February 24, 1954

MEMO OF UNDERSTANDING

At a luncheon conference today attended by Secretary of the Army
Stevens and Senators McCarthy, Dirksen, Mundt, and Potter, the following memo of understanding was agreed to:

1. There is complete accord between the Department of the Army and
the Senate Committee on Investigations that Communism and Communists must be rooted out of the Armed Services wherever and whenever
found.

2. There is complete agreement among us that the Secretary of the
Army will order the Inspector General to complete the investigation which
he ordered upon his return from the Far East on February 3, in the Peress
case, as rapidly as possible, and that he will give the committee the
names of everyone involved in the promotion and the honorable discharge of Peress, and that such individuals will be available to appear
before the committee.

3. In view of the fact that Senator Symington has requested that the
calling of Zwicker should be postponed until his return from Europe, the
appearance of Zwicker will be deferred. If the committee then decides to
call Zwicker, Secretary Stevens stated that at that time Zwicker will be
available.

In view of the foregoing memorandum of understanding the hearing
scheduled for tomorrow [where Stevens had planned to defy McCarthy]
has been cancelled.

When the luncheon was over, Stevens asked Dirksen to walk down
the corridor. Avoiding newsmen, he told Dirksen that he had misgivings about the understanding. Dirksen assured him that it was a fine
settlement—fine for the senate, fine for the Army. And, he said, Stevens had agreed to it.

When Stevens returned to the Pentagon, he asked BeLieu to call the
members of the Army Policy Council to his office so he could report
on the lunch. Into his office filed a dozen or more of the highest-
ranking Army officers then on duty in the Pentagon. There was Chief
of Staff Ridgway, Vice-Chief Bolte, Secretary of the General Staff
William Westmoreland, and two other future chiefs of staff. All of
them were much-decorated officers of World War II and of Korea. The
group was stony faced. All had read, or heard, what the wire services
were saying: Victory for McCarthy, surrender by Stevens.

At the conclusion of the "Chicken Lunch," Secretary Stevens sits among the barracudas. Shown are Senators Everett Dirksen and McCarthy on Stevens's right, and Senators Karl Mundt and Charles Potter on his left. Mundt, standing, holds a copy of the Memo of Understanding, by which Stevens "surrendered." COURTESY PHOTOWORLD (F.P.G.).

Stevens had not seen these reports, however. So he launched off on a proud, if somewhat labored, speech saying that he had worked out a satisfactory agreement, and that there would be no more abuse of Army officers. Though uninvited, Deputy Defense Secretary Roger Kyes, Assistant Defense Secretary Fred Seaton, and Department of Defense Counsel Struve Hensel also attended, sitting at a conference table on the side. Hensel read the "Memo of Understanding" with dismay, and passed it on to Seaton with a warning nod.

Stevens's speech was greeted with looks of disbelief. General Ridgway, always the soldier, then stood up ramrod straight and made a stirring speech in support of the secretary. The stunned officers left in complete silence.

The three Defense officials remained. Both Hensel and Kyes were two-hundred-pound men, over six feet tall, each with a commanding voice. They were forceful men, and they represented the Defense Department, the superior agency.

Seaton, though not as large physically, had an incisive and steely quality, and he was the President's man at the Pentagon. He walked over to the Army secretary and said, "Bob, don't you know what you've done?"

The other Defense officials bore in, yelling at Stevens. He yelled right back, hotly defending his "settlement." Then one of them told him what McCarthy had just told newsmen and thus the American public. "Stevens," gloated McCarthy, "could not have surrendered more abjectly if he had gotten down on his knees."

Stevens was struck speechless. Then he burst into tears.

CHAPTER XXI

_____/

"Boy, We Really Have a Commander in Chief . . ."

. . . yesterday, Senator McCarthy accomplished what Generals Burgoyne and Cornwallis failed to do—the surrender of the American Army.

The London *Times,* February 26, 1954

SURRENDER . . . CAPITULATE . . . RETREAT—the headlines were all the same. The bitter jokes began: "Private Schine is the only soldier in the Army with any morale today" was a favorite. In the New York *Times,* James Reston did have a compassionate word for Stevens. He accused Stevens of making "the worst deal since Yalta, but

> in an administration that comes to office pointing copy book maxims, he was the one man who tried, however ineffectually, for the right and moral thing. He became the goat because he placed too much faith in the moral pronouncements of the President. . . .

At the Pentagon, the telegrams poured in: "Resign," said one. Said another: "Boo, boo, boo, boo, boo, boo. . . ." It was widely rumored that officers were greeting each other in the hallways by waving their handkerchiefs. I never saw the handkerchiefs, but Stevens, who had been dubbed Fighting Bob by some newspapers before the "Chicken Lunch," was referred to by some at the Pentagon as Retreating Robert.

McCarthy, meanwhile, strutted around the Capitol, boasting of his successful humiliation of the Army. To one reporter, he said, "Want a commission? I can get it for you!" Then he gave a wink, a grin, and a small kick.

Stevens was brokenhearted. He called various senators and White House aides and indicated that he would probably resign. Repeatedly, he said: "Yesterday I was a hero; today I am a dog."

The entire administration seemed astounded by the press reaction to the "Chicken Lunch." As soon as the headlines began appearing, White House and Defense Department officials began a series of feverish meetings, trying to decide how to recoup some of Stevens's lost ground. Vice-President Nixon, the man who had set up the "Chicken Lunch" to begin with, chaired the meeting. Stevens later told me how emphatic "Dick" had been, wadding up and hurling the various drafts until the group settled on just the right mix of forcefulness and restraint.

At last a statement was worked out and read by Stevens from the White House press room:

> I did not at that meeting (recede) from any of the principles upon which I stand. I shall never accede to (officers of the Army) being browbeaten, humiliated. . . . From assurances which I have received from members of the Committee, I am confident that they will not permit such conditions to develop in the future.

The White House spokesman, Jim Hagerty, then stood up and said:

> On behalf of the President, he has seen the statement. He approves and endorses it 100 percent.

Grinning happily, like an overage Boy Scout, Stevens chimed in:

> Boy, we really have a Commander in Chief. He stepped up to the plate and knocked a home run.

**"Okay, Bud.
When I Want You Again
I'll Send For You"**
2/25/1954

"Okay, Bud. When I Want You Again, I'll Send For You." From *Herblock's Here and Now* (Simon & Schuster, 1955).

The press was doubtful. The prevailing attitude was that the lost ground had not been regained, and that Stevens had been seriously crippled—not only by the surrender, but by his lack of awareness of what he had done when he walked into it.

But there was one very valuable side effect. President Eisenhower was furious. His administration had been struck an extremely damaging blow. Stevens he could forgive as a political neophyte swimming with sharks. But his own White House operatives and his Senate allies like Mundt, Knowland, Dirksen, even his own Vice-President—had let him down. They had either been at the "Chicken Lunch" or had been aware of it, yet no one had stopped McCarthy from rubbing the administration's face in the dirt.

Eisenhower was not amused to read in a respected political column that the President was now sharing the command of the Army with McCarthy. His anger rose when he called for and read the transcript of the Zwicker hearing.

There was malaise in the administration; McCarthy had reached the apogee of his power. The polls showed that half the country approved of him and less than one third disapproved. The worldwide press had been grumbling for some months about Eisenhower's Munich-like policy of appeasement. Something clearly had to be done; the administration had to find a tool, a weapon it could use to fight back.

The weapon was sitting in my drawer. It was the forty-page diary I had prepared on McCarthy's abuse of the Army, focusing on the incessant demands for special treatment for G. David Schine. By now a number of top government officials, senators, Army officers, and newsman, were familiar with it. Sherman Adams, the President's chief aide, had asked me to send him a copy, so Eisenhower probably was aware of it.

Marder of the *Post* and Potter of the *Sun* came in again about ten days after they had first seen the diary. Their mission was to urge me to sacrifice myself by distributing the diary to the press.

I suspected that I had already made the sacrifice, but I didn't say so. I didn't agree to their plea, because I felt that by then such a step wasn't necessary. I could sense by that time that the entire situation was ready to explode. Just let things alone, I thought; the fuse is already burning.

Showing my diary to these newsmen heightened the pressure for its release. Alsop had dropped hints about it to Fred Seaton, the assistant defense secretary; the latter was convinced that the document was ready to burst forth in print. This unease reached the White House.

On one of the first evenings in March, I had already gone home when I received a call summoning me to the office of the secretary of defense. I was not told why, but I suspected that events were about to come to a head.

At 7:00 P.M., I entered the office of Defense Secretary Wilson. The assembled group looked like a planning session for an invasion. Even the Chairman of the Joint Chiefs of Staff, Admiral Radford, was there. The room was full of uniforms covered with stars.

The questions put to me were to the point. They wanted to know exactly what my part had been in refusing to hold Peress for court-martial. What had I done with the letter?

I told them in a short narrative. Then I said, "If you are trying to fix responsibility or blame for the fact that he wasn't held in the service in response to McCarthy's demand, it rests entirely with me. I did talk to General Weible, and we were in agreement that we saw no court-martial grounds, but I was from the secretary's office, and General Weible had every right to assume that I was speaking for the secretary.

You can put no blame or responsibility any place other than right on me and on me alone. I alone am responsible.''

I was not asked to stay at the war council after I finished discussing the Peress decision. But I knew what they were deciding: whether to go ahead in the fight against McCarthy or just throw me to the wolves.

The next morning, Assistant Army Secretary Hugh Milton came by my office. He said that my statement the previous evening had been ''courageous and honorable.'' His little speech irritated me; but I thanked him nevertheless. As I watched him walk down the hall, I hummed to myself the refrain I had been required to memorize in order to advance from Tenderfoot to Second-Class Scout in the Sioux Falls Boy Scouts in 1925: ''Boy Scouts are marching, loyal, clean, and brave! From East to West with banners on the wave. . . .''

Not long after the council of war in Wilson's office, Struve Hensel, the Defense Department counsel, called me and said that he thought my diary of McCarthy's pressure of the Army should be revised into a chronological order. It was going to be out in the open before long, he said, and the Defense Department wanted to be ready.

I knew then that the decision had been made. The Army was going to counterattack against McCarthy, and my diary was the ammunition. Stevens and I were obviously going to lead the charge.

First, however, the administration was taking no chances. The FBI was asked to see if there were any skeletons in my closet they might have missed on earlier security checks. They dared not risk as lead man someone who could be ''exposed'' by McCarthy.

A few days later, Fred Seaton came to me and said that I should feel proud that the FBI hadn't found any dirt on me. I told him that if he had an FBI report on me I wanted to see it. I said that I had as much right to see it as Seaton did, or his boss Defense Secretary Charles E. Wilson. ''Oh, no,'' said Seaton. ''It's confidential. The FBI says we can't show it to you.'' I said, ''You mean because I might find out what I've been doing?'' a remark that he did not consider funny.

So it was all arranged. No dirty linen on me, my diary reordered into a ''Chronology of Events,'' the administration ready to strike back against McCarthy. I was not included in any of the conferences at which my fate was decided, but I knew it was only a matter of time. On March 10, the chronology was finished. Miraculously, Senator Potter sent a letter to the secretary of defense that very same day, asking for a report on those rumors he had been hearing. This was a

phony exercise, of course; Potter had been fully apprised of all these
goings-on for a long time. By early afternoon, the chronology had
been shipped off to Potter and the other senators on the Investigations
Subcommittee, McCarthy included.

The war was on. By 3:00 P.M., my offices were overrun with reporters seeking copies of this precious document. Work was hopeless. I
sent home the secretaries, and told my associates to close up for the
day.

I walked into the office of Norman Dorsen, one of the lawyers who
had worked on the McCarthy conflict from the beginning, and said to
him:

"Well, it's out now. I don't know how it's all going to come out,
but one thing I'll guarantee, and that is when it's all over, I'll be lying
flat on the floor."

CHAPTER XXII

The Eleven Memoranda

The morning after the "Chronology of Events" was released, I got up and turned on the radio for the 7:00 A.M. news. The announcer began:

"Well, the roof fell in on Senator McCarthy last night. . . ."

That day, the corridor outside McCarthy's Senate office on the third floor of the Senate Office Building was jammed with newsmen. By afternoon, it was virtually impassable.

Late in the day, a McCarthy staffer emerged in the hall with a stack of carbon flimsies. They were memoranda—eleven in all—dating back through the winter and fall. Just "discovered" in a filing cabinet, they appeared to be memos dictated by McCarthy, Cohn, and Carr after various phone conversations, lunches, or meetings with either Secretary Stevens or me. They were McCarthy's answer to the Army's "Chronology of Events." The reporters grabbed for them.

"Memorandum for File," dated November 6, for example, described the luncheon in Stevens's office in the Pentagon that day:

> Mr. Stevens asked that we hold up our public hearings on the Army. He suggested that we go after the Navy, Air Force, and Defense Department instead. We said first of all that we had no evidence warranting an

investigation of these other departments. Adams said not to worry about that, because there was plenty of dirt there, and they would furnish us with leads. Mr. Stevens thought this was the answer to his problem.

A memo from Roy Cohn to Senator McCarthy on December 9 stated:

> John Adams said today that following up the idea about investigating the Air Force he had gotten specific information for us about an Air Force base where there were a large number of homosexuals. He said that he would trade us that information if we would tell him what the next Army project was that we would investigate.

A memo from Frank Carr to McCarthy on the same day:

> I couldn't get you on the telephone. What I want to tell you is that I am getting fed up with the way the Army is trying to use Schine as a hostage to pressure us to stop our hearings on the Army. . . . (Adams) constantly lumps together all talk about Schine with suggestions that we stop holding hearings on the Army. I am convinced that they will keep right on trying to blackmail us as long as Schine is in the Army. . . .

A memo from Roy Cohn to Senator McCarthy on January 14:

> Adams said this was the last chance for me to arrange that kind of law partnership in New York which he wanted. One would think he was kidding, but his persistence on this subject makes it clear to me that he is serious. He said he had turned down a job in industry at $17,500 and needed a guarantee of $25,000 from a law firm.

A last example, this from Carr to McCarthy, dated January 15:

> Maybe one of these days you should speak to John Adams in a friendly way. I've tried. He is baiting Roy pretty much lately on the "hostage" situation. They get pretty heated before Roy buys lunch, but it's going to lead to trouble.

That night McCarthy appeared before the press. He told reporters that I had come to his home on January 22 and had tried to blackmail him into calling off the Fort Monmouth investigation by threatening to otherwise issue a damaging report about Cohn and the committee. The next morning the New York *Times* headline read: "MCCARTHY CHARGES ARMY BLACKMAIL."

And then it proceeded with a full story of McCarthy's version of my crime.

Mysteriously, there were no original copies of McCarthy's memos, where the typewriter ink could be scientifically tested to determine the exact age of the document. Only the carbon copies were available.

The memoranda were never proved to be false, but I believed that they had all been created after the Army report had been sent forward, and distorted events to embarrass the Army. At the time, I told the press they were "fantastic."

At first I felt certain that the memos would be McCarthy's undoing. "Blackmailing" McCarthy to drop the hearings? Offering him Navy and Air Force homosexuals instead? Holding Schine "hostage"? I thought McCarthy must be absolutely desperate to think up such a scheme. This is suicide, the politics of desperation. How could he even dare to do such a thing? But as others had learned before me, McCarthy could get away with almost anything, as long as everyone let him.

The Army chronology and the McCarthy memoranda provoked a steady and growing drumbeat for a Senate investigation. Somebody had to be lying. Either McCarthy would be finally exposed, or the Army—or rather Stevens and Adams—would fall. And at first it seemed so clear to me: There was no way the truth could not come out. It seemed to me impossible for McCarthy to sustain those memos. Then I began reading them, and I became less confident. I realized that McCarthy, in almost every instance, had me in a two-on-one or three-on-one situation. It was always their word against mine. In a court of law, at best it could be very awkward; at worst, it could mean a perjury charge against me.

The more I thought about it, the more uneasy I became. Only one thing sustained me. McCarthy had blundered by bringing in Stevens. It was only two small sentences, alleging that Stevens had tried to sick McCarthy on the Navy and Air Force, but it was enough to save me. McCarthy could have extracted himself from trouble by a quick settlement: firing Adams. But the administration was not about to sacrifice Stevens. McCarthy had foolishly attacked a member of the President's official family, calling him a near criminal. Now a negotiated settlement that included the firing of an underling was impossible. Stevens would have to face a full investigation.

I was not the only one feeling a little nervous by now. Joe Alsop, the columnist to whom I had first shown my forty-page diary, asked me over the phone if I could come and see him. He said he did not want to be seen coming to my office. On March 15, Alsop had written a column in the Washington *Post* entitled "MCCARTHY-COHN-SCHINE TALE WAS HALF-TOLD." The piece said that the final version had been sanitized of Cohn's "disgusting obscenities," which had "studded" my version. "Second," the column went on, "the original document also contained certain suggestions as to the nature of the McCarthy-Cohn-Schine relationship; here again, of course, there are clear hints in the published version."

When I arrived at his home, I found a very uneasy man. Alsop said that when Cohn had read Alsop's column he had threatened to sue Alsop for libel. Cohn no doubt well remembered what he had said to me, and the "disgusting obscenities" would have been primarily the one word "shit," which he had used time and time again. But as to all else, that was pure Alsop fantasy.

Alsop pleaded with me to give him a copy of the forty-page document. He pledged that he only wanted to protect himself in case Cohn sued. He even swore that he would put it in his safe-deposit box.

I refused. I was already irritated with Alsop for having gone to Fred Seaton, the assistant defense secretary, hinting that he had seen the document, and stating darkly that "there are lots of them about." I felt that Alsop had stretched his promise of confidentiality, and that since everyone was sweating a little now, Alsop could just sweat a little, too.

I did tell him that if he got sued, I'd bring out the document in his defense. Little did I know that in a few days I'd lose possession of all the copies.

Within a week after the Army's "Chronology of Events" was sent to the Senate, Fred Seaton appeared in my office and demanded that all the copies of my diary of the Schine pressure be handed over to him on the spot. He was operating under White House orders, he said; those documents were to be suppressed. Accordingly, every copy I could locate was removed from my office.[1]

Out the door walked all of the written backup proof I had. I would sorely miss it in the months to come. I would particularly miss written

---

1. Nearly a year later, as I was shaking hands to say good-bye to my lawyer-colleagues in the Army counselor's office, one of them handed me an envelope as a farewell present. It contained a complete set of all the suppressed documents. They have been the basis for much of this narrative.

proof of McCarthy's reference to the "miserable little Jew," a document, I believed, that might have affected Cohn's loyalties to McCarthy.

At about this time, I flew up to New York and had dinner with General Lucius Clay, one of the war's great generals, who was now a corporate executive. He was a sage and sympathetic man and he had some very direct warnings:

> You'll have to be ready for the most violent and devastating sort of counterattacks. You'd better be searching your soul, because you'll probably be explaining some indiscretion of your college days you can't even remember. Even if that is not the technique, they'll hit you, and hit you so hard you'll be on your knees, and it will be in ways and in areas you haven't at all anticipated. It will be savage, and they'll show no mercy.

Not long after that dinner, I was told that McCarthy had asked the Internal Revenue Service for and had received my past tax returns. Fortunately, I didn't make enough money for them to be of much use to McCarthy, even with his creative imagination. McCarthy also dug into Stevens's and Struve Hensel's tax returns.

Hensel, the general counsel of the Defense Department, had signed the letter of transmittal by which the Defense Department sent the Army Chronology to the Senate. That made him a target. On hearing that McCarthy was preparing an attack on Hensel, Defense Secretary Wilson summoned Hensel into his office. As Hensel reported it to me, the conversation went something like this:

"Are you clean?" Wilson asked.

"What?" asked Hensel, startled.

"I said, are you clean?"

"Well, I bathed this morning," said Hensel, making an uneasy joke.

"No, I mean personally, your background. Can you stand it if they pry? Have you any skeletons in the closet?"

"Well, I was divorced a few years ago, and I'm remarried. But that's no skeleton. What are you driving at?"

"McCarthy," said Wilson.

On April 20, the attack came. McCarthy had decided that the "Eleven memoranda"—accusations that the Army was holding Schine "hostage" and "blackmailing" McCarthy while trying to deflect his aim to the Air Force and Navy—was not enough. So he added some more dirt to his "countercharges." Among them was a nasty swipe at Hensel.

He claimed that during World War II, Hensel had been a partner and dominant force in a very profitable shipping supply firm that sold priority goods to the Navy—this while Hensel was serving as assistant secretary of the navy. If true, the charges represented a serious conflict of interest.

The charges against Hensel were false. They were based on an old complaint that had been found meritless by both the IRS and McCarthy's own investigating committee under a previous chairman. Indeed, McCarthy had known about the charge when he voted to confirm Hensel in his new post as assistant secretary of defense for International Security Affairs a few weeks earlier. But McCarthy nevertheless, managed to spread this false accusation over the newspapers.

As usual, McCarthy made his charge during a "committee" meeting, thereby insulating himself against a libel suit. Hensel, however, refused to roll over like many other McCarthy victims. He denounced McCarthy's charges as "barefaced lies," and challenged McCarthy to repeat them outside the protection of congressional immunity.

McCarthy had gone down to Houston to visit some of his Texas oilmen supporters. He tried to slither around the challenge, announcing that he saw no harm in publicly restating the charges in the future, but "not now." Joe was a little taken aback by a Defense official who would not seek clearance from above before saying that McCarthy had "reached a high mark of scandalous cowardice and the low mark of cowardly irresponsibility."

Weeks later, the charges against Hensel were quietly dropped. In a secret meeting, McCarthy admitted to the other members of his subcommittee that he had been "only guessing" when he charged Hensel. When Hensel heard McCarthy admit this, he asked him why he would do such a thing. McCarthy responded that he had learned from an "old Indian friend" named "Indian Charlie," that "when anyone approached him in a not completely friendly fashion, (to) start kicking that person in the balls and continue to kick until there was nothing but air where the balls used to be."

CHAPTER XXIII

"He Dons His War Paint"

McCarthy was swinging wildly in that early spring of 1954. That, in itself, was not unusual. What was unusual, however, was that now people were beginning to swing back, and not just the Army and the White House.

In early March, a senator from Vermont, Ralph E. Flanders, stood up and launched one of the most biting attacks on McCarthy ever heard on the Senate floor. "He dons his war paint," said Flanders in a mocking voice. "He goes into his war dance. He goes forth to battle and proudly returns with the scalp of a pink Army dentist. We may assume this represents the depth and seriousness of the Communists' penetration at this time."[1]

On the same day a popular television voice turned on McCarthy, a voice familiar to millions of Americans. Edward R. Murrow devoted an hour of his show, *See It Now,* to an exposure of McCarthy's method of ruining lives by preying on fear.

1. Eisenhower cautiously congratulated Flanders: "I was very much interested in reading the comments you made in the Senate today. I think America needs to hear from more Republican voices like yours."

At the end of the show, Murrow came before the TV camera and said to twenty million viewers:

> We must not confuse dissent with disloyalty. We must remember always that accusation is not proof, and that conviction depends upon evidence and due process of law. . . .
> We will not walk in fear, one of another. We will not be driven by fear into an age of unreason if we dig deep in our history and our doctrine, and remember that we are not descended from fearful men.

Meanwhile, in the less exalted world of politics, efforts were being made to avoid the Senate hearing. McCarthy's friends sensed that he had gone too far, and they were searching for a face-saving way out. One advance was made by Postmaster General Arthur Summerfield to his fellow Michigander, Defense Secretary Wilson. Summerfield, a former GOP national chairman and great McCarthy friend, suggested that Cohn be fired—and that if the Army in turn would fire me, there could be a settlement without a public hearing. The answer from Wilson was "No."

Summerfield's next feeler was that Cohn should be fired, and that I should be retained, and that the hearing be called off. Again the answer was no. By now Stevens was demanding that either McCarthy withdraw his "Eleven memoranda," and admit that they were false, or that hearings be held to vindicate the honor of the accused Army officials.

McCarthy could not very well concede that his "Eleven memoranda" were false. The Senate would be compelled to take serious disciplinary action against him, perhaps even expulsion. The Army and McCarthy were at an impasse. The hearings would go forward.

CHAPTER XXIV

The Tortured
Mushroom, et al.

Finding a committee that was willing to hold the hearings, however, was not easy. The logical choice was the Armed Services Committee, which was responsible for overseeing all military matters. But the chairman of the committee, Republican Leverett Saltonstall of Massachusetts, was up for reelection that year, and wanted nothing to do with the coming brawl. Another possibility was the Government Operations Committee, the parent committee to McCarthy's Investigations Subcommittee. But the members of the full committee—which McCarthy also chaired—had no taste for the fight, either. In fact, no one in the Senate was eager to be seen passing judgment on McCarthy. The Senate Republican leadership which controlled the Senate, was unwilling to establish a select committee of impartial senators (like the Watergate committee years later), in part because practically no senators could be found who were willing to serve.

After much Senate maneuvering, it was decided that the Investigations Subcommittee would investigate itself. It was, of course a suspect and unworkable solution.

As a concession to objectivity, McCarthy agreed to step aside as chairman, knowing that he didn't have to worry about the loyalty of the four Republicans who formed the majority. Karl Mundt, the next senior member of the committee, stepped up to replace McCarthy as chairman. Alone among the committee members, Mundt had argued that the controversy should be investigated by some other committee. When he lost that argument, he added that he was not the man to preside over the hearings. As Michael Straight, the editor of the liberal *New Republic,* wrote, "His reasoning proved sound."[1]

An ardent Red hunter from the day he volunteered for the House Un-American Activities Committee, Mundt fully approved of McCarthy's witch-hunts. He disliked having to act as a referee between the Republican administration and a Republican senator, and he said and did as little as possible, preferring to puff great clouds of smoke from his pipe. He was totally incapable of controlling McCarthy, who was supposed to be a defendant in the dock but became instead a quasi-prosecutor. Mundt was so weak that reporters began referring to him as the Tortured Mushroom and the Leaning Tower of Putty.

Sitting beside Mundt on the Republican side was Everett Dirksen, another McCarthyite and mouthpiece for the right-wing Chicago *Tribune.* Dirksen had been McCarthy's self-proclaimed "best friend" in the Senate ever since McCarthy helped put him there. It was McCarthy's campaign against Scott Lucas of Illinois that supposedly put Dirksen over the top of his 1950 upset victory.

Standing on principle was not Dirksen's style. "He had been on more sides of more issues than any man in Washington," wrote Straight. On such issues as the New Deal, national defense, the Marshall Plan, and the draft, he had never formulated a consistent ideology. He began as an isolationist in 1935. He first opposed, then supported the draft. He supported, then opposed the Marshall Plan, first saying of Marshall "Thank God we have leadership like that," then joining McCarthy in denouncing Marshall as one of the greatest villians in American history.

He had been a strong supporter of Thomas E. Dewey in the 1944 and 1948 presidential campaigns when Dewey had been the party's

1. Straight, who was then the editor-publisher of the *New Republic,* wrote almost weekly articles devoted to the Army-McCarthy clash, and then, in the early autumn of 1954 published a book about the hearings, *Trial by Television* (Boston: Beacon Press). It is from that work that Straight's quotes are taken.

standard bearer. But in the 1952 Eisenhower-Taft conflict at the Chicago convention, Dirksen, then a Taft supporter, set off an hour-long uproar with his attack on Dewey. "I see you down there smiling, Tom Dewey. We followed you twice and you led us down the road to defeat."

Dirksen was sanctimonious and fickle. With his mellifluous voice and nickle-plated oratory, he would protest that issues had been "ventilated" enough and would try to sweep them under the rug if they could harm McCarthy. Even Dirksen's hair style was contrived: once neatly parted and combed down, it was now carefully rumpled, and stood up straight, giving him a garish and theatrical visage.

McCarthy dominated Mundt and Dirksen, meeting secretly with them almost every day throughout the hearings to plot strategy. While Mundt's role was to let McCarthy say whatever he wanted during the hearings, Dirksen's role was to get the hearings shut down before they could do McCarthy any real damage.[2]

The two other Republicans on the committee were ciphers. One was Charles Potter of Michigan, a former social worker who had lost both legs in World War II and who had won two House elections with a large sympathy vote, and then stepped up to the Senate to replace the late, great Arthur Vandenberg.

On Potter's recommendation, I had hired his best friend, Lewis Berry, as deputy Army Counselor many months before. I asked Berry to keep Potter fully informed about all that went on hoping that Potter would stand up to McCarthy. Although he was more independent than the other committee Republicans, mostly he laid low.

No one on the committee, Republican or Democrat, had a lower profile than Henry Dworshak of Idaho. He had been designated to fill McCarthy's place on the committee while McCarthy temporarily stepped aside. Dworshak clearly wanted to be anywhere else but at the hearings, and he said as little as possible, save to vote "yes" on any motion to cut off the hearings.

The three Democrats stood in sharp contrast. The senior man, John McClellan of Arkansas, was angry and forceful. He tried to be impartial and to give some semblance of order to the proceedings when Mundt abdicated his role. A Southern conservative from one of the

2. Having failed to get the hearings called off entirely, Dirksen wanted them to be at least closed to the public. But Lyndon Johnson and others successfully pushed to have them open, and televised.

nation's poorest states—McClellan was inclined to be suspicious of "pinkos" and the Eastern Establishment. But he had the basic integrity that McCarthy utterly lacked. "I can be as hard as anybody in rooting out Communists but I'll never violate the Bill of Rights," he would say. It had been McClellan who led the Democratic walkout when McCarthy began treating the committee as his personal plaything the year before.

W. Stuart Symington was McCarthy's most vocal foe. Scion of a prominent family, he had been a successful businessman in his own right and two years later than Bob Stevens at Yale. He had one Yale man's regard for another. He had also been secretary of the air force, and felt he had to protect the military. Symington did not flinch before McCarthy's tirades. "I'm not afraid of anything about you or anything you've got to say, any time, any place, anywhere," he said to McCarthy after one particularly bitter exchange in the hearings. At another juncture he told McCarthy to "go see a psychiatrist," and told him, "the American people have had a look at you for six weeks. You are not fooling anyone."

The junior Democrat was Henry Jackson of Washington. A former prosecutor, he asked direct, probing questions. He was the only committee member who publicly scorned the McCarthy committee's "need" for Schine after he had been drafted. He and Cohn frequently locked horns, but throughout, Jackson remained upright, tenacious, and disgusted. The same could really be said about all three Democrats. Unfortunately, they were in the minority.

The rules of the proceeding were as poorly chosen as the man who ran it. For reasons I never knew and certainly never understood, the hearings were turned into a quasi-criminal trial rather than an ordinary congressional fact-finding inquiry. The Army's "Chronology of Events" was rewritten without my participation and now included a long list of charges against McCarthy, Cohn, and Carr. This meant that McCarthy was allowed to respond with counter-charges of his own, a collection of lies beginning with his eleven memoranda and continuing through specious slurs, like his swipe at Struve Hensel.

McCarthy insisted upon, and was given, the right of unlimited cross-examination—a right he had denied others appearing before his committee—which the McCarthyites used as a vehicle to pour in unsworn and false information as part of their long-winded questions. Mundt was unable to stop McCarthy from interrupting whenever he wanted, and McCarthy seized the openings to turn the hearings into a farce. Finally, there was no rule of relevancy. McCarthy, as might be expected, had a fertile imagination for tirades and digressions that had nothing to do with G. David Schine or the Army.

Perhaps the most amazing aspect of this circus was the role of the committee's counsel. His job was to elicit testimony from the witness and then, in effect, switch sides and cross examine him. He became a lawyer trying to discredit his own client.

It would have taken quite a dexterous, fair-minded lawyer to play this role, and the lawyer the committee chose was anything but. Ray Jenkins of Knoxville, Tennessee, was totally unsuited for the job. He was a hulking man with a gray crew cut and a large jaw, which he thrust at witnesses. His voice was deep and grating, with a mountain man's twang, and he interrogated witnesses as if he was prosecuting moonshiners in a mountain courthouse. His awkward transition from advocate to adversary was enough to make any objective observer wince.

Everett Dirksen had found him. An earlier choice to act as committee counsel, a Bostonian named Samuel Sears, had bowed out when the press accused him as a McCarthyite. Dirksen had to find someone who appeared neutral, even if he wasn't. While visiting his daughter, Mrs. Howard Baker, Jr., in Knoxville, he had met Jenkins, a well-known trial lawyer in East Tennessee. As Straight later wrote, Jenkins "was to demonstrate that he had come to Washington with the firm conviction that Senator McCarthy was a great American engaged in practical work, and that neither McCarthy nor anyone else could induce Jenkins to change his mind. . . ." This was quite clear to almost everyone by the time the hearings were over. Lest there be any remaining doubt, however, Jenkins announced on *Meet the Press* that, should he run for senator from Tennessee, he would be only too happy to have McCarthy campaign on his behalf.

The Army also needed a lawyer, since I—the Army counselor—was in effect a defendant. The first man selected came to Washington, spent a day, and then withdrew. He said that he felt the counterattacks against any opposing counsel might be so vicious that only a person of impeccable past credentials would dare risk the assignment. In his past, he said, he had been associated with a person who might be vulnerable to a McCarthy smear.

I never met this man, or even knew his name. The Army's second choice was a Boston lawyer named Joseph Welch, who took the case for no fee. Welch was little known outside the tight legal world of Boston, but he was about to become so famous that Hollywood would hire him as an actor. Welch, too, was associated with someone vulnerable to a McCarthy smear—a young lawyer in Welch's firm named Fred Fisher. But Welch's extraordinary showmanship was able to turn that "liability" into a weapon that helped lead McCarthy to self-destruction.[3]

At first, Bob Stevens had no idea of Ray Jenkins's pro-McCarthy bias. About a week before the hearings began, he interviewed Jenkins at the Pentagon. From Stevens's point of view, it went swimmingly. "Jenkins is as nice as he could be," he told me. I was scheduled to see Jenkins next. "You're really going to enjoy this interview," predicted Stevens.

I did not. I sensed hostility right away. From the Army mess I had arranged for some cookies and coffee to be sent in as a midafternoon break, and Jenkins looked at me as if I were trying to bribe him. I felt he was my adversary, which indeed he proved to be. His coolness made me uneasy. So did my fear that McCarthy and his cronies would gang up on me in a war of their word against mine, with the attendant risk of a perjury charge. Still, I was not pessimistic before the hearings began. I thought there was a chance to vindicate my role publicly, to prove that McCarthy was a liar and that his "eleven memoranda" were pure fiction. I figured that I would lose my job sooner or later both for having defied McCarthy and for having showed my written record to the press, but I thought that I could at least clear my name. The prospect of testifying, even before television cameras, did not bother me. In my years at the Pentagon I had testified dozens of times at congressional hearings.

I had no idea how different these hearings would be from any that had ever come before. They were to be a twisted, brawling confrontation, a sometimes baffling but often vivid drama that drew twenty million viewers to their television sets every day. The *New Republic* accurately pinpointed my problem in its March 22 issue: "If the oath prevails over truth, then Adams may well be framed." McCarthy, fortunately, had an even bigger problem: himself.

3. I was not part of the administration's efforts to find an Army counsel. Years later I learned that Thomas E. Dewey was the person who had originally suggested Welch.

[IV]

SPRING 1954

CHAPTER XXV

Point of Order

The New York *Times* called the hearings "a proceeding without precedent in America's history." Joe McCarthy disdainfully called them "this television show of Adams versus Cohn."

The television technicians arrived first. Shortly after dawn, they began lugging wires and lights and cameras into the ornate, high-ceilinged splendor of the Senate Caucus Room. Beneath the soaring Corinthian columns, they set up scaffolds to hold the bulky TV cameras of the day. Before the graceful windows that admitted the soft light of the courtyard, the men raised four powerful floodlights. Anyone who chanced to glance out the window would be blinded, his focus wrenched back to the proceedings at hand.

Shortly before 10:00, the great oak doors were opened to the public. In streamed politicians, lawyers, generals, photographers, reporters. There were, joked one reporter, even some "people" in the crowd. Built in 1909 to accommodate an audience of 300, the 74-foot-long caucus room was wedged tight with 800 spectators, participants, witnesses, and hangers-on of all types. One enterprising lobbyist for the American chinaware industry was busily passing out china ashtrays inscribed with the slogan, "If it's American, it's worth protecting."

"Here Goes." Copyright
1954 by Herblock in *The
Washington Post*.

The Capitol police officers soon picked them up—no advertising was
allowed.

Around a coffin-shaped table sat the principals, the subcommittee,
various lawyers, and Counsel Jenkins. At the end of the table were
McCarthy, Cohn, and Carr, protected by two plainclothesmen. Immediately next to the McCarthy group sat the Army group, Stevens,
myself, and Special Counsel Welch. Behind Stevens sat a phalanx of
generals. Struve Hensel, still one of the accused, sat next to us, with
his lawyer.

The chairman of the committee, Karl Mundt, had been staring into
the snouts of the TV cameras. When their little red lights told him
America was watching, he picked up a glass ashtray and rapped for
order. At 10:35 A.M., April 22, 1954, the Army-McCarthy hearings
began.

The issue, said the chairman, was whether Senator McCarthy and
his aides, Roy Cohn and Frank Carr, had "sought by improper means

to obtain preferential treatment for one Private G. David Schine,'' and whether the Army, in turn, had held Schine ''hostage'' in an attempt to ''force a discontinuance of further attempts by (McCarthy's) committee to expose Communist infiltration in the Army.''

Mundt promised: ''It is the purpose of this investigation to make a full and impartial effort to reveal that which is true and to expose that which is false.'' This was to be done, he vowed, with the ''maximum degree of dignity.''

The committee listens to Secretary Stevens. Left to right: Senators Charles Potter (R. Michigan), and Everett Dirksen (R. Illinois), committee counsel Ray Jenkins of Knoxville, Tennessee, Senator Karl E. Mundt (R. South Dakota) the chairman, and Senators John McClellan (D. Arkansas), W. Stuart Symington (D. Missouri) and Henry M. Jackson (D. Washington). Beside Jackson is McCarthy's staff chief Frank Carr and then Senator McCarthy. Two Army officers are next: Lieutenant Colonel Jean Wood, a Stevens aide, and Major General George Back, chief signal officer of the Army. I am seated at the extreme right. The only Senate member of the committee not shown is Henry Dworshak (R. Idaho) whose place was at the extreme left, next to Potter. COURTESY WIDE WORLD PHOTOS.

After some pleasantries with the ranking minority member, John McClellan, Mundt announced, "Our counsel, Mr. Jenkins, will now call the first witness."

Jenkins opened his huge mouth to speak, but before he could, a voice whined out: "A point of order, Mr. Chairman; may I raise a point of order?"

McCarthy's "point" was that the Army brief was labeled "filed by the Department of the Army." This was misleading, insisted McCarthy. The real Army—from "generals with the most outstanding combat records down to privates recently inducted" was resentful "that a few Pentagon politicians attempting to disrupt our investigation are naming themselves the Department of the Army. . . . The Department of the Army is not doing this. It is three civilians in the Army and they should be so named."

Senator McClellan quietly noted that the counter-charges had been signed by "Joe McCarthy, Chairman." But Mundt quickly earned his nickname as the Leaning Tower of Putty. At first he waffled by post-poning judgment until Stevens had been called as a witness. Then, after Stevens had taken the stand, he decided in favor of McCarthy, ruling that Stevens spoke only for himself.

McCarthy smirked at his little victory. Eager not to offend "our boys in uniform," he tried to relabel the hearings as the "Stevens-Adams hearings." Everyone else called them the Army-McCarthy hearings.

As McCarthy whined into his microphone, I began to feel uneasy. McCarthy is in charge, I thought. He may be sitting here along with the others being investigated, but really he's in charge. And if Mundt and Jenkins can't control this "point of order" nonsense, the hearings are going to go on forever.

After McCarthy finished with his first preemptive strike, Jenkins was finally allowed to call the first witness. Major General Miles Reber, Commanding General of the Western Area Command in Europe, took the stand. Reber had been the Army's congressional liaison chief in the summer of 1953, and Cohn had gone to him to obtain a commission for his friend David Schine. Reber outlined Cohn's requests and his own attempts to get Schine a commission during that July and August.

The Army's lawyer, Joseph Welch, stood up. Nattily dressed in bow tie and tweeds, he tooked like a large, round penguin. He affected an appearance of overwhelming innocence, betrayed by an occasional knowing smile. He had a few questions for General Reber.

"Were you actually aware of Mr. Cohn's position as counsel for this committee?" he asked.

REBER: I was, Mr. Welch.

WELCH: Did that position . . . increase or diminish the interest with which you pursued the problem?

REBER: . . . I feel that it increased the interest.

WELCH: Disregarding the word "improper" influence or pressure do you recall any instance comparable to this in which you were put under greater pressure?

REBER: . . . I recall no instance in which I was put under greater pressure.

Finished, Welch sat down.

Now it was McCarthy's turn. He engaged in some pointed, but restrained, dialogue with General Reber that got him nowhere. Suddenly, his tone of voice changed.

MCCARTHY: Is Sam Reber your brother?

Immediately, the one hundred eighty-odd reporters in the room began scribbling. They sensed from the irrelevant question that McCarthy was about to launch his specialty, the personal smear.

Sam Reber had been deputy high commissioner of Germany. When Cohn and Schine had conducted their infamous whirlwind tour of Europe the prior spring, they had briefly tangled with Reber over the status of one of the commissioner's subordinates. McCarthy claimed this dispute made General Reber biased against both Cohn and Schine. He said that the commissioner had made an "attack" on Cohn, and accused him of "appointing a man to shadow" Cohn and Schine throughout Europe. The "shadow" had actually been the Visitor's Bureau, which had made some travel arrangements for Cohn and Schine at their request.

This nonsense, ostensibly offered to show General Reber's "bias" against Cohn and Schine, was really just an excuse for McCarthy to make a wild accusation. What he really wanted to ask was:

"General . . . are you aware of the fact that your brother was allowed to resign when charges that he was a bad security risk were made against him as a result of the investigation of this committee?"

A storm of procedural wrangling ensued, with Mundt and Jenkins both agreeing that the question was "perfectly legitimate," but with McClellan strenuously objecting to McCarthy's bullying. The Democrat from Arkansas pointed out that McCarthy was pouring in unsworn testimony in the guise of a question, and extremely damning testimony at that.

McCarthy, as usual, did not really want an answer from Reber. He just wanted to smear Reber's brother on television. He vehemently objected when Welch asked Reber if there was any truth to this allegation.

For two hours the squabbling continued. General Reber sat silently, his knuckles turning white as he gripped the table. Finally, he was allowed to speak.

> REBER: I merely wanted to say that as I understand my brother's case he retired, as he is entitled to do by law, upon reaching the age of fifty. That is all I wanted to say.

The diversion finally over, the Army continued its testimony. Stevens took the stand, nervously licking his lips and forcing a smile. ("His was the bemusement of a gentleman caught in a wharf brawl," reported *Time*.) He recounted that between July 1953 and March 1, 1954, McCarthy and his staff had made sixty-five phone calls to the Army on the subject of Schine. The draftee's future had been discussed at no less than nineteen meetings between Army or government officials. Under Secretary of State General Walter Bedell Smith, former director of the CIA, testified that Cohn had asked him for a direct commission for Schine, though not with the CIA, which Cohn regarded as "too juicy a subject for investigation."

There was "no record that matches this persistent, tireless effort to obtain special consideration and privileges for this man," said Stevens.

It had been the Army's day, outlining McCarthy's sorry record of pressures on behalf of a private. Yet McCarthy, too, had gotten in his licks, disrupting and distracting the hearings almost at will with his constant cries into the microphone, "Mr. Chairman! Mr. Chairman! A point of order!"

At home, millions watched. *Newsweek* reported a surge of television

sales; MCCARTHY-ARMY TELECASTS DISRUPT HOUSEWORK
ROUTINES headlined the Washington *Times-Herald*. The viewers
were confused by much of the procedural jousting, the points of order,
and the frequent objections (McCarthy even objected to Mundt thank-
ing Reber for his frankness). But they sat riveted by the figures flickering across the shadowy screen. The participants in the hearings,
McCarthy and Stevens alike, went home that night feeling that they
had scored points against the other side. But the millions watching
sensed something different. They wondered why the Army went to
such extraordinary lengths to satisfy the McCarthy-Cohn complaints
over the standard treatment of one draftee. And in hearing McCarthy's
whining, and seeing his blatant smear of Sam Reber, many were
repelled.

CHAPTER XXVI

A Simple Trial Lawyer

The story Stevens told on the witness stand over the next few days was supposed to be about McCarthy's pressure on the Army. Instead, due to Stevens's innate courtesy and his eagerness to keep peace, which struck many as weakness, his testimony appeared to appease McCarthy.

From Stevens's very first telegram to McCarthy, offering to help him root out subversives in the Army, the Army secretary seemed to be catering to McCarthy's every whim. When McCarthy wanted a plane to take his entourage to Boston, Stevens gave him his DC-3, and took a smaller plane home instead. When McCarthy was unhappy because Stevens told reporters that there were no spies at Fort Monmouth, Stevens took McCarthy to lunch at his club—and changed his story to suit McCarthy. When Roy Cohn was angered after being kept out of a secret radar lab and declared "war" on the Army for such a slight, the secretary soothed the young man's feelings with an apology. Did McCarthy and his staff need a place to eat lunch downtown? Use my club, offered the secretary, and just charge it to me.

To his credit, Stevens had refused to get Schine a direct commission, and told Schine that boot camp would be good for him. But he gave Schine an extra two weeks to report to Fort Dix, and he allowed him to go through boot camp like no other draftee, giving him frequent weekend and evening passes for "committee work" with Cohn. The testimony revealed that Schine had promptly abused his privileges, hiding in a truck cab on rainy days, leaving almost every night to dine in Trenton with Cohn, and excusing himself from drill practice to make an enormous number of long-distance phone calls.

Ray Jenkins, the committee's counsel, elicited the story of McCarthy's pressure on the Army from Stevens, and then clumsily switched hats and cross-examined Stevens on the special treatment he accorded Private Schine.

YOU ARE FAIR AND IMPARTIAL. MAY GOD GIVE YOU STRENGTH, a woman wired Jenkins when he finished with Stevens's direct testimony. When Jenkins began cross-examination, the woman sent a second wire: DISREGARD WIRE ASKING GOD TO GIVE YOU STRENGTH.

Jenkins was heavy-handed and blunt; with his huge jaw working he would demand, "Why? Why? Why?" as if trying to break Stevens and make him confess to some awful crime. His booming courtroom voice hit the microphones so hard that technicians had to install a special guard to keep his mouth two inches away.

Jenkins's treatment of Stevens was mild compared to what McCarthy did to him, however. By the end of the fourth day, Stevens had finished testifying, Jenkins had finished his cross-examination, and the senators on the committee had exhausted their questioning. Yet McCarthy managed to keep the Army secretary on the stand for ten more days.

He was able to do it because he was allowed unlimited cross-examination. Under rules insisted upon by McCarthy, every senator was given ten minutes of cross-examination. When each one had finished, the questioning would go around the table again. Long after everyone else had run out of anything to say, McCarthy kept flailing away at Stevens, taking small bites out of him, ten minutes at a time. And when McCarthy felt like making a statement, rather than asking a question, he would simply interrupt whoever was talking to make a "point of order."

Under the rules of parlimentary procedure, a "point of order" is to be used to correct improprieties in the proceedings. McCarthy, typically, turned the point of order into a tool of impropriety, and made a shambles of order. His Republican colleagues just sat back and let him.

In effect, McCarthy conducted a filibuster. He asked Stevens one hundred forty-three versions of the same question: "Did you want to stop the Fort Monmouth hearings?" Most of his questions were designed not to elicit an answer, but to utter as much unsworn testimony as possible before the TV cameras. When McCarthy got tired, then Roy Cohn took over. For instance, on May 6, Cohn asked Stevens:

> My question to the Secretary, Mr. Welch, is whether he knows that the day before the report was released the Secretary's office was asked to produce before this committee six additional Communists then currently in the military. . . .

Cohn was trying to show by this question that the Army had released my "Chronology of Events" to stop McCarthy from exposing Communists in the Army. There had been a request to produce six people, but there was no proof that they were Communists. Yet Cohn managed to imply, on national TV, that the Army was rife with Reds. Cohn followed up this question with another:

> . . . Did Mr. Adams likewise inform you that he had told Mr. Carr that if we would stop the hearings and call no more of these Communists, or people who had covered up for them, this report would not be issued?

It was all fiction. I had offered Carr no such deal; there were no Communists or "people who covered up for them."

Another McCarthy tactic was to ask Stevens questions he couldn't possibly answer. Unfortunately, that did not stop Stevens from trying. Painfully, he would grope to justify decisions made by others, or to recall this or that document which may or may not have crossed his desk at some time. There was an entire warehouse in Baltimore full of several acres of filing cabinets, each stuffed with security files on Army personnel. McCarthy presumed before the cameras that Stevens knew the contents of each file.

Under questioning by McCarthy, Stevens sometimes found himself boxed in by his own prior policy of appeasement. One of McCarthy's charges was that Stevens punished General Lawton, the commandant at Fort Monmouth, because Lawton had cooperated with McCarthy's committee.

Stevens sputtered incoherently while trying to reply. McCarthy's charge was not true. But the truth was just as damaging to Stevens. In

McCarthy's efforts to use Fort Monmouth commander Major General Kirke
Lawton to support his charges that Stevens sought to discipline Lawton for
supporting McCarthy was continuous, as were his efforts (unsuccessful) to
get Lawton on the witness stand to so testify. Here Lawton is shown with
most of McCarthy's major aides. Seated, left to right, are consultant G. David
Schine, Senator McCarthy, and General Lawton. Standing, left to right, are
McCarthy's chief investigator James Juliana, chief counsel Roy Cohn, and
chief of staff Frank Carr. COURTESY UNITED PRESS INTERNATIONAL.

fact, on October 2, Stevens had *ordered* Lawton to cooperate with
McCarthy. Lawton had taken the order to heart, and begun suspending
in droves employees suspected of subversion. Then, almost two months
later, Lawton had shown his Red-hunting zeal again in a series of
speeches to top-level employees at Fort Monmouth. According to the
local papers, Lawton had blamed some respected universities (Columbia, Harvard, the Universities of Minnesota and Chicago, CCNY, and
MIT) for the spread of communism in the United States.

This attack on the universities upset Stevens. He told me that he
intended to relieve Lawton if the newspaper accounts were true. But,

he added, he wanted me to check first with McCarthy, and tell him that if Lawton was relieved, it had nothing to do with Lawton's cooperation with McCarthy.

I was not keen on the idea of having McCarthy "preclear" personnel actions by the secretary of the army. I also recalled that Stevens had accommodated McCarthy's displeasure with General Partridge, the chief of Army Intelligence, by banishing him overseas when he was caught not knowing about "subversive" books in his library. So I lightly asked Stevens, "What are we going to do with all those surplus generals we relieve?"

Stevens did not appreciate my flippancy. He exploded. "I am the secretary of the army! I don't care for that sort of talk! If any of my officers are making improper remarks that I can prove, they'll have to go!"

But Lawton stayed. It may have been because General Ridgway changed Stevens's mind, or because Stevens was afraid to cross McCarthy. In any event, McCarthy was able to twist the incident around at the hearings, insisting that I had repeatedly begged permission to fire Lawton.[1]

McCarthy and Stevens made an odd match through this long ordeal. McCarthy looked grotesque close-up, his face covered with cream-colored pancake makeup to disguise his heavy beard for the television cameras. Though he was fleshy with whiskey weight, and his shirt would be soaked through by noon, his sharp nose made him look like a hawk as he descended on Stevens. His voice was usually a tight whine, and he occasionally emitted a strange, high giggle.

Stevens on the stand looked like Stevens under any other circumstances. His cheeks were chubby and pink and freshly shaven; his gray hair was neatly combed; and his suit—always gray double-breasted—was beautifully cut and neatly pressed. He looked like the men who pass the collection plates at prosperous Presbyterian churches, which he did when he was home in Plainfield, New Jersey.

1. At the hearings, McCarthy claimed that Stevens had punished Lawton by blocking his promotion and forcing his retirement. McCarthy wanted to get Lawton on the stand to support this assertion, but there was a slight catch. Stevens had nothing to do with Lawton's missed promotion; what's more, Lawton had applied for a medical disability retirement. He could not very well claim that Stevens had driven him out of the Army, lest he lose his medical benefits. On the day Lawton was to testify, John Pernice, the Signal Corps chief counsel, met Cohn in Karl Mundt's office and asked the two of them, "Are you gentlemen prepared to do that to General Lawton?" Lawton was not called.

Stevens was unfailingly polite before McCarthy's crude browbeating. To McCarthy's condescending, "Oh come on now, Bob," he would reply, "Yes sir" and "No sir." Not once did he raise his voice or lose his temper, although McCarthy did everything humanly possible to provoke him.

Many admired Stevens for his calm graciousness under pressure. STEVENS, A LATTER-DAY JOB, HANGS GRIMLY TO HIS PATIENCE, headlined the Washington *Star*. Wrote the *Star*'s Mary McGrory:

> If they give out any good conduct medals when the Army McCarthy hearings are over, Robert T. Stevens should be first in line to get his. For eight days, the Army Secretary had been having his honesty questioned, his motives impugned, and his patriotism challenged. He has been bullied, baited, and patronized. He has been treated like a stubborn and not very bright child. Throughout his ordeal, moreover, he has been subjected to the rather jostling familiarity of Senator McCarthy, who calls him "Bob."
>
> Mr. Stevens had not once shouted, lost his temper or cast aspersions on any character. He has not—and this is probably the full measure of his forebearance—turned on the junior senator from Wisconsin and said through set teeth:
>
> "And don't call me Bob, either!"

Other newspapers, however, saw in Stevens's gentlemanly forebearance the Army's policy of appeasement. "He acts like a man born without a snarl," reported a North Carolina newspaper, "as mild as a duck on a rock." After two weeks of hearing Stevens grope on the stand, most shared the assessment of Stevens's boss, Secretary of Defense Charles E. Wilson: "If a gunman held him up in an alley, he would hand over his wallet and then write the man a check to buy a new suit of clothes."

Andover, Yale, and a textile business were not the proper training grounds for street fighting with McCarthy. "My background hasn't fit me for this sort of thing," he moaned one night to Norman Dorsen, one of my young associates in the Army counselor's office.

Gradually, McCarthy's browbeating took its toll. In the late afternoon, Stevens's answers began to falter, and his weariness began to show. He answered one question, "I don't think that I did, probably." Even his sartorial splendor slipped: A newspaper photographer caught his feet crossed under the witness table, shod in mismatched shoes. By the fourteenth day, his right eye blinked uncontrollably, his right cheek twitched; his voice broke, and tears welled up in his eyes. The double-dose of penicillin he had taken that morning could not ward off a rising fever. He was done in.

While Stevens kept his temper in public, it grew shorter and shorter at the Pentagon after his testimony. Any criticism of his testimony would bring a sharp rebuke. Eventually, I stopped saying much of anything to him.

But my frustration began showing in public. The following appeared in the Washington *Daily News,* May 7, 1954 in an article by Anthony Lewis:

EVERYBODY'S GETTING RAGGED

Intense frustration is becoming apparent as the Army-McCarthy carousel grinds around and around.

Army Secretary Robert Stevens, who has been fabulously earnest and polite during most of his saga on the stand and once seemed near tears, yesterday showed an undertone of desperation. His jaw worked between questions, his eyes were glazed, and he looked as if something might suddenly snap.

But Army Counselor John G. Adams is the really frustrated man. Quite apparently he's much more familiar with the subjects on which Secretary Stevens has been quizzed. When Mr. Stevens is asked a question, Mr. Adams often answers to himself in a hoarse whisper.

"No, no, no" he mourned at one point yesterday, as if in anguish. Another time he exclaimed, "Jesus. . . ."

Sometimes Mr. Adams half rises out of his chair in the row behind Secretary Stevens, as if to plunge into the proceedings.

On other occasions he laughs sardonically to himself at what he appears to consider absurd remarks by Sen. McCarthy.

Put on the defensive by McCarthy, Stevens missed his few opportunities to take the offensive. McCarthy would taunt Stevens, almost begging him to hit back. He openly invited Stevens to describe McCarthy's pressure on the Army. "Just try to tell us what you objected to," demanded McCarthy.

STEVENS: I objected to the hammering over the head of the Army and the unfair publicity.

MCCARTHY: You talk about "hammering over the head." It sounds rather rough.

STEVENS: I think that.

MCCARTHY: Who up to that point had been hammered over the head?

STEVENS: I think the New York *Times* editorial this morning gives a pretty good picture of what I am trying to talk about here.

To the millions of television viewers who had not read the *Times* that morning, Stevens's "picture" was meaningless. McCarthy moved right in to get the last word. "You mean a few Communists in the Army were hammered over the head, don't you, Bob?"

Stevens did not get much help from his lawyer at such moments. While McCarthy taunted and browbeat Stevens, Joe Welch sat back, for the most part, quietly listening. During recess, he could be found standing alone, hands thrust in his pockets, toes pointing out, silently watching. At the hearings, he would cup his chin in the palm of his hand, and trace the deep furrows on his forehead with a long, bony finger.

Most of the accounts of the Army-McCarthy hearings portray Welch as overwhelmed during the first few days. He was depicted as just a little Boston lawyer in the big, bad world of Washington politics, blinking innocently into the TV lights, no match for the bluster of McCarthy or the quick jabs of Cohn.

Welch did his best to reinforce this impression. "I came down from Boston in the guise of a simple trial lawyer. I supposed I try to think up some questions and then, if I did not like the answer, ask another one." Welch wanted reporters to believe this, and by and large they did.

But it was all a big act. Welch was a great trial lawyer, and he was simply biding his time, waiting for the right cues.

His background was indeed humble. His parents were English; his mother had been a domestic servant while his father was an enlisted man in the Royal Navy, which he had run away to join at fourteen. They emigrated to America and settled in the tiny town of Primghar, Iowa, where Joseph was born in 1890. After graduating from Grinnell College Welch had made his way to Harvard Law School, where he scraped to pay his tuition, waiting on tables and selling maps and flagpoles.

By the time he undertook to represent the Army gratuitously (pro-

Joseph Nye Welch of Boston, Massachusetts, at the age of sixty-four, when he served as the Army's special counsel. A quintessential Victorian gentleman, he dressed like a middle-aged dandy. He was unfailingly courteous and at the same time shrewd and brilliant in his rapierlike thrusts and counterthrusts. He endeared himself to millions of televiewers during the hearings and inflicted severe damage on McCarthy in numerous exchanges, where McCarthy's blunderbuss crudeness was exacerbated by his losing skirmishes with Welch. COURTESY U.S. ARMY.

testing that he had no political experience and wouldn't know how to comport himself in the presence of television), Welch was a senior partner in the old-line Boston law firm of Hale and Dorr. Along the way, he had become a Brahmin. When I met him, he looked the perfect cross between a prep school headmaster and the sort of man who serves as a trustee for old and distinguished institutions and families. Somewhat of a dandy, he was resplendent in tweeds and bow ties (he owned one hundred fifty of them) and he had picked up a slight aristocratic lilt along with a perfect command of the English language. He exuded courtliness and Old World charm, and had that elusive something now called television charisma.

Welch had long since learned the value of detachment, of stepping back and showing nothing but quiet integrity. It was as much an act for Welch as appearing effortless is for the rich, but it was an act that he had thoroughly mastered.

Welch was not really sitting back while McCarthy devoured Stevens. He was waiting for a chance to strike. I think McCarthy sensed

how dangerous this quiet, slightly awed-looking, elderly man was.
While McCarthy called everyone by their first names (Stu Symington,
Scoop Jackson, Ev Dirksen, Bob Stevens, and so forth), he greeted
Welch coolly as Mr. Welch.

Welch found his chance before long. The first was a photograph,
the second was a letter. They were to become famous as the "Purloined Letter" and the "Doctored Photograph."

CHAPTER XXVII

Midmorning Madness

Stevens had done much to please McCarthy and his men in the fall of 1953. One of his lesser acts was to pose in front of his airplane at McGuire Air Force Base with a smiling Dave Schine.

On the fourth day of the hearings, Counsel Jenkins asked Stevens about this picture. When Stevens couldn't recall it, Jenkins thrust at him a large reproduction of the photograph, showing the Army secretary and the private smiling at each other. Stevens mumbled in confusion, and Jenkins jumped him:

> JENKINS: Mr. Stevens, isn't it a fact that you were being especially nice and considerate and tender of this boy Schine—?

McCarthy, it appeared, had scored. But the public relations officer at McGuire Air Force base thought something was not quite right about the picture, and he dug through his files to get the original. That picture showed something different: Stevens was not smiling at Schine, but at a Colonel Jack Bradley, who was standing next to Schine. Colonel Bradley had been cropped out of the picture so triumphantly displayed by Jenkins at the hearings that afternoon.

The McGuire PR man immediately called Welch. By morning the whole picture—blown up and displayed on a large board, was in Washington and ready for presentation at the hearings.

Welch began that day's hearing by quietly attracting Chairman Mundt's attention. "Mr. Welch, a point of order?" inquired Mundt. Welch went into his soft-shoe, little-Boston-lawyer-lost-in-parliamentary procedure routine.

> WELCH: I don't know what it is but it's a point of something. I have—
>
> MUNDT: If it is a point of order, you may state it.
>
> WELCH: My point of order is that Mr. Jenkins yesterday was imposed upon and so was the Secretary of the Army by having a doctored or altered photograph produced in this courtroom as if it were honest.
>
> MUNDT: This is a committee room, Mr. Welch.

Welch blinked at him, but the reporters were scribbling by now. McCarthy saw trouble, and immediately launched a point of order on an obscure point.

He was flailing, and Senator Symington—his prime antagonist among the Democrats—taunted him: "I would like to say if this is not a point of order, it is out of order."

"Oh, be quiet," snapped McCarthy.

"I haven't the slightest intention of being quiet," reported Symington.

McCarthy, as usual, couldn't stand to be treated the way he treated others. "I am getting sick and tired," he whined, "of sitting down here at the end of the table and having whomever (sic) wants to interrupt in the middle of a sentence."

The debate went downhill from there, as various McCarthy minions danced around while avoiding blame for cropping the picture. Welch retreated, watching the spectacle as he rested his chin in the palm of his hand. Only when Roy Cohn took the stand did Welch, for a moment, unsheath his rapier.

> WELCH: Mr. Cohn, I assume you would like it understood that although I sit at the same table, I am not your counsel.
>
> COHN: There is not a statement that has been made at this hearing with which I am in more complete agreement . . . Roy Cohn is here speaking for Roy Cohn, to give the facts. I have no counsel and I feel the need of none.

McCarthy attempts to defend the cropped photo. The lower photo, as presented by McCarthy to the committee, shows Secretary Stevens smiling,
apparently at Private Schine. The larger photo, presented to the committee
the next day by the Army, showed that the photo had been cropped to cut
out Colonel Jack Bradley, at whom Stevens actually was smiling. From left
to right are Senator Henry Jackson, McCarthy's staff chief Frank Carr, and
McCarthy (standing). Next to him is Struve Hensel, the Defense Department
general counsel. Between McCarthy and Hensel in the rear row, wearing
glasses, is Colonel Jack Murray, a judge advocate officer assigned as a
Welch special assistant. I am seen at the extreme right of the picture. COUR-
TESY PHOTOWORLD (F.P.G.).

> WELCH: In all modesty, sir, I am content that it should appear from
> my end that I am not your counsel.

Cohn was a little slow to join in the general laughter.

Welch then asked McCarthy's assistant, James Juliana, where the
cropped picture came from. "Do you think it came from a pixie?" he
asked. McCarthy thought he saw an opportunity to divert and tweak
Welch:

> MCCARTHY: Will the counsel for my benefit define—I think he may be
> an expert on that—what a pixie is?

WELCH: Yes, I should say, Mr. Senator, that a pixie is a close relative of a fairy. Shall I proceed, sir? Have I enlightened you?

McCarthy had exposed himself for a second, and Welch had struck. Many viewers were also stirred by a distant memory of a "Doctored Photograph" of Millard Tydings of Maryland, apparently posing with Earl Browder, the former head of the Communist party. McCarthy had been behind that low blow, too.

Welch's sharp barb had been but a brief diversion. For the next week, he resumed his detached posture, chin in hand, fingers rubbing his blue-veined temples. But then on May 5, almost two weeks into the hearings, another chance came.

Late in the afternoon on May 4, McCarthy had thrust a new document at Stevens. It was the two-and-a-quarter-page "letter" from J. Edgar Hoover to General Bolling, chief of Army Intelligence, revealing the names of the thirty-five Fort Monmouth employees suspected of subversion. This was the letter that had been slipped to McCarthy by one of his "young patriots"; it had set McCarthy off on his investigation of Fort Monmouth in September, 1953.

Stevens had been caught by surprise. He had never seen the letter, a fact McCarthy emphasized as further proof of the Army's lack of vigilence at Fort Monmouth. Welch had but one question: Was the letter authentic?

An overnight check with the FBI showed that indeed it was not authentic. The original Hoover-to-Bolling letter had been fifteen pages. The "young patriot" apparently had condensed the "good parts" into a two-and-a-quarter-page version and slipped it to McCarthy. The excerpted version was really not much different from the original, and McCarthy repeatedly insisted that it was a "verbatim copy," an "abbreviated report," "an accurate summary" of the real thing.

Nonetheless, the fact that information had been extracted from it and retyped was a legal issue. Retyping a classified document amounted to "publication"—which was a criminal act. McCarthy, for the first time, was put on the stand in order to explain how he came into possession of this "Purloined Letter."

He defiantly protected his "young patriot,"[1] indeed his network of informants:

1. I have often wondered who the "young patriot" was. At times, I suspected J. Edgar Hoover himself. A book by Hoover's aide, the late William Sullivan (*The Bureau*, New York: W.W. Norton & Company, Inc., 1979), disclosed that Hoover regularly and secretly supplied McCarthy

Welch challenges the "Purloined Letter." Robert Collier, one of Ray Jenkins's aides, is testifying that the FBI director has labeled the document as
spurious. I am seen between them, in the row behind. Welch's assistant, Jim
St. Clair, is seen to the left of Welch in the rear. COURTESY CBS FILMS.

> MCCARTHY: I want to notify the people who give me information that
> there is no way on earth that any committee, any force, can get me to
> violate the confidence of these people.

McCarthy was skating on thin ice. Welch watched, finger crooked
on cheek, brow furrowing, waiting. He stirred himself to ask a few
questions:

> WELCH: Senator McCarthy, when you took the stand you knew of
> course that you were going to be asked about his letter, did you not?
> MCCARTHY: I assumed that would be the subject.
> WELCH: And you, of course, understood that you were going to be
> asked the source from which you got it.
> MCCARTHY: I won't answer that. . . .
> WELCH: The oath included a promise, a solemn promise by you to tell
> the whole truth and nothing but the truth. Is that correct sir?
> MCCARTHY: Mr. Welch, you are not the first individual that tried to

---

with confidential FBI information. Hoover and McCarthy were friends, often vacationing together,
and their admiration was mutual. Still, I am inclined to believe that the "young patriot" was—
as McCarthy testified—an official in the Army. Though we have no proof to this day, those of
us who worked closely on the Fort Monmouth matter believe we know who the person was.

get me to betray the confidence and give out the names of my informants. You will be no more successful than those who have tried in the past.

WELCH: I am only asking you sir, did you realize when you took the oath that you were making a solemn promise to tell the truth to this committee?

MCCARTHY: I understand the oath Mr. Welch.

WELCH: And when you took it did you have some mental reservation, some Fifth or Sixth Amendment notion that you could measure what you could tell?

MCCARTHY: I don't take the Fifth or Sixth Amendment.

WELCH: Have you some private reservation when you take the oath that you will tell the whole truth that lets you be the judge of what you will testify to?

MCCARTHY: The answer is that there is no reservation about telling the whole truth.

WELCH: Thank you, sir. Then tell us who delivered the document to you!

Incredibly, Senator Dirksen managed to save McCarthy by claiming that his refusal was justified because he was a "law enforcement officer . . . ferreting out crime."

But McCarthy had been exposed by Welch's artful questions. The same Joe McCarthy who taunted witnesses for hiding behind the Fifth Amendment, was now hiding himself. Furthermore, he had declared himself above the law. He had taken possession of a "Purloined Letter" that violated the law, and then contemptuously defied Congress by refusing to answer when asked where he got the information. Such defiance, "if sustained," wrote Walter Lippmann, "is a license to lawlessness and an invitation to anarchy. . . . It was in accord with this very principle—that their own consciences were superior to the laws of the land—that . . . the Rosenbergs acted."

It was a damning moment for McCarthy, and he proceeded to make it worse by vowing to publicly release the letter. No "Truman directive" banning disclosure of FBI loyalty-security reports was going to stop him, he cried, growing hysterical. He demanded that his colleagues in Congress overrule a decision not to release the letter made by "someone in the executive department." The someone happened to be the attorney general, the nation's highest law enforcement officer.

McCarthy's allies on the committee watched this performance with dismay. Dirksen, in particular, was always searching for a way to call off the hearings. Watching McCarthy shoot himself in the foot made him redouble his efforts. He proposed a compromise: After Stevens finished testifying, McCarthy would take the stand—as the last public witness. That way, the two major principals would get their say, but the public would be spared an unseemly but apparently endless brawl. If any more testimony was necessary, it could be in closed sessions before the committee.

The hearings had indeed degenerated. When McCarthy was not asking Stevens the same rhetorical questions again and again, he was squabbling with his Democratic antagonist, Stuart Symington. McCarthy had learned that the Army had gone to Symington in February for support without Joe's knowledge, and McCarthy naturally saw this as a foul plot. He made much of a transcribed conversation between Stevens and Symington in which the Democratic senator had warned the secretary of the army that he "better forget the Marquis of Queensberry Rules" if the Army was going to "play" with McCarthy because McCarthy played "rough." Symington was not chastened by this revelation; he yelled right back at McCarthy: "You better go see a psychiatrist." Mundt, the chairman, who was supposed to keep order, just sat back and smoked his pipe. Occasionally, he publicly despaired of "this midmorning madness," this "miserable business." But he seemed incapable of doing anything about it.

The press began to share Mundt's assessment. While most newspapers thought a public airing was healthy, they began to be disgusted by all the dirty linen and pointless diversions. "Endless repetition and hopeless obfuscation," lamented the Washington *Post*. Wrote a British columnist in the London *Daily Mirror:* "I have been watching a circus so fantastic, so degrading, so puerile, and so recklessly dirty that the disgust one feels is matched only by the alarm over the behavior of our closest ally in the conduct of their domestic affairs." Out in the American heartland, the view was just as grim: "Talk about circuses!" exclaimed an editorial in *The People's Voice* of Helena, Montana. "There never had been anything like this since they sat a midget on J. P. Morgan's lap." The editorial recounted the various low points ("Here's a Senator filibustering a hearing into charges of his own misconduct with speeches poorly disguised as points of order, with grandstand plays and extraneous charges. . . .") and sighed, "O, brother! And the newspapers used to talk about the mess in Washington under Harry Truman."

Against this backdrop of public disgruntlement, Dirksen thought he could "ring down the curtain," as he put it. Stevens, wracked with fever after fourteen days on the stand, was finally finished. Now if McCarthy would just say a few closing words. . . .[2]

The Democrats didn't want McCarthy to get off so lightly, and presented three solid votes against calling off the hearings. But on the Republican side, Dworshak and Potter were eager to forget what Dworshak called "the circus" and Potter termed "this public brawl." So all Dirksen needed for a 4 to 3 majority was Mundt, a McCarthyite.

Mundt may have been pro-McCarthy, but he was also spineless. He thought he saw a way out of the hearings without having to take responsibility for it.

When Dirksen's settlement resolution was publicly offered at the committee hearing, Mundt passed the buck by deferring to Stevens. With a great show of fairness, the chairman said that he could not agree to the Dirksen resolution unless Stevens would say such a resolution would do no inequity to the Army side.

The press, for once, was impressed by Mundt's honorable performance. In fact, Mundt thought he was on safe ground. Over the past few days, he had been secretly meeting with Fred Seaton, the assistant defense secretary, who had close White House ties. Seaton, perhaps reflecting the White House view, was also eager to see the hearings shut down and the country's attention diverted from such embarrassing squabbles. Mundt felt confident that Seaton could use his White House standing to bring Stevens around and persuade him to call the hearings off.

But Mundt was mistaken. Stevens, though striken with fever and now bedridden at home, was intransigent. Twice, Mundt sent Welch off to telephone Stevens to get his acquiescence, but both times Welch returned shaking his head. Stevens had earlier told Welch that he would not be a party to any more deals, that he had eaten chicken once and that was enough, and that while he could not stop the committee from voting to end the hearings, he wasn't going to participate in the deal. His honor had been impugned and the hearing could go on all year if needed, unless the charges against the Army were withdrawn.

While the parleying was in progress, Stevens roused himself from his sickbed and came to the Pentagon, where we went to Seaton's

2. Dirksen wasn't the only one who wanted to call off the hearings. Dr. Charles Mayo, the famous medical authority, wanted to end the inquiry because, he said, it was raising the nation's blood pressure. "I look at it," said Dr. Mayo, "but I don't agree that it should be happening."

Roy Cohn testifying on April 27. Behind him on his extreme right, is Major
General Miles Reber, against whose brother McCarthy made an under-
handed and false attack on the first day of the hearing simply because Reber
had testified as to the efforts by the McCarthy group on Schine's behalf.
Next to Reber is Major General Robert Young, chief of Army personnel,
and between Young and Cohn can be seen Assistant Army Secretary Hugh
Milton. To the left of Cohn in order are Joe Welch, Secretary Stevens, and
James St. Clair. COURTESY UNITED PRESS INTERNATIONAL.

office. Seaton asked us, Would it be agreeable to us, to have the whole
matter dropped? I said I thought it was Stevens's prerogative to decide;
he was the secretary. Stevens said no again, not unless McCarthy con-
cedes the falsity of his charges. When Seaton got this answer, he stalked
angrily out of his own office and slammed the door. How dare Stevens
value his honor!

Mundt was trapped. He grumbled, but cast his vote to keep the
hearings going. Dirksen was crestfallen, and McCarthy accused Welch
of "welching," an expression he enjoyed using.

So the hearings would continue. Stevens had managed to salvage some honor by refusing to call it quits. His counsel, Joseph Welch, had stood by while McCarthy had abused Stevens, but he had also tricked the demagogue into wounding himself. The Army had not exactly covered itself with glory, but McCarthy had shown his true colors.

Now it was my turn.

CHAPTER XXVIII

"It's Mr. Adams
to You, Senator!"

On May 7, under a photograph that showed me clenching a pencil in my teeth, Mary McGrory of the Washington *Star* wrote:

> When Mr. Stevens steps aside and Mr. Adams takes over the change of pace is terrific. The proceedings shift at once from an inquisition to a fight.
>
> A slight, sharp-nosed, green-eyed man, Mr. Adams has been simmering on the sidelines during the 11 days of the hearings. Every time his name is mentioned—and that happens a good deal—he looks up sharply, wordlessly answers the question involved, glares around the room and then goes back to his furious left-hand doodling. Sometimes he rolls up a little piece of paper and chews on it tensely. In all, he gives the impression of a man who is sore and who furthermore doesn't care who knows about it. . . .
>
> When Mr. Adams relieves Mr. Stevens on the witness stand, it probably won't be any lawn party.

From time to time during Stevens's testimony, I was called to the stand to answer a few questions. One question concerned a press release

I had drafted back in October for McCarthy's possible use. According to McCarthy, I had tried to persuade him to issue a statement calling off the Fort Monmouth investigation. Of course I would have liked that, but that's not what the press release stated. It said the Army was ready to take over the investigation on the conclusion of McCarthy's own investigation. It praised the "many thousands of competent, able, and completely loyal Americans" working at Fort Monmouth, and regretted that there were "a few bad apples who are tainting the barrel." But it said nothing about halting the hearings. Indeed, the last paragraph announced that McCarthy would soon begin open hearings on Fort Monmouth. I had drafted the release after Cohn told me that McCarthy was going to end his closed hearings. We were all meeting in New York in a day or so, and I had put it together in case McCarthy wanted to make such an announcement.

Six months later, at the Army-McCarthy hearings, McCarthy tried to use this draft press release as further evidence of the Army's campaign to frustrate his search for subversives. I was briefly put on the stand to testify about my role.

McCarthy had been all smiles during the hearings, playfully squeezing my shoulder one day as he walked by my chair. But I was in no mood for his friendship, and I was disgusted when he called Stevens "Bob" in a patronizing tone of voice. So when McCarthy called me "John," I snapped at him:

"It's Mr. Adams to you, Senator."

Thereafter, whenever I saw McCarthy and Cohn and Carr in the elevator, they would mockingly say, "Good morning, Mr. Adams. Good morning, Mr. Adams." But at least McCarthy didn't call me "John" during the hearings.

McCarthy began reading aloud from my draft of the press release, but in his usual fashion he omitted the last paragraph announcing new hearings. With some vehemence, I interrupted him: "Read the whole memorandum in context!" I flung the document across the table. The paper flipped up, making it appear that I was throwing it at his face. "Let us keep our tempers," said McCarthy, in his most unctious voice. He said that he was "not accusing" me "of wrong intent." I glared at him across the table, and demanded "You are not accusing me of anything?" Jenkins hastily interrupted with a point of order, and the confrontation quieted.

It left an impact on the viewers and the press. I received a good

I rest my cheek on the microphone as the wrangling over the subject of
executive privilege continues. Jim St. Clair is on my right and seated immediately behind me is Colonel Ken BeLieu, Stevens's senior military aide.
COURTESY WIDE WORLD PHOTOS.

many congratulatory telegrams, though one old war buddy wired me
from Houston telling me not to lose my temper.

When I finally did take the stand on May 12 to begin my direct
testimony, however, I looked a good deal less combative, according
to the newspapers. McGrory wrote that I looked tired and gray, and
one reporter joked, "If Stevens needed penicillin when they finished
with him, Adams will need a blood transfusion." In truth, I felt well
enough, though I had not been sleeping well, and, according to one
reporter, had sunken eyes. I was no newcomer to congressional testimony. My only concern was that the Republican majority was more
interested in saving McCarthy than in establishing the truth.

The first day was fairly easy and straightforward. For weeks I had
been poring over the "Chronology of Events" since I first took the

Army job, and I was able to simply recount, day by day, the abuse heaped on me by Cohn—when he ordered me out of a car in the middle of Park Avenue, his phone call to get Schine off KP duty at Fort Dix, the endless phone calls and vituperative language (though I did not recite Cohn's "making Dave eat shit" line for the television audience). "If you would pile together all the abuse that I had from all the Members of Congress and all of the congressional employees over a period of five years," I testified, "it would not compare to the abuse I took over this situation."

At the end of the day, a newspaperman wrote:

> His manner was incisive and often icy. Feeling seldom tinged his voice. At times, he spoke in such low tones that he was asked to nuzzle up to the microphone. As he made his most serious charges against the McCarthy camp—"pressure . . . vituperative language . . . obscenity . . . abuse" . . . his manner suggested a man testifying more in sorrow than in anger. As the hearings wore on, a deep frown notched between his eyes.

McCarthy, for the first time during the hearings, remained quiet. He affected disinterest, making a great show of reading the newspaper while I talked.

What captured the headlines that first day, however, was not Cohn's abuse or McCarthy's silence. It was my revelation, at the end of the day, that the White House played a role in the fight against McCarthy.

The news came out while I was recounting how McCarthy had tried to subpoena the members of the Army Loyalty-Security Boards. I had been dead set against McCarthy's demand, and I had gone to the Justice Department on January 21 for their support. There, in the attorney general's office, I found Sherman Adams, the President's chief aide, and three other White House insiders—U.S. Ambassador Henry Cabot Lodge, Special Counsel Gerald Morgan, and General Persons, the congressional liaison chief. It had been Sherman Adams who suggested that I begin to make a record—the "Chronology of Events" that became the basis for the Army's counterattack.

There was a sudden stir in the committee room when I dropped the names of Sherman Adams and Ambassador Lodge. The next morning the New York *Times* had a three-column headline, ADAMS SWEARS TOP WHITE HOUSE AIDE URGED LISTING OF PLEAS FOR

SCHINE. The Washington *Post*'s two-decker ran: ADAMS SAYS IKE
URGED SCHINE RECORD.

The news was to cause a new turn in the hearings when the senators
got a chance to question me two days later. In the meantime, Counsel
Jenkins clumsily switched hats and began his "cross-examination,"
which lasted a full day.

"Those who hear only part of Counsel's questions may think he has
chosen sides," said Chairman Mundt before Jenkins began. "He has
a Jekyll and Hyde personality." Jaw jutting, eyes bulging, Jenkins did
his best to bully me. For about an hour we danced around trying to
establish my "attitude" toward McCarthy's investigation of Fort Monmouth. My attitude, of course, had been abhorrence. But I couldn't
very well express those sentiments now without giving McCarthy an
opening to exploit his "blackmail" charge. So Jenkins and I finally
settled on "indifference." I had no "enthusiasm" for the hearings,
but I didn't try to get them called off, either. Like Stevens, I objected
to the manner, not to the fact, of the hearings. The Army was receiving
a very bad and unfair press, I said, and I was uneasy "about the headlines and how they compared with what was going on in the 'executive
sessions.' "

Looking back at the transcripts of those hearings after twenty-five
years, I regret to see what an apologist I was for Stevens and the
administration. I felt compelled to say that it was "gracious" of Stevens to apologize to Cohn after Cohn had thrown a temper tantrum
when he was barred from entering a secret lab at Fort Monmouth.
"Wasn't that appeasement?" Jenkins asked me. "I don't think that's
appeasement," I replied. "That's living with people." Jenkins asked
me whether it wasn't appeasement for Stevens to back off his "no
spies at Monmouth" statement after the Merchants Club lunch. "Well,
I don't know;" I said, "everybody would interpret it differently." I
saw "nothing wrong" when Stevens allowed McCarthy and his boys
to charge their meals at the Merchants Club. Wasn't it appeasement
for Stevens to grant Schine a long weekend from Fort Dix? It was "for
the purposes of preserving good relations with the committee," I
answered. Mundt, in particular, was eager to get the charges dropped
against Frank Carr, the mild-mannered ex-FBI agent. Over my angry
objections, Carr's name had been added as a co-respondent in the Army
charges prepared by Welch and the faceless superiors in the administration who were running the show. Yet during the hearings, I found

myself the only Army witness defending the decision to include Carr among the principals accused. "Don't let Carr off the hook," I had been urged before I went to testify—after Stevens had already done so!

Why I just didn't say that I had no part in this or that decision by Stevens or somebody else, I do not know. Perhaps I suffered from some of the same mentality that White House aides showed when they mindlessly tried to protect their Commander in Chief during Watergate. Perhaps I just let Jenkins bully me into it.

Jenkins wanted me to admit what a great job McCarthy had done in exposing subversion. To do so, he had to get me to lump together spies, subversives, and security risks. "Isn't a subversive or poor risk an embryonic spy?" he demanded. I drew a distinction that was too often lost in those days. "A security risk may be a person who drinks too much or talks too much," I told Jenkins. "Not a spy." "Well," Jenkins blundered on, wasn't it "salutary" to expose these people? "It does a great disservice to them as individuals, and in some cases wrecks their lives," I said. In many instances, I added—as in about a dozen at Fort Monmouth—"the charges fail to stand up, and the people are reinstated," although their names were first dragged through the newspapers by McCarthy.

This was an essential point. Indeed, it went to the heart of all that was wrong with McCarthyism. The terrible harm done these people— not the petty privileges granted Private Schine—should have been the subject of the Army-McCarthy hearings. But my testimony that day was the only time the subject came up. It represented a couple of pages in over seven thousand pages of typewritten transcript.

I spent more time denying McCarthy's ridiculous charge that I had offered to give him the names of Navy and Airforce homosexuals and subversives if he would leave the Army alone. "Did you ever do that, Mr. Adams?" asked Jenkins. "I did not," I said. "We got a definite answer in that, didn't we?" said he. "That is correct, sir," I said. "You will always get a definite answer on that."

There actually had been a homosexual scandal brewing on an Army base in the South, and I had been scared to death that McCarthy and Co. would find out about it. In December, Cohn and Carr had been hinting around about a "big new investigation" of the Army, and I had been afraid some "patriot" had tipped them off. To try to find out what they knew, I had drawn a crude map of the country for them, dividing it into the nine geographic zones used by the Army. I had asked them to point out the zone of their investigation. When they did not point to the South, I had breathed a sigh of relief. But they remembered the incident, and McCarthy had trumped it up as an offer to trade.

As I described this incident at the hearings, some senators, as well as Jenkins, began to look concerned. "Well, it wasn't in Tennessee, Mr. Adams," said Jenkins. "No sir, it was not," I answered to laughter from the audience. Senator McClellan interjected, "Point of order, point of order. Let's exclude Arkansas, too." I said I could. Then Mundt jumped in and demanded to know about South Dakota. I finally had to reassure all the senators on the committee that their states were safe from the homosexual threat.

With this weighty issue out of the way, Mundt turned to allegations that I had accepted favors from Cohn. In the fall Cohn had bought both theater and prize fight tickets for me, and then refused to take my money when I offered to pay him back. I finally stuffed the money in his jacket pocket in January. "You didn't pay until the jig was up, did you?" sneered Jenkins in his most abrasive voice, jaw thrust forward.

Then there was the twenty-five-thousand-dollar law partnership I allegedly tried to extort out of Cohn. My facetiousness had opened me up to this one. I had once jokingly told Cohn, "If you know somebody in New York who wants to pay about twenty-five thousand dollars a year for somebody who is not worth half that money to come here and practice law, send him around." Cohn had replied, "Oh, I might know somebody." I told him to forget it because I knew I didn't have the right training and background for such a venture. He knew there had never been a serious discussion of the subject, but all the same, I got pretty well smeared by Jenkins, who had been well coached, for this "favor seeking."

In the late afternoon, Jenkins let his assistant, Thomas Prewitt, finish up on me. He gave me a rough time trying to explain why I had let Joe Alsop and the other newsmen read my diary. I was not successful in convincing them that the diary was simply the story of how one taxpayer-supported-body—a congressional committee—was mistreating another taxpayer-supported body—the Army. It was not classified. There was no reason to keep it secret, except for the longtime expectation of members of Congress that executive branch employees were not to tattle about congressional misbehavior.

CHAPTER XXIX

Executive Privilege

While Secretary Stevens was still testifying, I went to see Struve Hensel, the former Defense general counsel and a friend, with a dilemma. I knew I was going to have to testify about my meeting in the attorney general's office. "I'm worried about it," I told Hensel, "I don't see any way I can keep the White House out of it if they ask the right questions. How do you think I should handle it?"

Hensel was a big, blunt man. He was a fighter who had told McCarthy to go to hell when he came up with the trumped-up charge that Hensel had been a war profiteer. Because of his combativeness, I had been sorry to lose him as a co-"defendant" when the charges against him were dropped.

Hensel looked across his half-glasses at me and said: "How should you handle it? Pull 'em all in! Why should you be stuck out there all by yourself? Hell, pull 'em all in!"

Bolstered by Hensel's blunt advice, I called Bill Rogers, the deputy attorney general who had known about the Army's problems with McCarthy, and told him that if I were asked, I intended to tell who was there that day in Brownell's office. He listened without comment, and I didn't hear another word about it—until I actually testified about the meeting, and the New York *Times* splashed it all over the front page.

The next morning, as I was leaving the Pentagon to go up on the Hill for my third day of testimony, I got a call from Fred Seaton, the assistant defense secretary. His message was simple: Don't talk anymore about that meeting. These are orders. Written instructions would follow.

Jenkins had finished his cross-examination, and now it was the committee's turn. Symington was the first to bore in:

> SYMINGTON: Why was Ambassador Lodge at the meeting on January 21?
>
> ADAMS: I don't know, sir. I did not arrange for his presence.
>
> SYMINGTON: Was there anything that you discussed that had to do with the United Nations?

Welch stirred beside me and interrupted:

> WELCH: This was a high-level discussion of the executive department, and this witness has been instructed not to testify as to the interchange of views on people at that high level at that meeting.
>
> SYMINGTON: Does that mean we are going to get the information about low-level discussion but not about high-level discussion?

Symington's sarcasm aside, the issue was serious. Symington wanted to know where I got my instructions. I told him that I got them through the Defense Department, but I did not know where they originated. Clearly the finger was beginning to point at the White House. A constitutional confrontation loomed. But first came a moment of terror for me.

At the conclusion of the meeting on January 21, Gerald Morgan, the White House special counsel, and I, had paid a visit to Senator Dirksen. Our purpose had been to tell him about McCarthy's improper pressures on the Army, and to get him to stop McCarthy from subpoenaing the Loyalty Board members. I had told the committee all this. Senator Dirksen, however, decided to give his own version of what happened in his office that evening. The way he said it—implying that he wanted to tell firsthand what *really* happened that evening, nearly knocked me out of my chair. It could only be that he intended to impeach my testimony, to testify that I hadn't told the correct story of the incident. He demanded that he be put under oath. My God, I thought. I could hear my heart pumping. It sounded like a plumber pounding on a pipe with his wrench, at about two hundred strokes a minute.

Dirksen was his usual unctious self as he began:

> DIRKSEN: Mr. Chairman, let me just say . . . for the benefit of those who may be watching this proceeding that there arrived at my office about 2,500 letters and telegrams today. Some of them are so intemperate and abusive and so unrestrained that my office force is afraid that they might affect my finer sensibilities and they don't even show them to me. It would occur . . . that I have been charged with being belligerantly partial to one side or the other.

He was about to show just how partial. He had a few kind words for Gerald Morgan of the White House, a "fine citizen and a brilliant lawyer" whom he "esteemed like a friend." As for me, however, he said, "I know of no reason why Mr. Adams shouldn't have come on his own. My door is always open." It was the "first time I have ever been honored by a visit from Mr. Adams, notwithstanding the fact that it appears that this controversy was in the development stage for a period of nearly two and one-half months."

By having Dirksen take the stand, McCarthy had seen an opportunity to destroy me. Like a black-jowled hawk, he began circling his prey. Wasn't it true, he coaxed Dirksen, that I had threatened to release my report on the Schine affair unless the committee quashed those subpoenas? In other words, wasn't this the moment of blackmail?

As I watched Dirsken's huge mouth open, I thought I was going to have a heart attack. I was almost paralyzed with fright. If Dirksen answered yes, he would support McCarthy's charge of blackmail, and another powerful senatorial voice would be added to my prosecution for perjury. I looked at Dirksen sitting there, his hair carefully crumpled and his thick, rubbery lips working, and I saw the power of the Senate, the power of the Chicago *Tribune,* the force of McCarthyism. And I suddenly saw myself, a once reputable government official indicted for perjury. I had to cup my jaw in the palms of my hands and brace my elbows on the table, so afraid was I that I would simply crumble in front of the television cameras if Dirksen turned on me. Dirksen had only to say yes to McCarthy, and I could go to jail.

He almost did. He went right up to the edge—and pulled back.

DIRKSEN: May I say that my recollection is slightly vague on that point. I am not sure that it was said that a report was going to be circulated. It may have been. But I know what my own agitation and spirit was when I first heard it. I thought if such a report were going to be issued and ventilated on the front pages, that it would seriously reflect upon the credibility of this committee and its usefulness in the future.

Of course, there was no "report" then in existence. Sherman Adams had suggested that I prepare a record of our running fight with McCarthy in the attorney general's office less than an hour before Morgan and I had called on Dirksen.

Again and again, McCarthy tried to lead him into a flat accusation. But each time, Dirksen stopped just short of an accusation. He would talk about his "distress of the spirit," and his fear that the story would be "ventilated." But he never actually accused me of threatening to release the story if those subpoenas weren't quashed.

As I listened, it slowly dawned on me why he was hesitating. I had been saved by the presence of Gerald Morgan in Dirksen's office that evening. Indeed, it had been Morgan, not me, who had done all the talking. Dirksen knew that if he accused me, Morgan—his "esteemed friend" on President Eisenhower's staff—could contradict him. In a sense, Morgan was present in the hearing room as Dirksen spoke. He was like Banquo's ghost—only Dirksen could see him, but he was there.

I survived Dirksen's hints and innuendos, but the day was far from over. In the afternoon, Senator Henry Jackson read the federal perjury statute aloud to me and then asked me twenty-six direct, yes-no answers about my testimony. It was a grim, sobering business, but I was able to answer in good conscience, and Jackson seemed satisfied.

At day's end, as I sat drained by three days of testimony and the heart-stopping events of the morning, Roy Cohn drew the microphone near him to take his turn at cross-examination.

We had hardly spoken in three months. I could recall only a day in mid-February when we had come across each other at the Capitol. Cohn had shrugged and smiled ruefully, as if to ask, "What went wrong? How did this come to pass?"

Cohn returned to our lost friendship as he cross-examined me. He brought up the theater and fight tickets he had bought for me, as well as his invitation to dine at his parents', and getting a table for me at Sardis. He would have mentioned the Drake Hotel bill he had once paid for me—but when he subpoened the hotel's records, he learned that I had insisted on paying it myself.

How was it possible, Cohn wanted to know, that he had been so abusive and vituperative to me at the same time he was taking me to the fights and buying me theater tickets?[1]

> ADAMS: . . . when we had difficulties over the telephone or face-to-face, it would ebb and flow.
>
> COHN: I see.
>
> ADAMS: There could be some pleasant conversation and then it would erupt.
>
> COHN: During the ebb, you think you might have asked me to get those theater tickets for you?
>
> ADAMS: It is conceivable.
>
> COHN: I see. Did you cancel the order during the flow?

It was excruciatingly embarrassing. He had me.

Michael Straight called this thrust "exquisite, a brilliant tour de force," and he concluded by likening me to a whore for letting myself be in such a position.

The senators were not satisfied with my refusal to say anything more about the January 21 meeting at the Justice Department. They wanted to know precisely who had muzzled me, and why. I was given the weekend to find out.

I had been gagged, of course, because the White House wanted to stay out of this unseemly brawl. President Eisenhower had made that clear during the very first week of the hearings. At a press conference on April 29, a reporter had asked the President if he had discussed the Schine affair with the secretary of defense, Charles Wilson. Eisenhower had said he'd never heard of it. The reporters at the press conference had laughed openly at the President, who had flushed and balled up his fists until his knuckles turned white. A second reporter had asked him, "As a former Commanding General of the United States Army, what do you think of all the excitement at the Capitol over the privileges granted this private?" Eisenhower had been silent for a moment. Then he had drawn up his shoulders and begged forgiveness

---

1. As I testified at the hearings, I had taken my two aunts to the theater to see Rosalind Russell in *Wonderful Town*. The next day one of my aunts was lunching when a man said, "I knew Adams was lying when he said he took two aunts to the theater when he had a night out in New York." She flared at him, "*I* am one of the aunts."

for declining to talk about the matter. He just hoped it would be concluded quickly, he said. "The President, nearly speechless with emotion . . . strode from the room," reported the New York *Herald Tribune*. "The scene was unique in Presidential press conference history. The President was flushed. His jaw was set. His eyes appeared moist. The atmosphere as he walked out was electric."

The passage of time had not made the President any more eager to get involved. Over the weekend, I heard nothing from the White House, the Justice Department, or the Defense Department. But as I stepped into an Army car to go up to the hearings on Monday morning, I was handed an envelope with two documents. One was a letter signed by Eisenhower to the secretary of defense. I read it as we drove to the Capitol:

> Because it is essential to efficient and effective Administration that employees in the Executive Branch be in a position to be completely candid in advising with each other on official matters, and because it is not in the public interest that any of their conversations or communications, or any documents or reproductions, concerning such advice be disclosed, you will instruct employees of your Department that in all of their appearances before the Subcommittee of the Senate Committee on Government Operations regarding the inquiry now before it they are not to testify to communications or to produce any such documents or reproductions. The principle must be maintained regardless of who would be benefited by such disclosures.
>
> I direct this action so as to maintain the proper separation of powers between the Executive and Legislative Branches of the Government in accordance with my responsibilities under the Constitution. This separation is vital to preclude the exercise of arbitrary power by any branch of the government.

The letter was accompanied by a long memorandum from the attorney general citing history and precedents.

The President was invoking Executive Privilege to shut me up. The principle was to become famous to a later generation, when Eisenhower's Vice-President—Richard Nixon—used it in a futile effort to save his own presidency. Nixon's Watergate lawyer, James St. Clair, was familiar with the argument. In fact, he was sitting in the limousine with me that morning while I read Eisenhower's letter. St. Clair, then a young lawyer at Hale and Dorr in Boston, had come to Washington to assist his law partner, Joseph Welch, in the Army's defense.

White House Chief of Staff Sherman Adams, the former governor of New Hampshire, shown at left, with President Eisenhower and New York governor Thomas E. Dewey, the 1944 and 1948 Republican presidential candidate. It was Sherman Adams who, on January 21, suggested that I make a record of my experiences with the McCarthy committee during the previous months. Governor Dewey is credited with having suggested Joe Welch to be the

Army's special counsel. COURTESY UNITED PRESS INTERNATIONAL

When I took the stand, I read the letter aloud in its entirety, ending by saying, "The letter is signed Dwight D. Eisenhower."

McCarthy was nonplused by the White House's stonewalling. "I must admit," he muttered, "that I am somewhat at a loss to know what to do. . . ." He even seemed conciliatory toward me: "I fear that maybe in my mind I was doing an injustice possibly to Mr. Adams. . . ." What he was really doing was building up his rage against the White House. Finally, he exploded against this "Iron Curtain."

> MCCARTHY: Who. . . . Who was responsible for the issuance of the smear that has held this committee up for weeks and weeks and weeks and has allowed Communists to continue . . . with a razor poised over the jugular vein of the nation?

The White House, naturally. But there wasn't much McCarthy could do about it, except rant. He did just that for a while, but finally stalked out of the hearing room—never to return, some thought.

He did return, though, and asked for a week's recess to figure out how to proceed. The Democrats were worried that the hearings would be recessed for good without a chance to put McCarthy on the stand. But they were outvoted, and the hearings were adjourned until the following Monday.

CHAPTER XXX

"Over There"

What the senators wanted to know was what the White House didn't want to tell them: the role played by the President's men in releasing the charges against McCarthy. McCarthy thought he could prove that he was set up, "framed" by the White House—if only he could force White House officials to testify.

I have never been precisely sure of the White House role. I never was told exactly what went on "over there."

"Over there" was an expression of Fred Seaton, the assistant secretary of defense for Legislative and Public Affairs. He had been a successful Nebraska newspaper publisher who had entered politics when the Nebraska governor appointed him to fill an unexpired U.S. Senate term in 1951. Seaton had been an early Eisenhower supporter, and his support was doubly important because he came from the exact center of the rock-hard political territory of Senator Robert A. Taft. During the 1952 campaign, Seaton managed the Eisenhower campaign train, one of the most difficult, exasperating, and thankless of all campaign jobs, and he did it well. Eisenhower came to depend on Seaton's political advice. After the election, he was a White House pet, and Secretary of Defense Wilson—whose own legislative skills were atrocious—

jumped at the chance to bring Seaton to the Pentagon. When Seaton made frequent reference to "over there" and "across the river," he wasn't bragging. He was the White House man at the Pentagon.

After Stevens surrendered at the infamous Chicken Lunch, it was Seaton who brought Stevens to the White House, where a hasty effort was made to recoup losses with a supportive press release. That evening, Seaton had growled at me, "Don't let this happen again. Don't get into these things and wait until there is a mess and expect *us* to get you out." I thought that *us*—if that included Vice-President Nixon and the eager-to-appease White House liaison chief Jerry Persons—had played a big part in setting up the whole Chicken Lunch surrender, but I didn't say so. Besides, I was never quite sure who "us" was. Sherman Adams? The President himself?

I did know that Sherman Adams had obtained a copy of my Chronology of Events, the basis for the charges, in mid-February, a month before its release. It was Governor Adams who had suggested that I prepare such a document on January 21, and on February 16 he telephoned me to ask for a copy. After the "surrender" of February 25, I tried to get the document back, and telephoned him twice to see if he was finished with it. Each time he put me off, never saying why he wanted it, never saying whether he had read it, or whether anyone else had; only saying that it was locked up "in a good safe place."

I had no part in the decision to release the chronology. But I felt that Fred Seaton had pressed Defense Secretary Wilson to send it up to the Hill, and I also felt that he had carefully touched base "across the river" before doing so. Maybe "over there" had pushed Seaton.

My assumptions are based on hints, knowing looks, unfinished sentences, and all the other techniques people use to get a point across without using words. I still don't think the White House completely orchestrated the whole thing from the beginning. I just think that "over there" they had come to the conclusion that there was a wild horse rearing in the Pentagon stable (the Adams diary), and that the time had finally come to open the barn door.

Did Eisenhower himself give the order? I can only guess. At the time of the press conference following the Chicken Lunch, he was out on the White House lawn practicing chip shots. But Eisenhower's indifference was deceptive; he could be in control while appearing to loaf. Certainly he knew what was going on. Writing in 1965, Senator Potter told of being summoned to the White House on the eve of the hearings. The thrust of the interview, not quoted verbatim by Potter, was that the President was concerned about whether Stevens would be able to stand up to the assault he faced in the days ahead. Periodically thereafter, Potter would go secretly to the White House and report on the hearings. At the hearings, Potter publicly agreed with McCarthy that the decision to release the Adams chronology came from the White House.[1]

In his memoirs, Sherman Adams wrote of the concern in the White House about McCarthy's demands for the Loyalty Board members back in January. "Henry Cabot Lodge suggested that it was high time for the Administration to take a more thoughtful look at the situation," wrote Adams. "He and I arranged to meet with (Attorney General Herbert) Brownell and John Adams on January 21 in the Attorney General's office to talk about McCarthy." Obviously, my pleas for support to the Justice Department had been relayed to the White House at a fortuitous moment. The President's men were becoming anxious about McCarthy, and arranged to be in Brownell's office when I came to tell my story.

The memoirs of Potter and Sherman Adams, and the winks and nods of Fred Seaton, lend some support to the impression that there was careful, but subtle, orchestration of all that occurred in order to bring the Army's conflict with McCarthy to an end.

In any case, one thing is certain. They did not want anyone to know about their involvement, whatever it was. The Army, in the person of Stevens and Adams, was to be the stalking horse. If we won, it would be a great victory for the administration. If it was a standoff, only we would be damaged. If, in his adroit manner, McCarthy managed to give more than he got, somebody could be fired: Adams, if McCarthy just barely scored, both Adams and Stevens if he really scored.

I said to Seaton one day that this was how the picture looked to me. I spoke about the lack of any outward manifestation of support from "across the river," despite the hints that "over there" everyone was with us. Such suggestions usually provoked Seaton's anger, and this time was no different. "Now don't try to threaten me, boy," he said. "I just don't go for that at all. . . ."

In some ways, gagging me at the hearings made no sense because I didn't *know* any more than I had already told the committee. I told

1. Most observers thought Vice-President Nixon had asked Potter to make the March 10 request to the secretary of defense for the release of the Army Chronology of Events.

them that I had simply asked for a meeting with the attorney general, and found the four top White House aides there when I arrived. Therefore, the gag was not a gag; it prevented me from telling what I didn't know in any case.

The real purpose of the gag was not to shut me up. It was to stop the committee from summoning and interrogating the President's men—Sherman Adams and Co.—about their role in the whole affair. The committee did question Fred Seaton in a secret "Executive Session" about *his* role, but the wily Seaton successfully stonewalled. For instance, Mundt wanted to know why Stevens had repudiated the Chicken Lunch settlement after he had seemed so satisfied with it. Seaton professed ignorance, even though Seaton had been at the Pentagon showdown after the lunch when Stevens had realized his surrender and had burst into tears. Indeed, Seaton was one of the first to tell Stevens what a fool he had been. About my diary, he professed more innocence. He told the committee that he didn't even know about it until March 1, and that as far as he knew, it was all my idea. His only part, he said, had been to tell Secretary of Defense Wilson that pressure was growing on the Hill for the release of the report. But the Defense Department's only role had been to redraft my diary into the Chronology of Events which was sent to the Senate.

What Seaton neglected to tell the committee in that closed session could fill a book, I'm sure. But as a result of his protestations of ignorance, I was the one left looking like a cover-up artist, the man who knew all but would tell nothing.

When the hearings resumed after a week's recess, Senator McClellan berated me for not being forthcoming: He accused me of wasting the committee's time with a week's recess when I didn't know any more after a week than I knew when the committee recessed. There was little I could say in response; at the Pentagon, no one was talking to me. I had no instructions other than simply "don't talk." The gag order was handed to me a few minutes before it was made public.

If the fall guy role for me was hard, it was even more difficult for Secretary Stevens. Before the recess, Stevens had flatly stated in testimony before the committee, "I don't know who decided to prepare it (the Army chronology)." When asked by McCarthy if he had ordered the chronology put out to Congress and hence the public, Stevens flatly stated, "No, sir; I did not order them put out."

Now, after the recess and the White House gag, Stevens had to eat his words and take responsibility for releasing the chronology. It was not easy in light of his earlier testimony. The Democratic members tried hard with helpful leading questions, and Stevens struggled with his answers to make it appear that the responsibility was all his. McCarthy, naturally, jumped all over him, saying that Stevens either had a "bad memory"—or that he was committing "perjury." Stevens snapped back at that and denied a cover-up. But the going was hard. In the afternoon, the senators wanted to know whether Sherman Adams had ordered me to prepare the chronology. I responded that it was more of "suggestion" than an "order," but most of the committee seemed unconvinced. Symington was curious as to why I had even mentioned the presence of the White House aides in the first place. "Was it carelessness, loneliness, or a plot?" he asked. "I don't think it was any of the three," I answered. "I was narrating the incidents as they occurred."

It had been a wearing day. In the late afternoon, I went to Stevens's office in the Pentagon for the daily posthearing discussion with the Army's lawyer, Joseph Welch. "We didn't do so well today," I said. Stevens exploded and gave me a drill sergeant's dressing down. I left the room, not to return thereafter for these discussions unless I was invited. I rarely was. From then on I could feel Stevens's hostility toward me; our relationship, never easy, was permanently ruptured.

I was alone now. Seaton avoided me. I tried to reach him countless times during and prior to the hearings, but he was always "busy." I was told by Stevens that Welch was to be my lawyer as well as his, but in fact, that was not really true. I could never understand the Welch-St. Clair operation. They stayed at the Army's VIP headquarters at Fort McNair; they were chauffered about in an Army car, but they didn't seem to have much to do with the Army defendants—at least this one. After Stevens's testimony there were late-afternoon sessions to review the day's events and prepare for the next round; there were no such sessions after mine. I later learned that Welch was having secret conferences with the committee and making certain deals which I would have repudiated had I known about them. No lawyer has a right to make deals without his client's consent, assuming, that is, that I was his client.

On the whole, although Welch didn't do a very good job in defending the Army, he was brilliant at exposing the ugliness of McCarthy's tactics. In the light of history, that is what really mattered. But I had little sense of history in May 1954. I had only the sense that I was facing serious trouble, and was not getting much help.

Dirksen and Mundt wanted to find perjurers to save McCarthy. If they could prove that Stevens or Adams was lying, then the heat would be off McCarthy. I feared that I was the easier target because Stevens was a part of the President's official family, and I was not.

Before the hearings even began, Mundt gave a message to Fred Seaton. It was a warning that the record of the hearings would undoubtedly be reviewed by the Justice Department for perjury. Perhaps this was intended as a friendly message, but I didn't like it. Nor did Stevens. When I told him about it he was even more angered than I had been. "I don't appreciate that one bit," he said.

Mundt, a fellow South Dakotan for whom I had once campaigned, was supposed to be a friend of mine. But he was petty enough to put a "temporary hold" on a planned salary raise for me until the hearings were over—"to see how things turned out," he explained.

Now as I finished my testimony, Mundt excused me from the stand with a parting question he asked no other witness at the hearings:

> Mr. Adams, before dismissing you, I would like to revert to a practice that the Chair followed back in 1948, when we had a very serious and controversial set of hearings over which the Chair was called upon to preside. I would like to ask you before you are dismissed and unsworn whether you feel that you have now had a complete and full and fair opportunity to testify before this Committee?

Every working newsman in the room knew that in 1948 Mundt was chairman and Congressman Richard Nixon was the second-ranking Republican on the committee that investigated Alger Hiss. Mundt had given the same warning to Hiss, shortly before Hiss had gone to prison for perjury.[2]

2. I answered the question with a courteous affirmative, but inwardly I was seething with anger to have been so singled out. I left the hearing room and went directly home instead of returning to the Pentagon. It took me the rest of the day (and more than one stiff drink) to calm down. Mundt remained in the Senate until 1972, and while I reestablished a relationship with him in subsequent years, I could never really forgive him for that parting shot.

CHAPTER XXXI

Paranoia

I needed help and I didn't feel that I was getting much from Joe Welch. So I decided to look elsewhere. Before the hearings, Morris Ernst, a famous civil liberties lawyer of the Roosevelt era, had come down from New York to offer us help against McCarthy. Stevens had received him courteously, but that was all. He told me he didn't want the Army case to get help from any liberal New Dealer. I saw Ernst briefly a few other times, feeling somehow guilty for doing so. As much as I needed counsel, and as much as he wanted to help, it was clear that Ernst did not fit in the Army's plans.

I turned to Francis Sayre, Woodrow Wilson's grandson and dean of Washington's National Cathedral. Sayre had spoken critically of McCarthy before, and his remarks had been widely noted. I thought perhaps he would have some advice for me. The gentle churchman was interested, and he hoped that the power of prayer might help. Perhaps, but I was seeking more than that. I needed a good lawyer. A South Dakota friend of mine named Harvey Gunderson, who was a successful Washington banking lawyer, thought that Covington and Burling, the most powerful law firm in Washington, might be the answer. We went to see Ed Burling, and he took us to see the firm's senior counsel, John Lord O'Brian, then quite old, but a lawyer who had seen everything since the pre-Roosevelt days. The elderly sage immediately spotted a problem that would backfire against both me and his firm if they agreed to assist. One of the firm's partners was a brother of Alger Hiss.

I was running out of places to look when I called Marx Leva, a former assistant secretary of defense who had hired me for the Defense Department legal office after I had lost my Senate job in 1949. He was ill at the time, but he sent me to talk to his partner, Joe Fowler.

Fowler did help. In the evenings, after the hearings, I would go to see him and his associate, Bob Martin, at their office or at Fowler's home.[1] We reviewed the law on perjury and discussed the day's testimony. Fowler tried to reassure me, but it was hard to comfort me.

By the second or third evening, convinced that I was being followed, I started leaving my cab, walking in one door and out the other of the Mayflower Hotel, and picking up a second cab. Another time I walked through an alley, into the back and out the front of the Statler Hotel. I slunk by side streets to Fowler's office, and stood in the shadows for some time before I entered the darkened building. Clearly, paranoia was setting in. The Pentagon leaked like a sieve during this period, and matters we, at the Army secretary's office, thought we were discussing in confidence, had a way of reaching the McCarthy side in short order. We heard of a dinner at an out-of-the-way restaurant where one of our trusted employees, who had access to all our files, was seen whispering intensely with a Pentagon employee known for his pro-Dirksen sympathies. We suspected the worst.

Everyone thought their home phones were being tapped. We took to conversing in double-talk over the phone, and during the latter days of the hearings in the evenings I usually walked to a neighborhood drugstore (but never the same one twice) to make calls.

I didn't even trust the telephone operator of my own apartment building. I was stunned to read in a Drew Pearson column one day that I had been receiving regular late-night phone calls from Joe McCarthy. Then I recalled that my brother, a Naval officer on duty in Washington, called me often during the hearings, and thought it was a great joke to identify himself as Senator McCarthy. I'd usually answer, "Oh,

---

1. Fowler later became secretary of the treasury in Lyndon Johnson's cabinet. Martin, a Columbia Law School classmate of Roy Cohn's, became one of my law partners seventeen years later.

yes, Senator.'' The telephone operator thought the caller was the *real* Joe McCarthy and obliged Pearson's legman by telling him of our collusion. It was all very amusing, except that if she was willing to tell Drew Pearson about my private phone calls, what was to stop her from telling Joe McCarthy's henchmen?

One day Colonel Ken BeLieu, Stevens's military aide, walked into my office and announced, ''Your telephone's being tapped.'' ''How do you know?'' I asked. ''My wife saw a repairman working on a telephone pole outside our house,'' he replied. He had just assumed that since that probably meant his phone was bugged, then mine surely was, too.

Our jumpiness was not completely unjustified. One night during the hearings, John Simon, one of the young attorneys in my office, was asleep on a couch in the room next to my office. He and his colleagues sometimes worked so late that they just slept on a sofa until dawn rather than go home. At about 3:00 A.M., hearing noise in my office, he got up and switched on the light.

There was a man rummaging through my desk. Simon demanded to know what he was doing there. The intruder said he was a G-2 building security officer checking to see if I was violating security regulations by locking classified documents in the desk instead of in the safe. We later learned that G-2 had keys to every office, every desk, and the combination to every safe in the building. There was no way of knowing whether a McCarthy ''patriot'' in G-2 was using them to spy on us.

When I heard about the incident the next day, I tore off a sheet of paper and wrote in red pencil: ''Fuck You G-2.'' I sealed the paper in an envelope which I stamped in red letters, SECRET and put it in my top desk drawer. On the insistence of my associates, I later tore it up and put it in the ''Burn'' basket, agreeing that the office already was in enough trouble.

Through all of May, I received anonymous phone calls, many of them insulting, even a bomb threat. I received hundreds of letters, some scurrilous, some rude, some outrageously filthy, and some threatening.[2]

2. I also received some fan mail. A Cleveland woman wrote that she had fallen in love with me, and that if I would wear a striped tie next Monday when I was before the camera, she would interpret it as a signal and would fly into my arms. I was careful to wear a solid-color tie that Monday.

Ten-month-old Rebecca Adams seems to recognize her father as, seated on Margaret's lap, she watches the image on our rented television set. Because Rebecca suffered from colic, croup, allergies, and an unusual number of the maladies of very small children, Margaret would never leave her with a sitter, and thus attended none of the hearings. The hearings were a most popular spectacle in the spring of 1954, attracting a large number of usually jaded Washingtonians. The wall seats behind the committee members were usually occupied by senatorial friends and social contacts, many with gaily decorated hats. Perle Mesta, Washington's "hostess with the mostest" during the Truman era, was a regular. COURTESY UNITED PRESS INTERNATIONAL.

On May 13, while I was on the stand as a witness, my car, parked right in front of my apartment building, was stolen. It had been locked, and the police surmised that it was the work of a professional. A month later, the police found the car, hidden in an alley less than a mile from my home; my golf clubs and our child's baby seat were still in the car. It seemed clear to me that it had been stolen just to harass me.

My wife began to fear for my safety. Margaret was a gentle young woman from rural Virginia who had gone to a woman's college and had led a sheltered life. She was appalled by McCarthy and frightened of him, but never, for a moment, did she waver in her support. Her background had not prepared her for sitting at home with her baby, while watching Joe McCarthy try to destroy her husband on national television.

McCarthy did have some pretty unsavory types working for him. One, an early McCarthy spy sent to Switzerland to dig up dirt on John Carter Vincent (one of the State Department hands who had, it was charged, "lost China"), managed to get himself convicted of political espionage by the Swiss. He had been dropped by the Navy as an alleged homosexual and later admitted to being a member of the Communist party; but he found a job with McCarthy. McCarthy hired another who, while employed by a committee investigating McCarthy, leaked the committee's findings to McCarthy. Two New Jersey attorneys, representing Fort Monmouth employees, later complained of getting threatening phone calls from this man, who had a thirty percent psychiatric disability by the Veteran's Administration. J. B. Matthews, a Red-baiting, former Methodist minister with ties to the Hearst press, was McCarthy's first chief of staff. Unfortunately, he had just published an article alleging that most of America's Protestant clergy had been infiltrated by Communists. The national outrage was so great that McCarthy had to fire him after just two weeks.

Then there was Don Surine, another ex-FBI agent. He had lost his FBI job for some violation of bureau regulations, and while J. Edgar Hoover refused to take him back as an agent, he recommended him to McCarthy. Surine became a close and trusted McCarthy aide and investigator thereafter.

Men like these made one wonder. But I was more afraid of a perjury indictment than getting harassed by one of McCarthy's boys. It was not so much the fear of a prison sentence. I could live with that. But I simply could not bear the thought of doing that to my wife and child.

I began to have trouble sleeping. I would rack my brain for some transgression that McCarthy might seize upon. Had I made some facetious remark that Cohn could twist into an accusation? I rued my flippancy. I would toss and turn, thinking back over my career. Once, seven years earlier, I had received free meals on a Senate junket. That woke me up. Four years earlier, after speaking at the University of Wisconsin, I had received a fifty-dollar-honorarium. Would that somehow haunt me? As I lay awake, I lost all sense of proportion as I searched for skeletons. I recalled that I had helped my wife's sister get a commission in the WACs by telling her who to call. My God, I thought, I'm dragging my wife's sister through this!

I had never been much of a drinker, but I began drinking that spring. Every day when I came home, Margaret would have two old-fashioneds waiting for me. I would gulp them down. And sometimes I would have a couple after dinner, so that I could face the night.

CHAPTER XXXII

"... A Handful, a Handful, Sir ..."

The Roy Cohn I knew could be haughty, abusive, and sullen. He could also be the perfect gentleman. The Roy Cohn who took the witness stand after me was almost angelic in his injured innocence.

He was pale and mild, and ended every sentence with "sir." He did not even want to refer to McCarthy's charges against the Army as "charges." "We did not make charges," he insisted. "We told what the facts were as we saw them." Stevens, he said, was a "fine gentlemanly person." Even I was not so bad. "There was a good deal of joking between us," said Cohn. Cohn's mission—rousting communism out of the government—was taken on with a kind of sad nobility, it seemed. The exorcism was hard and painful for the country, but necessary. Somebody had to do it. It seemed tragic to him that this small band of patriots should be criticized:

> COHN: . . . the staff—a handful, a handful, sir, hardworking boys who work night and day up against probably hundreds and thousands of people who work over in the Army and in other places, this handful of

Cohn and McCarthy at the hearings. COURTESY CBS FILMS.

people has brought about the removal from defense plants of Communists.

They have brought about the removal from government agencies and from the Army of Communists and spies, sir, and it is hard to hear them criticized for having done the job.

Cohn's sweet demeanor was carefully calculated. In his memoirs of his McCarthy days, Cohn states that he realized that he had appeared "arrogant, self-righteous, and condescending" in his early appearances during the hearings. He knew that when he took the stand to tell his story in direct testimony, he would have to change his image. So, says Cohn, he practiced a new image in front of his hotel room mirror. "Instead of being talkative, I would speak to the point," vowed Cohn. "Instead of being aggressive, I would be withdrawn. Instead of being smart-alecky, I would be deferential. Instead of being excitable, I would be unruffled."

Cohn added that "Whenever possible, I gave simple 'yes' or 'no' answers." He said that I called Schine a "hostage" more often than I called him by his real name. He denied losing his temper when Schine was given KP duty. He even denied using "vituperative language." Said Cohn: "In my opinion the statement that I used vituperative language is false. I think the language I used is the same as anybody else uses. There might be an occasional word I would not want to repeat on television."

But Cohn stepped somewhat gingerly when it came to repeating, under oath, the allegation made in one of the Eleven Memoranda that I had offered him the names of homosexuals and subversives in the Air Force and Navy. The way Cohn put it on the witness stand was that I had made the suggestion that if we could sort of spread around the investigation to include other parts of the military it would not look so bad for the people in the Army. He said, "There was no dramatic thing about saying, 'Stop the investigation about us and go ahead and blow up the Navy and the Air Force.' "

Cohn tended to sidestep the Army charges. And it seemed to me that if there had been witnesses on-the-scene who could now contradict him, Cohn became evasive. Throughout his testimony, he gave such answers as: "I have no recollection of the words I used." "Specifically to answer you, I do not remember using these words." "I can't give you a categorical yes or no." Asked once, "Well, you don't deny it?" he responded, "Well, I come pretty close to denying it." Asked if he had said, "We will investigate the heck out of the Army!" he gave a long and vague answer. Elsewhere he said, "Sir, again I can come pretty close to denying that this is the type of thing I said." And, later, "I don't have the remotest idea of all I said."

There were some clear denials. To the Army charges that he had threatened to "wreck the Army" and had said that "Stevens is through" as Army secretary if Schine were sent overseas, he firmly said he had made no such threats. Calmly and skillfully, never losing his well-known temper, Cohn avoided traps and pitfalls laid before him by the various questioners. He managed to tell his version of the story to the satisfaction of McCarthy's supporters.

Cohn's testimony was overshadowed by a more fundamental issue that had emerged briefly once before, and that now threatened to expose McCarthy's astounding arrogance. When McCarthy had refused to identify his source of the "Purloined Letter" in early May, he had revealed that he felt himself to be above the law. Now, when they hinted at other secret sources of information, Senator McClellan focused in on McCarthy's essential lawlessness.

"I do not believe," he told McCarthy, "you can receive information that is obtained by criminal means and hold it in your possession without the probability of you too being guilty of a crime."

McCarthy was defiant—and outrageous—in his response:

> I'd like to make it clear that I think that the oath which every person in government takes to protect and defend this country against all enemies . . . towers far above any Presidential secrecy directive. If any administration wants to indict me . . . they can just go right ahead . . . I would like to notify those 2,000,000 Federal employees that I feel it's their duty to give us any information which they have.

McCarthy could not have been more explicit. Not only was he above the law, but he declared that the entire federal bureaucracy owed him a higher allegiance than it did to the law.

That was going too far for the White House. The next morning the attorney general "with the approval of the President," issued a statement insisting that it was the responsibility of the executive branch alone to enforce the laws. In a pointed reference to McCarthy, the statement continued: "That responsibility cannot be usurped by any individual who may seek to set himself above the law."

McCarthy was unable to contain himself, as usual, and poured more gas on the flames. "I hope to remain in the Senate and see many Presidents come and go," he said loftily. And, he insisted, government employees are "duty bound to give me information even though some bureaucrat may have stamped it secret."

Cohn's testimony was interrupted a second time so as to resolve a mystery that had haunted the hearings. In all the charges and counter-charges between the Army and McCarthy, the truth was not easily divined. In almost every case it was the Army's word against McCarthy's, with no concrete proof to back up anyone's word. Except, that is, for a series of monitored phone calls between Stevens and McCarthy or Cohn.

The existence of these monitored calls had been known since the second day of the hearings. Under questioning from Senator Symington, Stevens had admitted that his secretary monitored his calls. The revelation caused a sensation, and gave many reporters and neutral observers hope that some solid evidence would tip the scales one way or another.

McCarthy was worried about the monitored calls. He denounced them as "the most indecent and dishonest thing I have heard of," "completely indecent and improper," and "indecent and illegal under the laws."

For five weeks, McCarthy managed to stall the release of the transcripts of these calls by insisting that all or none be released. The Army was reluctant to air certain tapes that were irrelevant to the hearings but reflected poorly on General Lawton, the Fort Monmouth base commander, but eventually the Army gave in. On June 3, the public was finally plugged into the conversations between the Army and the McCarthy committee.

McCarthy's fears, it turned out, were groundless. In fact, the transcribed calls *favored* McCarthy's side. There were, unfortunately for the Army, no recordings of any of my conversations with Cohn. My calls had not been monitored until February, by which time Cohn and I were no longer communicating. But Stevens's calls had been recorded all along, and they showed more placation from the Army secretary than pressure from McCarthy.

The worse was a conversation between Schine and Stevens on October 21. Schine was a few days away from his induction into the Army, and he was personally lobbying the Army secretary for a way out. Stevens was firm about basic training, but then he tempted Schine with the prospect of better things. "I think there is an excellent chance that we can pick you up and use you in a way that would be useful to the country and to yourself. Just what that would be, I don't know. . . . I personally would like to arrange it . . . in such a way that you could use the knowledge and ability you have in certain fields. . . ." Stevens finished by saying, "If you come down, I will be delighted to see you."

After a conversation like that, it is no wonder that Schine and Cohn thought they could wrangle concessions out of the Army, perhaps using Schine's "knowledge and ability" to purge the West Point library of subversive books. Hearing it, I began to understand why Cohn had continued to harp about an "original agreement."

The transcripts did offer a few revealing glimpses of Cohn and McCarthy. Cohn told Stevens, for instance, that it "would have been a lot of fun" to make a fool of General Partridge, the former head of Army Intelligence. The twenty-six-year-old Cohn said, "You know, I'm an old big-game hunter." And McCarthy, threatened, in another call, to "kick the brains" out of the secretary of the army. But then again there was Stevens's eagerness to please: "Do you want me to call Allen Dulles [the CIA director]?" a helpful Stevens volunteered to Cohn, presumably thinking that the CIA would be able to make use of Schine's talents. "It would give us a start. . . ."

There was surely no smoking gun in the recorded calls that could be aimed at McCarthy or Cohn. "Those highly touted monitored calls turned out to be duds," pronounced the Washington *Post*. "If anything they were more damaging to the Army than to the subcommittee."

The invocation of executive privilege, the revelation of recorded conversations, the kleig lights and smoky hearing room, the daily televised melodrama . . . the hearings were full of premonitions of a later summer, when the lawlessness of almost an entire White House staff was laid bare. Nor do the similarities stop there. For in the first week of June, Mary Driscoll, McCarthy's faithful secretary took the stand.

CHAPTER XXXIII

"The Real McCoy
or Not"

Throughout the hearings, McCarthy and Cohn made scant mention of
their "Eleven Memoranda," the basis for their counter-charges that
the Army tried to blackmail McCarthy's committee. I suspected that
by their silence on the subject the McCarthyites wanted to avoid any
probes into their authenticity. But during Cohn's testimony, the subject of the memoranda inevitably came up. And with it came questions
about their origins.

Cohn testified that the memos were dictated to, and typed by Mrs.
Mary Driscoll, McCarthy's personal secretary. On the afternoon of
June 1, Mrs. Driscoll was summoned to the stand.

A middle-aged woman, she looked scared to death. Her small chin
trembled; her voice could barely be heard.

Mrs. Driscoll did not answer questions by saying "yes" or "no."
Instead, she replied, "I couldn't." She couldn't say much about the
memos because she remembered almost nothing about preparing them
and she had destroyed her stenographic notebooks. She was also unable
to tell which copies were the originals, or whether the originals had

somehow been lost. Without the originals, it was impossible to date or authenticate any of the memos.

All eleven, and nothing else, were filed in a folder that was labeled simply "Investigations Committee." Reams of material on the Investigations Committee were filed in McCarthy's office, yet Mrs. Driscoll seemed easily capable of finding this particular folder. "How did you know where to go look for that file, Mrs. Driscoll, when you were called upon to produce it?" asked Counsel Jenkins.

> MRS. DRISCOLL: I can't tell you that, Mr. Jenkins.
>
> JENKINS: How is that?
>
> MRS. DRISCOLL: I can't tell you that. That is my way of filing. (Laughter)
>
> JENKINS: And so without any index or anything of the kind you just consulted Mrs. Mary E. Driscoll's mind and knew where it was and went and got those memoranda?
>
> MRS. DRISCOLL: That is right. (Laughter)

The test as to what went into the file was "conversations with Stevens," said Mrs. Driscoll. Mrs. Driscoll was asked why she then filed memos concerning conversations with Adams in the folder.

> MRS. DRISCOLL: It is the same general thing, Stevens and Adams.

Mrs. Driscoll was not doing very well, and an expectant hush fell over the hearing room. There was a sense among many of the newspaper reporters watching that if this very fragile-looking woman broke down, McCarthy and his men would come crashing down with her. With great anticipation, the press table awaited the cross-examination of the Army's counsel, Joseph Welch.

Welch began by saying that it was difficult to cross-examine a woman. He clearly meant it, for he questioned Mrs. Driscoll very gently and gingerly. Among other things he was curious that the memos had been typed on three different typewriters, and that none of those typewriters was the IBM now on Mrs. Driscoll's desk. Mrs. Driscoll was unable to recall what typewriters she used to type the memos, or even how long she had had the IBM.

> WELCH: You can't tell us whether you've had it a month or two or longer than that?

MRS. DRISCOLL: No.

WELCH: You have no memory at all?

MRS. DRISCOLL: No. A typewriter is a typewriter and I don't pay any attention to the type of typewriter.

Welch could not resist a dig at this:

WELCH: You are a paragon of virtue! My secretaries are always kicking about them and wanting a new one. You don't pay any attention to them?

McCarthy jumped in to rescue her, ridiculing Welch's questions as irrelevant and silly. But Welch turned on him. "I'm interested to know whether these memoranda are the real McCoy or not!" he exclaimed. "You know that, don't you!"

But Welch never found out whether the memos were the real McCoy. I thought he came close to cracking Mrs. Driscoll and was disappointed when he backed off. And at the close of her testimony, he simply observed:

I could not help being somewhat suspicious about these documents, and I am still unconvinced, because of some internal evidence in at least one of them. But in any event, I now say to you that if there is a riddle, it is wrapped in an enigma that we won't be able to solve.

I watched the Driscoll interrogation with great expectations. Here, I thought, was the chance to trap McCarthy. McCarthy's memos were highly vulnerable to attack, I believed, and I thought McCarthy and his men were holding their breath, hoping that someone—Welch in particular—did not home in.

There were so many soft spots. Why, for instance, did Cohn and Carr dictate just these memos to Mrs. Driscoll? They had their own secretaries, and their office, room 101 of the Senate Office Building, was two city blocks and three floors away from McCarthy's office, where Mrs. Driscoll tended her many typewriters. Mrs. Driscoll's remarkable filing system certainly deserved more scrutiny. How did she know how to put all those memos into one tidy package? Surely the label "Investigations Committee" was no guide. McCarthy tried to offer a way out by suggesting that "all of the memoranda have to do with the attempted pressure to call off the investigation." But how

Mrs. Driscoll could tell that from the wording of the memoranda is remarkable, even for a woman of her apparent intuition. The first memo in October twice mentions how ''very helpful'' Stevens was, and pressure is far from obvious in several others. I thought that someone else at some time must have helped her lump these memos together. Even McCarthy testified that he ''didn't take the pressure seriously until the 21st day of January or thereabouts.''

It was quite clear to me that the structure of the ''Eleven Memoranda'' was built not brick by brick, but all at once, when a shelter was badly needed. But Welch drew back from kicking the supports out from its shaky frame. In part, I think, he was genuinely reluctant to press a woman with unpleasant cross-examination. Welch was the quintessential Victorian gentleman, a man of exceeding civility. He also felt that rough treatment of a woman could backfire. Nonetheless, I thought he missed a great opportunity to deal McCarthy a mortal blow.

So it was with tremendous disappointment that I watched this opportunity slip away. I feared it was our last chance.

CHAPTER XXXIV

"Have You No Decency?"

On the afternoon of June 9, Counsel Welch mockingly explored the "committee work" of Cohn and Schine while Private Schine was supposedly taking basic training at Fort Dix. With Cohn on the stand, the sly Boston lawyer traced the meals and hotels, the hours on the road between Fort Dix and New York, and the minimal work product that came out of it all.[1]

Cohn remained polite and respectful throughout, maintaining that Soldier Schine had been home sleeping while Cohn nightclubbed alone at the Stork Club and Sardi's. Welch affected his perplexed look, and decided to have some fun with the serious young Mr. Cohn.

"Mr. Cohn, if I told you now that we had a bad situation at Monmouth, you'd want to cure it by sundown if you could, wouldn't you?" asked Welch. "Yes, sir," modestly replied Cohn. After a short exchange Welch pressed. "Mr. Cohn, tell me once more. Every time you learn of a Communist or a spy anywhere, it is your policy to get them out as soon as possible?"

> MR. COHN: Surely we want them out as fast as possible, sir.
> MR. WELCH: And, whenever you learn of one from now on, Mr. Cohn, I beg of you, will you tell somebody about them quick?"

1. Asked to produce all drafts or notes prepared by Mr. Schine during his association with the committee, Cohn came forward with two-and-a-half pages plus a few marginal notes.

Cohn mumbled humbly that he worked for the committee, and if they were displeased with his handling of Communists, he was sure they would so instruct him. Welch taunted him again.

> MR. WELCH: May I add my small voice, sir, and say that whenever you know about a subversive or a Communist or a spy, please hurry! Will you remember these words?

Across the table, McCarthy listened with a deep frown. Basically a humorless man, he despised being laughed at. He disliked Welch, hated his clever barbs. Suddenly, in his low, nasal monotone he interrupted.

> MCCARTHY: Mr. Chairman, in view of that question—
> MUNDT: Have you a point of order?
> MCCARTHY: Not exactly, Mr. Chairman, but in view of Mr. Welch's request that the information be given once we know of anyone who might be performing any work for the Communist Party, I think we should tell him that he has in his law firm a young man named Fisher . . . who has been for a number of years a member of an organization which was named, oh, years and years ago, as the legal bulwark of the Communist party. . . .

A hush fell over the room. Welch looked stricken. So, curiously, did Cohn. Welch silently formed the word "no," with his lips, and Cohn shook his head urgently. . . .

But McCarthy could not be swayed from his self-destructive course. His voice heavy with sarcasm, he licked his lips and continued:

> . . . . Knowing that, Mr. Welch, I just felt that I had a duty to respond to your urgent request that before sundown, when we know of anyone serving the Communist cause, we let the agency know. . . . I have hesitated about bringing that up, but I have been rather bored with your phony requests to Mr. Cohn here that he personally get every Communist out of government before sundown. Therefore we will give you the information about the young man in your own organization.

Fred Fisher was a young lawyer in Welch's law firm in Boston. He had once been a member of an organization called the Lawyer's Guild, which later had been put on various subversive lists as a Communist front organization. Welch's only misgiving about representing the Army had been that McCarthy would drag Fisher's name through the mud.

Indeed, Welch had struck a deal with Cohn which McCarthy had agreed to: if McCarthy did not mention Fisher, then Welch would not explore Cohn's nonexistent wartime military record. This no doubt contributed to Cohn's extreme discomfort when Fred Fisher's name was dropped into the hearing by McCarthy.

While Cohn blanched and looked beseechingly at McCarthy to stop, Welch looked desolate. He sat with his head in his hands, staring blankly at the table. After a moment, he quietly addressed Chairman Mundt:

> WELCH: Mr. Chairman, under these circumstances, I must have something approaching a personal privilege.

Even Mundt knew something was amiss: "You may have it, sir. It will not be taken out of your time."

The room was completely silent by now, except for McCarthy, who was loudly ordering his aides to get him the file on Fred Fisher. Three times Welch spoke to him, trying to get his attention, before McCarthy snapped, "I can listen with one ear."

"This time," said Welch, "I want you to listen with both." He began again, "Senator McCarthy, I think until this moment. . . ."

McCarthy ignored him again, and instructed his investigator to find a news clip on Fisher's affiliation with the Lawyer's Guild. "I think that should be in the record," said McCarthy.

> WELCH: You won't need anything in the record when I have finished telling you this. Until this moment, Senator, I think I never really gauged your cruelty or your recklessness. Fred Fisher is a young man who went to the Harvard Law School and came into my firm and is starting what looks to be a brilliant career with us.
>
> When I decided to work for this committee I asked Jim St. Clair . . . to be my first assistant. I said to Jim, "Pick somebody in the firm who works under you that you would like." He chose Fred Fisher and they came down on an afternoon plane. That night, when we had taken a little stab at trying to see what the case was about, Fred Fisher and Jim St. Clair and I went to dinner together. I then said to these two young men, "Boys, I don't know anything about you except that I have always liked you, but if there is anything funny in the life of either one of you that would hurt anybody in this case you speak up quick."
>
> Fred Fisher said, "Mr. Welch, when I was in law school and for a period of months thereafter I belonged to the Lawyer's Guild. . . ." I

said, "Fred, I just don't think I am going to ask you to work on the case. If I do, one of these days that will come out and go over national television and it will just hurt like the dickens."

So, Senator, I asked him to go back to Boston. Little did I dream you would be so reckless and so cruel as to do an injury to that lad. It is true he is still with Hale and Dorr. It is true that he will continue to be at Hale and Dorr. It is, I regret to say, equally true that I fear he shall always bear a scar needlessly inflicted by you. If it were in my power to forgive you for your reckless cruelty I would do so. I like to think that I am a gentle man, but your forgiveness will have to come from someone other than me.

Throughout this speech, McCarthy pretended to be reading the newspaper. When Welch was done, McCarthy continued to attack him for baiting Cohn and, incredibly, tried once more to rake over Fred Fisher's record.

WELCH: Senator, may we not drop this? We know he belonged to the Lawyer's Guild, and Mr. Cohn nods his head at me.

Cohn was visibly upset. Welch said to him, "I did you, I think, no personal injury, Mr. Cohn."

COHN: No, sir.
WELCH: I meant to do you no personal injury and, if I did, I beg your pardon.

Cohn nodded and McCarthy once again opened his mouth.

WELCH: Let us not assassinate this lad further, Senator. You have done enough. Have you no sense of decency, sir, at long last? Have you left no sense of decency?

It was a brilliant moment for Welch, a terrible wound for McCarthy. Yet McCarthy bulled ahead, whining on about Fisher's subversive affiliations. This time, Welch had nothing but cold disdain for McCarthy:

WELCH: Mr. McCarthy, I will not discuss this with you further. You have sat within six feet of me and could have asked me about Fred Fisher. You have brought it out. If there is a God in heaven it will do neither you nor your cause any good. I will not discuss it further. I will not ask Mr. Cohn any more questions. You, Mr. Chairman, may, if you will, call the next witness.

The debate was over. Despite Mundt's standing admonition against applause, the audience applauded long and loud. Mundt, who had threatened to eject anyone who clapped, just sat silently. So did McCarthy, his face set and grim.

Welch got up and walked out of the room, which emptied behind him as spectators and reporters reached for him, full of sympathy and congratulations. McCarthy stayed in the huge chamber, a bumbling figure, looking around for someone to talk to. He looked at some of his aides, spread his hands, and turned his palms upward. He asked, "What did I do?"

In the hallway, Welch announced to newsmen, "I am close to tears." They nodded sympathetically. A woman gently touched his sleeve. Other spectators turned away, to let him grieve for Fred Fisher in silence. Only another lawyer, an old acquaintance, followed him down the Senate Office Building stairway to a lower floor. When the crowd had thinned, Welch looked up at his friend and asked in an even voice, "Well, how did it go?"

Welch was a master actor. He was not pursuing issues at the hearings, but rather conducting a theatrical performance. I suspect that all of it may have been rehearsed, including the eloquent Fred Fisher defense and his final piercing thrust at Joe McCarthy—"Have you no sense of decency, sir, at long last?" There is at least one thing that Roy Cohn and I agree on, and that is that Welch set a trap for McCarthy that day. He taunted Cohn to come forward with the names of Communists. This finally brought McCarthy out, snarling about Fred Fisher. No real harm could come to Fisher from such a moment (indeed, he prospered as a lawyer and became head of the Massachusetts Bar Association in 1973) while inestimable damage was done to McCarthy. It was the telling moment of the hearings, and for McCarthy a devastating setback. The Fred Fisher incident was McCarthyism in its rawest form exposed.

Winston Churchill was once asked what he did in his spare time. "I rehearse my extemporaneous speeches," replied Churchill. So, I think, did Joe Welch.

CHAPTER XXXV

"Do You Want to Fight?"

After McCarthy had leapt into Welch's trap in the full view of millions, Counsel Jenkins clumsily tried to rescue him. For the first time in the hearings—then in their thirtieth day—McCarthy was sworn in as a witness to tell his story.

Before McCarthy began, a large colored map, showing McCarthy's version of the extent of the Communist menace in the United States, was hoisted in front of the television cameras. Then, in his most sympathetic voice, Jenkins asked McCarthy: "What had been your interest in Communists, espionage, subversives, poor security risks?" McCarthy allowed as how he was against them. "Your position on Communism then, I take it, is well known, Senator?" asked Jenkins. Said McCarthy, grinning: "I think so." Jenkins then asked McCarthy to tell the American public "just what the set-up of the Communists is." McCarthy obliged by lumbering over to his chart and speaking to it, pointer in hand like a grade school teacher in geography class. This chart listed the names and addresses of Communist leaders in every state except Texas, which was too patriotic to have Communists (and where, coincidentally, so many pro-McCarthy oil men lived). Some of the names were of dead men, and some of the addresses were wrong,

but no matter. McCarthy launched a long diatribe about the Communist threat. No part of his blackboard lecture, which ran on all afternoon, was related to any issue in the hearings. As 5 o'clock approached,
Jenkins had to step in to cut him off—with one last question:

> JENKINS: Senator McCarthy . . . it is about closing time. . . . Now,
> while you have an audience of perhaps 20 to 30 million Americans . . .
> I want you to tell . . . what each individual American man, woman, and
> child can do . . . to do their bit to liquidate the Communist Party.

And so it went for several more days. No member of the committee
had the courage to challenge this irrelevancy. When McCarthy finally
did turn to the issue at hand—the charge that the Army had "blackmailed" him to drop his investigation and offered up substitute targets
like the Navy and Air Force—he became at times quite mild and cir-
cumspect. He shied away from citing any of the "Eleven Memoranda" as proof.

Jenkins pursued the "blackmail" issue, and asked McCarthy to tell
the committee what he considered the most important evidence of Army
pressure to call off the Fort Monmouth hearings. McCarthy said,
". . . the most important . . . was the meeting of January 22 in my
apartment . . . Adams made it clear that if we persisted in calling the
(Loyalty Board) members . . . charges against Mr. Cohn would be
made public . . . I told him that we just would not be blackmailed that
way. . . . It was a combination of salesmanship and threatening . . ."

Then Jenkins asked McCarthy precisely what "threat" I had made
that evening when I was in his apartment. It was his word against
mine, and McCarthy lied. He said that I had told him that he had better
get off the Fort Monmouth investigation or have his committee wrecked.
McCarthy said he had discussed my visit with Cohn, and they agreed
that if they gave in to this sort of blackmail it would set the *modus
operandi* for the same type of blackmail whenever they tried to get rid
of Communists. Under no circumstances should they accede to it, he
stated righteously.

When McCarthy made these allegations, I toyed with the idea of
revealing the things he actually had said in his apartment that night—
that he couldn't fire Cohn without being accused of being anti-Semitic,
and also that Schine was "just a miserable little Jew." But I said
nothing.

As the hearings dragged into the second week of June, they degenerated once more into a farcical repetition of squabbles. At one point, Senator Jackson amused himself by asking McCarthy about a short document known as the "Schine Plan Outline." McCarthy had cited this as one of the reasons the committee hired Schine. The "Schine Plan" was a "global" scheme of "psychological warfare" that included such media weapons as "pictures, cartoons, humor, pin-ups." The audience giggled as Jackson read aloud from it. He asked McCarthy about Schine's plan to fight communism with "pin-ups." Even McCarthy grinned at that one.

Cohn was not amused, however. According to some witnesses, he sent for a folder marked "Jackson's record." At the end of the day's session, he grabbed the twenty-eight-year-old counsel for the minority—Robert F. Kennedy—and exchanged angry words. A few reporters gathered round. "Do you want to fight now?" Cohn demanded of Kennedy. It looked for a moment that there might be fisticuffs, but the two young hotheads were pulled apart. Kennedy's version of the story was that Cohn had said that he'd better tell Jackson that "we're going to get him on Monday. We're going to bring out stuff on his being favorably inclined toward Communists." Cohn denied saying any such thing.

Finally, on the thirty-sixth day, Chairman Mundt gaveled an end to the circus. The senators made a windy round of speeches about the search for truth, and set about writing a report that would largely ignore it. It didn't really matter. Because of television, millions had—for the first time—seen the true face of McCarthyism.

Perhaps they were more willing to really look than in McCarthy's early days. By 1954, America was beginning to feel comfortable again. Eisenhower—dependable, likable Ike—had ended the Korean War and brought a sense of tranquillity to the nation. In an age of growing complacency, McCarthy was becoming a jarring note. Communism had not diminished as a world threat, to be sure, yet somehow the Red Menace began to seem a little less close to home, and Red-baiting became tiresome.

Certainly, television had stripped McCarthy of his ability to manipulate the press. TV has been criticized as a superficial medium. Yet in this case, it showed McCarthy in the flesh, without the distorting filter of headlines and self-serving press conferences and phony "news events."

Over twenty years later, Alfred Friendly of the Washington *Post* who had recognized the power of TV, described a hearing in 1952 at which McCarthy had denounced Philip C. Jessup for his "affinity to Communist causes." Since Jessup was a former ultra right-wing American Firster, this was an incredible charge. Senator J. William Fulbright was presiding at the hearing, and during a recess he pulled Friendly aside in the corridor. "He was shaking with a rage born of incomprehension of how one man could be so evil, yet so impregnable," wrote Friendly.

"I didn't know, I didn't know," Fulbright kept repeating. Yet, wrote Friendly,

> Fulbright was far from being the least intelligent, least attentive, or least informed senator on the Hill.
> "Good Lord, Senator," I said. "Haven't you been reading about what he's been doing for the last two years?"
> "Yes, of course I have," he replied, "but you can't believe it until you've seen him in action yourself."

"He was right," wrote Friendly. "The American people could not know just how ugly that ugly man was until they saw him, finally, on television during the Army-McCarthy hearings."

The hearings had lasted thirty-six days. Thirty-two witnesses had spoken 2 million words which stretched over 7,000 pages of transcript. Little had been proved, yet McCarthy was finished. And so was I.

CHAPTER XXXVI

Last Chance

Like twenty million other Americans, I watched the last days of the hearings on television. With my own testimony over, I had no further reason to attend the hearings. Instead, I sat in my Pentagon office, watching a flickering gray screen, alone and brooding. My door was closed; my phone almost never rang; I had little to do. I just sat there, watching McCarthy posture in front of his charts, and contemplating my own bleak future.

My one remaining hope was the Army's brief. Carefully prepared by the lawyers in my office and Welch's aide, Jim St. Clair, it took apart McCarthy's counter-charges against the Army point by point, and, I believed, exposed the "Eleven Memoranda." There were, for starters, certain discrepancies in timing. For example: Cohn swore that he dictated all his memos in McCarthy's office, and Mrs. Driscoll, McCarthy's secretary, swore that they were all dated on or after the actual dictation. Yet Cohn was in New York the day he supposedly dictated a memo about the Merchants Club lunch (November 17), and that night he flew to Boston. McCarthy swore he dictated a memo about General Lawton to Cohn and Carr by long-distance telephone on the night of December 16. Yet all three were already in New York. A

Frank Carr memo of December 9 alleges "unfair" treatment of Private Schine by the Army, yet Carr testified at the hearing that as of December 9 the Army had treated Schine fairly.

There were more crucial inconsistencies, however. If the Army had offered McCarthy evidence of subversion and homosexuality in the Navy and the Air Force, why then did he not take us up on the offer? After all, McCarthy insisted that he had a sworn duty to accept such leads from patriots in the government, and thus ferret out subversion. The notion that Stevens wanted to "break" General Lawton for cooperating with McCarthy was absurd. It had been Stevens who *ordered* Lawton to cooperate. Finally, if I had tried to "blackmail" the McCarthy committee into dropping their planned subpoenas of Loyalty Board members by threatening to expose the Schine pressure, why hadn't Dirksen and Mundt so testified? They took the stand to testify in detail about my visits to their offices, yet they both backed away from accusing me of blackmail. And my conversation with McCarthy didn't sound much like blackmail. McCarthy had invited me to his home and he testified that it was "a not unfriendly conversation." Indeed, he sent me away with an armful of Wisconsin cheese and sausages. And if I had tried to blackmail McCarthy, why had he waited six weeks—until the release of the Army "Chronology of Events"—to tell anyone—in the Senate, at the White House, the Justice Department, or the Defense Department? There was considerable evidence of cooperation, even, unhappily, of some fawning by the Army, but not of blackmail.

These points and many more were brought out in great detail in the Army brief—and in a far more persuasive and orderly fashion than could be divined by listening to the rambling and regularly disrupted hearings.

But the Senate was to see no brief. It had been written all right, but it was never submitted. I was not told why.[1] Stevens had been giving

1. Years later I learned that Welch did not want to sign the brief himself because he feared he might be sued for libel in Massachusetts, where juries were likely to be pro-McCarthy. Stevens had been willing to indemnify him from that worry and let the brief go forward. But first Stevens wanted to check with his superiors. When he did, he was told there was to be no brief under any circumstances. Had I known all this was going on, as an interested and accused party I could have simply forwarded the brief as my own, whether Stevens or the higher-ups approved. They could hardly have stopped me from seeking to clear my name. I certainly had nothing to lose since I had known for some time that I was a goner. In signing the document as Army Counselor, I couldn't have been sued, because it would have been an official communication from the Army to the Senate.

me the silent treatment for weeks. While Welch and I remained on friendly terms (both then and for years afterward), he consulted almost solely with Stevens on strategy. Actually, after the "Chronology of Events" had been sent forward, I had been almost completely isolated from these conferences. I had never attended any of the "Executive Sessions" at which Welch, McCarthy, Jenkins, and the committee cut various deals, and never even knew of some of them. Only later I learned, for instance, that Welch had agreed not to bring up Cohn's lack of wartime military service if McCarthy did not bring up Fred Fisher.

I have always been baffled at the reason why Welch agreed that the hearings should be conducted as quasi-judicial proceedings with criminal overtones, and even more perplexed at the decision to have no closing arguments or written summations or briefs. I felt the lack of a closing brief doomed any chance of exposing the holes in McCarthy's case. I resented the efforts of Mundt and Dirksen (and many others) to save McCarthy and McCarthyism no matter what the cost. Nor was I happy with my silent treatment from the White House.

I thought Joe Welch had not agressively defended the truth of my testimony against the hedged and waffling story given by McCarthy. He was a great trial lawyer, but he wasn't really representing me. In a sense, he was not obligated to. Had this been an ordinary criminal trial, and Welch my lawyer, he would have been derelict. But this was no ordinary trial, and in many ways his real client was the national interest. Early on, I think, Welch perceived that he could best serve that interest not by dwelling on a squabble over Private Schine, but by trying to expose McCarthy's basic character.

And in that, of course, he succeeded.

I'm afraid that at the time I took only limited satisfaction from his success since I was going down the drain, too.

There was no winner at the Army-McCarthy hearings. Even sadder is the fact that the battle was fought on the wrong front. It is farcical that when the administration finally stood up to McCarthy, the fight degenerated into a squabble over an issue as petty as special favors to Private Schine. McCarthy himself said he really didn't care about Schine. The battle should have been fought over what McCarthy had been doing to the Army's employees at Fort Monmouth and his attempts to subpoena Loyalty Board members. His kangaroo court "Executive

Sessions'' and his attempts to interfere with the normal executive branch processes were the very essence of McCarthyism. But they were not explored at the hearings.

Instead, McCarthy managed to put the Army on the defensive by accusing it of holding Schine hostage and trying to blackmail McCarthy into dropping his investigation of subversion at Fort Monmouth. The Army spent its effort trying to vindicate itself.

It never was brought out that there was every reason to try to stop McCarthy's Fort Monmouth investigation. He had been trying to railroad a group of helpless scientists out of their jobs. And after having cleared them all in earlier reviews, when McCarthy started his investigation, the Army had "cooperated," suspending Fort Monmouth employees right and left. I had resisted those suspensions, but with only partial success. Then, to make matters worse, McCarthy tried to drag the judges of the Army Loyalty Boards before his committee so that he could pillory them for exonerating "subversives." That was destructive to the future of any sort of impartial adjudication, and I had resisted that bitterly too.

My resistance had helped provoke the confrontation between the Army and McCarthy. But the real stakes became lost along the way. By the time twenty million viewers turned on their television sets to learn what was going on, the issue had become Private Schine. No wonder everyone came off looking so badly.

[V]

ENDINGS

CHAPTER XXXVII

"Inexcusable"

Roy Cohn was the first to go. He resigned from McCarthy's staff a month after the hearings. Cohn had been "mantrapped in the rough game of politics we play down here," said McCarthy, who scowled at reporters and grumbled that Cohn's resignation was a "victory for Communism." Within a few weeks, McCarthyites had organized a huge testimonial dinner for Cohn at the Hotel Astor in New York, where 2,000 of the faithful paid tribute to the fallen warrior. One organizer said that 6,000 had to be turned away.

I read in the New York *Times* that I was being fired. Actually, it was a July 22, 1954 *Times* dispatch reprinted in a Winnepeg, Ontario, newspaper that quoted "administration and Congressional sources," as expecting my "early retirement." It was news to me, though not exactly unexpected. When I arrived home from a Canadian fishing trip with my family in August, I denied that I was about to leave. But I knew it was only a matter of time before the administration would ask me to go. Twice during the summer Deputy Attorney General Rogers told me that a move was afoot to have me fired, but, he said, that he had put a stop to it "this time." Throughout the autumn I heard rumblings from various Senate sources. Some House members joined the chorus. Congressman Gerald Ford, chairman of the House Military Appropriations Subcommittee, said I should be fired. No member of Congress wanted to deal with an official in a liaison position who might "tell" of congressional misbehavior.

McCarthy, meanwhile, pretended to be undaunted by the hearings. He promptly announced new investigations of subversives in defense industries and in the CIA.

But the tide had turned against him. State Republican leaders from the heartland expressed their dismay over the spectacle of the Army-McCarthy hearings, and began to worry that McCarthyism was hurting them politically. "It is now time for the Republican Party to repudiate Joe McCarthy before he drags them down to defeat," said Palmer Hoyt in Colorado. The politicians had their eye on the polls: Since January, nearly one quarter of the nation had changed its mind about McCarthy; over half the country now looked on him with disfavor.

In Congress, Senator Ralph Flanders of Vermont, saw his chance. Flanders had mocked McCarthy as Dennis the Menace during the hearings, and two days after the Fisher incident he introduced a resolution to strip McCarthy of his committee chairmanships. He called McCarthyism a "crisis of civilization," and cited McCarthy's "contempt of the Senate, contempt of the truth" and his "habitual contempt for people." McCarthy responded to Flanders by saying, "I think they should get a net and take him to a good, quiet place."

Flanders had been virtually alone in his criticism of McCarthy before the hearings. Now people were listening. Wisely, to placate Republican leaders worried about setting dangerous precedents, Flanders substituted a simple motion of censure: "Resolved, That the conduct of the Senator from Wisconsin, Mr. McCarthy, is contrary to senatorial traditions, and tends to bring the Senate in disrepute, and such conduct is hereby condemned." A special select committee was appointed to look into the charge.

Over the next few weeks, Flanders tacked on a list of specific charges. They covered almost all of McCarthy's transgressions in the Senate, from his calling Adlai Stevenson Alger, to threatening newspapers that they would lose their second-class mailing privileges, to taking questionable fees from lobbyists, to abusing his colleagues, to disclosing classified information. There were thirty-three charges in all, a long and damning record.

The first notice to McCarthy that he might face Senate disciplinary action occurred on June 11, 1954, when Senator Ralph Flanders (R. Vermont) (seen standing in the aisle behind McCarthy) casually walked into the hearing room while McCarthy was testifying and handed him an envelope. McCarthy said, "Oh, thank you, Ralph." He is shown reading the notification contained in the envelope that Flanders intended to introduce a resolution to discipline McCarthy that afternoon. Flanking McCarthy as he reads are Frank Carr and Roy Cohn, with James Juliana seen behind McCarthy in the second row.

The newspaperwoman facing Cohn with a note pad on her knee is Mae Craig of the Maine newspapers, one of the ablest and most effective exponents of women's equality of the era. COURTESY WIDE WORLD PHOTOS.

At the end of August, the Mundt committee made its report on the Army-McCarthy hearings. It should have been breathlessly awaited after two months of televised hearings, but it wasn't. The results were all too predictable:

The committee split 4 to 3 along straight party lines. Both sides agreed that both the Army and McCarthy had been at fault, but the

Republicans heaped more abuse on the Army, while the Democrats reserved their harshest judgment for McCarthy. McCarthy came in for criticism from both sides for letting Cohn get out of hand on the matter of Schine, while Stevens and I were blamed for appeasement and vacillation. The Republicans said it was "inexcusable" that I had shown my record of the McCarthy subcommittee's abuses of the Army to newsmen. Apparently I had broken the unwritten Code of the Hill that civil servants are expected to be silent about congressional impropriety. McCarthy was slapped by the Democrats for encouraging government employees to steal and disclose classified information. The Republican majority did not see any need to ask the Justice Department to review the record for perjury; the Democrats did. Not that it made much difference. Four months later, the Justice Department quietly announced that the record showed no grounds for grand jury action—only "differences of opinion."

The committee neglected to take note of its own negligence in dealing with McCarthy. Everything they criticized had been going on for months under the noses of the committee members. The Republicans had even assigned staff members to sit in on many of McCarthy's "Executive Sessions" and to report back to their senators. Yet they had done nothing. During the same period the Democrats walked out instead of fighting on the Senate floor so that proper procedures would be implemented. But when a committee investigates itself, noted the Washington *Post*, "the members of the committee (can) scarcely be expected to reproach themselves."

The report, issued in late August, went almost unnoticed. A few editorial writers lamented the whole sorry business, but most journalists and the public had already turned their attention to the next round: McCarthy's censure hearings.

CHAPTER XXXVIII

"The Senator Is Out of Order!"

Historically, Congress has been loath to punish its own. In the near century or so between the Civil War and the McCarthy era, Congress had not thrown out or refused to seat a single member. The Senate had censured only three: Hiram Bingham of Connecticut, who in the late 1920s brought a lobbyist from the Connecticut Manufacturers Association to executive sessions of the Senate Finance Committee; and Senators Benjamin Tillman and John McLaurin of South Carolina, who in 1902 had a fist fight on the Senate floor. Several other senators, accused or convicted of corruption, managed to avoid or survive disciplinary proceedings.

It was not an easy job to find senators willing to sit in judgment on another senator. Had McCarthy not been so damaged in the Army-McCarthy hearings, it might have been impossible. But in the fall of 1954, the Senate leadership put together a select committee of three Democrats and three Republicans that was everything the Mundt committee was not.

Three were former judges: Arthur Watkins of Utah (the chairman),

John Stennis of Mississippi, and Sam Ervin of North Carolina. Two—
Frank Carlson of Kansas and Edwin C. Johnson of Colorado—had
been state governors, and Francis Case of South Dakota had been a
seven-term veteran of the House. It was a basically conservative, experienced, and responsible group.

Chairman Watkins, a devout Mormon of unblemished integrity, made
it clear from the outset that he was determined to avoid the circus
atmosphere of the Army-McCarthy hearings. "Let's get off the front
page and back among the obituaries," he said. Television was banned.
Even smoking was forbidden. And so were McCarthy's constant dis-
ruptions. No longer was McCarthy allowed to sit at the same table as
his judges; this time he was stationed at a small table before the committee, like a true defendant. When McCarthy began that familiar
whine, "Mr. Chairman, Mr. Chairman," in the first session, Watkins
gaveled him into silence. "The Senator is out of order," intoned Watkins. "We are not going to be interrupted by these diversions and
sidelines. We are going straight down the line." Out in the hallway,
McCarthy sputtered his now famous line, "I think this is the most
unheard-of thing I ever heard of."

Watkins was aided in his effort to restrain McCarthy by McCarthy's
own counsel, Edward Bennett Williams. In his 1962 memoir, the
famous trial lawyer relates that McCarthy had asked him to represent
the McCarthy side at the Army-McCarthy hearings, but when McCarthy
refused to give him complete control, Williams turned him down.
McCarthy came back to Williams for the censure hearings, and Williams made the same demand. Perhaps sensing that he needed Williams even more this time, McCarthy went along. What Williams forgot
to get from McCarthy was control over his behavior outside the hearing room. This, Williams later wrote, was a "tremendous oversight."

The select committee quickly condensed Flanders's laundry list of
thirty-three charges into six categories: McCarthy's finances, his abuse
of his colleagues, his contempt of a Senate investigation committee,
his acceptance of classified information without authorization, his
encouragement of government employees to break the law, and his
abuse of General Zwicker.

Williams's defense was very skillful. It was essentially a pot-call-
ing-the-kettle-black argument. Williams claimed that everything
McCarthy had done, some other senator had done before, without getting punished for it. He knew that the senators were reluctant to estab-

lish precedents by which they might be judged. For instance, McCarthy
had said many abusive things about his colleagues. He had called Senator Robert C. Hendrickson "a living miracle without brains or guts,"
and Senator Flanders, "senile." On the other hand, Senator Flanders
had likened McCarthy to Hitler and hinted that he was a homosexual.

It is difficult to think of another senator who had done *all* the things
McCarthy had done. Still, Williams's defense almost worked. One by
one, the charges against McCarthy were dropped. The "Purloined Letter" could be considered as an attempt to get government employees
to break the law, reasoned the committee. On the other hand, there
was nothing wrong with a congressional committee receiving evidence
of corruption or subversion from a government agency. The committee
decided that McCarthy's pipeline to his "patriots" was "susceptible
of alternate constructions" and left it at that.

By the end of the hearings, the original thirty-three charges had
become just two: the Zwicker abuse and McCarthy's contempt for the
Gillette committee. The Zwicker abuse was dropped at the last moment
when Senator Case got cold feet. Case decided that the Army's refusal
to honor McCarthy's request that Major Peress be held for a court-
martial was sufficient "provocation" for his abuse of Zwicker. The
other five committee members wanted to keep the Zwicker charge, but
Democrat leader Lyndon Johnson, sensing some weakening among the
Democrats, told Watkins he had better just drop it.

That left only one count, McCarthy's contempt for a Senate subcommittee. In 1951, the Senate Subcommittee on Privileges and Elections, chaired by Senator Guy Gillette, had begun an inquiry into
McCarthy's finances. An early McCarthy foe, Senator William Benton, had called for an investigation to decide whether the Senate should
begin expulsion proceedings against McCarthy. Gillette's subcommittee had been assigned to the task. Specifically, the Gillette committee
had wanted to know if McCarthy had siphoned off for personal use,
money sent by supporters in his search for subversives; whether he had
accepted illegal campaign contributions; and whether he advanced his
own self-interest in his dealings with various special interest groups.
McCarthy had refused to cooperate with the committee in any way.
Instead, he had sent it an abusive letter: "I cannot understand your
being willing to label Guy Gillette as a man who will head a committee
which is stealing from the pockets of the American taxpayers tens of
thousands of dollars and then using this money to protect the Democrat

Party from the political effect of the exposure of Communists in Government.''

As the censure proceedings began, there were many serious charges against McCarthy. Abusive treatment of other senators was far down on the list. But as one charge after another was dropped, McCarthy compounded his problems by beginning an attack on the committee which was hearing the matter. The chairman, gentle Arthur Watkins of Utah, he singled out for particular abuse.

True to his agreement with lawyer Williams, McCarthy held his tongue-in-check in the hearing room. Outside, in the hallway, it was another story. McCarthy vented his spleen at this "lynching party" and called the Watkins committee the "unwitting handmaidens" and "attorneys-in-fact" of the Communist party. Such outbursts cost McCarthy another censure charge—this one for abusing the Watkins committee.

McCarthy's hard core had not deserted him. A group modestly called "Ten Million Americans Mobilizing for Justice," delivered to the Capitol a petition with 1,000,816 signatures in an armored truck. In November, 13,000 attended a "Who Promoted Peress?" rally in New York. The Hortonville High School band, flown in from McCarthy's hometown Appleton, played "On Wisconsin," a blues singer shouted that he would "shake, rattle, and roll" for McCarthy; and everyone sang "Nobody Loves Joe but the People." McCarthy himself was missing; an enthusiastic admirer had pumped his arm so hard that his elbow had cracked through a glass table.

McCarthy came back from the hospital full of bravado. "I can go 15 rounds!" he exclaimed to reporters. Meanwhile, his old defender, Everett Dirksen, joined forces with a rising Republican senator—Barry Goldwater—to try to save McCarthy with a deal. They urged the formation of a committee whose purpose would be to write some new rules of Senate conduct. If McCarthy proceeded to break those rules, then he would be censured.

But it didn't work. McCarthy's colleagues—the same ones who had voted almost unanimously a year before to give him all the money he wanted for his one-man Investigations Subcommittee—now wanted to chastize him. At the last moment, Vice-President Richard Nixon, exercising his prerogative as president of the Senate, struck out the word "censure" from the resolution, making it a "resolution relating to" McCarthy's conduct. On December 2, the measure passed the full

Senate, 67 to 22. Whatever the resolution was called, it was "not," as McCarthy himself observed, "exactly a vote of confidence."

In some ways, it seemed that McCarthy had escaped with a mild slap on the wrist. He had been convicted only of offending Senate custom and propriety, mild offenses compared to the original charges, several of which were criminal. Yet to be punished at all by the U.S. Senate was to be disgraced. Certainly, other senators saw it that way.

Now, when McCarthy stood up to speak on the Senate floor, the chamber would empty. "From here on out," said Senator Mike Monroney, "McCarthy will bear a scarlet C on his chest." When McCarthy would sit down with his colleagues in the clubby Senators-only dining room, his colleagues would make lame excuses and leave. McCarthy would be left alone, with a hurt and puzzled look on his face. He never forgave Senator Watkins. When he passed Watkins's desk on the Senate floor, McCarthy would lean over and whisper, "How's the little coward from Utah?"[1] The press began to sense McCarthy's leprosy. The self-proclaimed "goon squad" of reporters that had covered him for the last three years disbanded. McCarthy continued to make the same speeches, but he made them to a void. The headlines that had so long sustained McCarthyism, disappeared.

From time to time, a reporter would have a glimpse of McCarthy looking gray and drunk, stumbling down a Capitol hallway. Over at the White House, President Eisenhower greeted his Cabinet with a little joke. "Have you heard the latest?" he asked. "McCarthyism is McCarthywasism."

1. Nor did the Utah McCarthyites forgive Watkins. In the next election they ran a pro-McCarthy ex-governor as a third-party candidate for the announced purpose of splitting the Republican vote, so that Watkins was defeated for reelection by a Democrat.

CHAPTER XXXIX

The Education of John Adams

My own friends in Congress also disappeared. Those who were still willing to talk to me wanted me to come to their offices. It had been a great shock to Congress to learn that every call to Stevens since he had become secretary two years earlier had been monitored, and that mine as well had been monitored for four or five weeks. They were afraid it was still going on. My years of comfortable relations with a wide variety of congressmen and staff were clearly over, and with them, my usefulness.

My career, as Army counselor and before, had been built on cooperation. Now that few would talk to me, I wasn't much help to the Army. And I was clearly a canker to the administration.

I couldn't be fired right away, however. It would have looked unseemly to give in to the steady demands of the McCarthyites and run me out at the same time Congress was holding censure hearings on McCarthy. For the most part I just sat in my office, without much to do, although my colleagues would try to cheer me up.

Around Christmas, the ax fell. Stevens called me on his squawk box: "Can you come up?" Here it comes, I thought. Stevens looked just the same, the same double-breasted gray suit, same white shirt and dark tie, same thick glasses and highly polished black shoes, same carefully parted gray hair, same guileless boy scout smile. "I'd like to talk to you about your career, John," he said.

March 31 was set as my departure day. But first, I had to play out a last farcical chapter in the Army-McCarthy story. As a last gasp, McCarthy had persuaded his old Senate Permanent Subcommittee on Investigations to pursue the most ridiculous question of the whole Army-McCarthy fiasco: "Who promoted Peress?" The committee wasn't even supposed to have jurisdiction over subversion, but off it went on a last wild-goose chase, trying to find the villain who had protected the dangerous dentist.

The chief villain, of course, had been me. The real question was not who promoted Peress—an act of Congress had done that. The question was who let him slip out of the Army before McCarthy had a chance to force a court-martial. The answer was John Adams.

I had just gotten fed up that night in February, sitting in my Pentagon office staring at McCarthy's letter. We had been pushed around by McCarthy and his men for months, and I had just had enough. So I had let Peress go, thereby setting off a chain reaction that exploded in the Army-McCarthy hearings.

Now, over a year later, I was in no mood to apologize for it. About a week before my retirement date, I was called before the Permanent Investigations Subcommittee, which was now chaired by a Democrat, Senator McClellan. Senator Ervin, a new member on the committee, tried to pin me down on my great disrespect for the "Committee," which, of course, had been nothing more than McCarthy's committee-of-one.

ERVIN: Do you not think that a proper consideration for an agency of a legislative branch ought to have prompted you to at least contact the Chairman of the Subcommittee on Investigations and at least acquaint him with the fact that that was your final determination?

ADAMS: That could have been done, Senator, and it was not done in this case.

ERVIN: Do you think you ought to have done it?

ADAMS: I don't think it would have made any difference in what we did. . . .

ERVIN: . . . you allowed your personal feelings to cause you to take

an action which showed contempt, did it not, for a coordinate branch of
the federal government?

ADAMS: You can draw that conclusion if you wish, sir. . . .

Ervin and McClellan proceeded to threaten me for my lack of "common courtesy" to the legislative branch, that is, to the senator they had just finished censuring. But I was beyond caring. A couple of months later, the committee handed down a report finding forty-eight errors in the handling of Major Peress, or about one for every time Peress's papers landed on another desk. Error number forty-eight was:

> Failure of John Adams to suggest to General Weible that the honorable
> discharge be held in abeyance, or on his own responsibility to initiate
> action which would accomplish this end, after receipt of Senator
> McCarthy's letter of February 1, 1954.

I considered that no error.

There was an eerie quality to the Peress hearings. The committee was the same that had conducted the Army-McCarthy hearings, and many of the old players were back. McCarthy called me "John" again, and once again, I told him to call me "Mr. Adams." But this time around the hearing room was half empty, the TV cameras gone. McCarthy, sitting quietly at the committee table, looked ghostly and sick, a shadow of the terror he had been. According to a newspaper column by Stewart Alsop, I looked even ghostlier.

A few weeks after the Army-McCarthy hearings, a police officer had come up to me in New York's Grand Central Station. "You're Adams, aren't you?" he asked. I answered yes. "I hope you're satisfied, you son of a bitch," he said. A newspaper in Boston about that time called me a Communist. I asked Joe Welch if I could sue the paper for libel. He told me that I'd never win before a Massachusetts jury.

My critics were not just Irish hard hats. Michael Straight, the editor of the liberal *New Republic,* rushed into print a book about the Army-McCarthy hearings that compared me to Rosencrantz and Guildenstern. Like Hamlet's lackeys who died doing their master's bidding, I "did make love to this employment," wrote Straight. To me that meant he was calling me a whore.

He then sent me a copy of the book and an accompanying letter in

Lunching with my colleagues on the last day of my incumbency as Army
counselor. From the left: John G. Simon, now a professor of law at Yale,
and the late Charles Haskins, who left the Army counselor's office to
become a member of President Eisenhower's National Security Council
staff. To the left of me is Lewis Berry, my deputy, who also went to the
White House staff and then served for twenty years as a senior counsel at the
House of Representatives, and Norman Dorsen, now a professor of law at
New York University and, in 1981, the national president of the American
Civil Liberties Union. (Dorsen says that his experiences during the Army-
McCarthy fight are what sparked his lifelong dedication to civil liberties.)
COURTESY U.S. ARMY.

which he said "I hope you find it fair." He autographed the book,
"To John Adams with gratitude."

My mail wasn't all bad; in fact, most of it cheered me for standing
up to McCarthy. I also received a message from Dean Acheson, the
Red Dean, so villified by McCarthy, that he thought my actions
throughout had been "great." His praise meant a great deal to me.

So, too, did the support of my colleagues, the lawyers who worked in the Army counselor's office. Their long hours had helped sustain me through the dark days of 1954, and their good cheer had bucked me up in the low days after the hearings.

Now, on my last day at the Pentagon, I had invited the few who remained to have lunch with me in my office—a perquisite of the position. Mel Dow had already left to begin a very successful law career in Houston; Joe Sullivan had taken a post in Germany; Howard Sacks was off to teach at Northwestern Law School, then to become dean at Connecticut Law School; Peck Hill had taken a post at the Justice Department. Only four remained: my deputy, Lew Berry, who was to hold other high posts in the Eisenhower administration and then serve for twenty years as a senior staffer on the Hill; Charles Haskins, who was already scheduled to transfer to the National Security Staff at the White House; Norman Dorsen, who would go on to become Stokes professor of law at New York University and finally, president of the American Civil Liberties Union; and John Simon, who would become Lines professor of law at Yale. We had a cheerful lunch, reminiscing in a goodnatured way about our extraordinary times together.

As I was cleaning out my desk and getting ready to head home, a reporter showed up. It was Anthony Lewis, later a New York *Times* columnist, but then a young reporter for the Washington *Daily News*.

From the Washington *Daily News,* April 1, 1955:

THE EDUCATION OF JOHN ADAMS

A little after 3 o'clock yesterday afternoon John G. Adams, sometime Army counsel, television star and combatant with Sen. Joseph McCarthy, walked out of Washington.

Mr. Adams had a few possessions piled on his desk to take home. There was a musical plastic Easter egg given him by the secretaries for his 21-month-old daughter, and a book from his legal staff, Bernard DeVoto's "The Course of the Empire." The book was inscribed: "To John G. Adams who contributed so much to righting the 'course of empire'—from those who served with him throughout the great conflict." . . .

Mr. Adams whose resignation "for personal reasons" was announced some time ago said he had no immediate plans.

"I am going to spend April trying to get my golf score down from 145 to 125," he said. "I think every point I can get off my golf score my blood pressure will go down correspondingly. Perhaps I can get it back to where it was when -quote- all this started -unquote-. . . .

A member of his staff rushed up with a piece of paper. "I hate to do this, John," he said, "but there's one more official act before you go— sign my efficiency report." Mr. Adams signed.

His secretary . . . gave him a last note about airline schedules . . . Mr. Adams picked up his packages and walked out. . . .

He dropped in on Gen. Matthew Ridgway, Army Chief of Staff, and Deputy Chief, Lieutenant Gen. W. L. Weible, and then poked his head in some nearby doors to say goodbye to smaller fry.

"I have lots of friends on the Indian level here," he said.

Wasn't he surprised there were no other reporters around?

"No," he said "It's kind of like last year's hat. Last year's hat is last year's hat."

He walked up to the receptionist at the Mall entrance. "Well, Mr. A., is this the day?" she asked.

As he stepped into the sunlight a large middle-aged woman rushed up. "Mr. Adams," she said, "I'm from Excelsior, Minn. . . . Mr. Adams, I hope somebody in Government gives you a great big gold star," the woman said.

"You think I'm a gold star mother?" Mr. Adams said.

"I think you did something for all of us," the woman said seriously. "I think you're a gold star man."

"That was some ending," Mr. Adams said as he walked down the stairs. And he got into his car and drove away.

Epilogue

In November of 1954, Norman Thomas, the old Socialist, remarked that "in spite of" McCarthyism, "there has been a saving common sense about our Democracy. . . . The end has always been victory for comparative reason and decency." He continued:

> The struggle against demagoguery scarcely fits the St. George-against-the-Dragon myth. . . . Our democratic St. George goes out rather reluctantly, with armor awry. The struggle is confused; our knight wins by no clean thrust of lance or sword, but the dragon poops out, and decent democracy is victor."

In the spring of 1955, this particular knight was out of a job. I had become a little too controversial for the job market, even the jobs once offered to me by old friends. I didn't have much choice except to try to start a private law practice. Since I had never argued a case or filed a courtroom brief, the normal work of a lawyer was for me, at the age of forty-three, a novel, and difficult, experience.

I was napping on my living room sofa one Saturday afternoon when the phone rang in the next room. Margaret answered and tiptoed in. In a shocked whisper she said, "It's Joe McCarthy, for you."

He wanted me to come for dinner the following Monday, and to bring my wife. Roy Cohn would be there, he said, and Senator Symington and his wife. McCarthy was his old cheerful self; gone was the on-camera sneer he used when he called Senator Symington Sanctimonious Stu at the hearings. Still, I was pretty sure Symington would not be at McCarthy's home, and I didn't want to be there with McCarthy and Cohn and whoever else he would drag in as a surprise.

"Joe, I can't do that," I said. "I can't ask my wife to come to your home. She despises you. She wouldn't set foot in your door."

Joe giggled, that self-conscious giggle he used when something was more embarrassing than funny. "Heh, heh, you know the girls; they take these things seriously."

He said a few words, and I hung up. I thought that was the last I would hear from McCarthy. But I was to see him one last time.

I was sitting in my small law office near the District of Columbia courthouse, a few months later when he called me again. He wanted me to come to see him at his home. It was a bright, cool day, and my law business was making minimal demands on my time. McCarthy's home, a townhouse on Capitol Hill, was less than a half hour's walk away. I decided to go.

When I arrived, I shook hands with his wife Jean who was just leaving with her mother. McCarthy offered me a drink; I said no thanks. I followed him into the kitchen where he made one for himself. He poured about six ounces of Fleishman's gin into a glass, added a little tonic and a lump of ice, and lumbered back into the living room.

He looked awful. He had lost about forty pounds, and his hands shook. He was having trouble drinking, and gin trickled from the corners of his mouth when he took a sip.

McCarthy said that he had admired my integrity during the Army-McCarthy hearings. He said that I had behaved honorably throughout. He then suggested that I now show my integrity by repudiating the Army position. He wanted me to join with him in some sort of statement which, he believed, would help him reestablish himself.

He did not explain how, if one show of "integrity" repudiated another show of "integrity," either could be believed. Nor did he explain how a disavowal of former testimony under oath would be anything other than an admission of perjury. But then, logical consistency had never been McCarthy's aim. If day had to become night to reestablish McCarthy, then so be it.

"It's no good, Joe," I said. "It won't work. It's over and finished; that's all. You can't change the truth."

We talked for a little while longer. McCarthy seemed not to regret, or even remember, what he had done to Stevens and me. It was as if the Army-McCarthy hearings had never happened, as if Dave Schine had enthusiastically spent his basic training doing push-ups, as if Major Peress was still drilling Army teeth, as if the sight of scientist "Z," gasping before McCarthy's interrogation like a drowning man, had been only a bad dream.

After about an hour, I got up to leave. McCarthy walked with me to the door and stood there until I reached the sidewalk. I said, "So long, Joe" to the cadaverous visage of McCarthyism, standing silently in the shadows, slowly dying.

A few months later I stood alone on the corner of Third and Constitution Avenue and watched Gawler's funeral coach and a small procession of black limousines roll slowly up Capitol Hill. They were taking McCarthy to his last appointment on the Senate floor.

Retrospect

RAYMOND E. BALDWIN, a senator from Connecticut, had in 1949 the dubious distinction of being the first high public official to be attacked by McCarthy. Baldwin resigned from the Senate shortly after McCarthy's brutal attack over the Malmedy prisoners. He was appointed to the Connecticut Supreme Court of Errors immediately following his resignation from the Senate, serving there for fourteen years. He retired from that court as its chief judge in 1963. Now eighty-three, he is living in Connecticut.

MILLARD E. TYDINGS, defeated for a fifth term as Maryland's senator in 1950 by the McCarthy-orchestrated "despicable back street campaign," tried a comeback in 1956. He won the Democratic nomination to again face McCarthy's selection, John Marshall Butler, but a disabling attack of shingles forced him to withdraw from the general election race. He died five years later at the age of seventy-one.

ANNA M. ROSENBERG HOFFMAN, attacked by McCarthy in 1950, served until 1953 as assistant secretary of defense for Manpower and Personnel and then returned to her New York business advisory firm which she still heads, an energetic and active eighty-year-old. She told me in 1981 that even thirty years after McCarthy's attack on her, she has never forgotten the anguish and suffering that she and her family endured during the ordeal, and that what sustained her most throughout was the never-wavering support she got from General Marshall.

GENERAL OF THE ARMY GEORGE CATLETT MARSHALL retired from the Defense secretary's post in 1951, his third retirement since 1945, first from the post of Army Chief of Staff, and then as secretary of state.

Writer Richard Rovere stated that McCarthy's attack finished Marshall's career, but I think not. Marshall had already retired twice: he was in failing health, and he had reluctantly accepted the Defense post on President Truman's insistence—and then with the understanding that he need stay only a year. Marshall had been the Allies' great strategist as Chairman of the Combined Chiefs of Staff (US-UK); then as secretary of state his Marshall Plan to revitalize Europe won him the Nobel Peace Prize in 1953.

Robert A. Lovett, who had been Marshall's deputy secretary of defense, and who succeeded him as secretary in 1951, told me in 1979 that the only impact of McCarthy's attack on Marshall was to fill him with disgust. Marshall retired to Pinehurst, North Carolina, where he died in 1959 at the age of seventy-eight.

AARON H. COLEMAN spent 14 months looking for a job in private industry after he was fired from the Army as a security risk. He had to start over as a $75-a-week engineer. In 1958, he regained his federal employment rights after his long court struggle. Reinstated in the Army, he immediately resigned to remain in private industry, where he could now do classified work. In 1973, he was offered the same job he had held at Fort Monmouth 20 years before. The final review and approval of his security clearance for access to "Secret" matters was made by the same official who had run the Loyalty Security program in the McCarthy era. Coleman retired from government service in 1978, and is again working on classified matters in private industry. He says he has recovered financially but not emotionally. He is now 63, and lives in Pennsylvania.

"Z" was immediately harassed in his neighborhood after his October 1953 appearance before McCarthy. His family received threatening phone calls, his home was decorated with a hammer and sickle, and even his three-year-old son was told his daddy was a spy. A few months later he was charged as a security risk and ultimately fired. He regained his employment rights through litigation. Whether he reentered government service, and how he spent his life subsequently, I do not know. I have had no direct contacts with him and know only that he wishes to be left alone.

IRVING PERESS was vilified after McCarthy began trumpeting "Who Promoted Peress?" His family received obscene and threatening calls day and night, many neighbors avoided him, rocks were thrown through his daughter's bedroom window, and his children were ostracized by playmates. Peress lost his dentist's office when his landlord kicked him out, and 80 percent of his patients deserted him.

Yet there were people who stood up for the Peresses. The local PTA refused to remove Mrs. Peress as editor of the school paper, despite intense neighborhood pressure. Others—particularly Quakers—volunteered to help the Peress family, babysitting for them, even scrubbing the kitchen floor when the Peresses were out. Many nights near-strangers would sleep in the Peress living room to protect the house from attack. Then there were the 20 percent of Peress's patients who stood by him, and helped him rebuild his practice over the years as the anti-Red hysteria died down. "I will always feel proud of, and grateful for, that twenty percent who dared to have me in their mouths," Peress says today.

Age sixty-seven, he is now semiretired after forty-two years of practice, and lives in New York.

BRIGADIER GENERAL RALPH W. ZWICKER, whose abuse by McCarthy in February 1954 helped set off the Army-McCarthy conflict, was promoted to major general in 1956, an action which required Senate confirmation. McCarthy, already condemned by the Senate, sought to block the nomination on the grounds that Zwicker had lied to the Permanent Investigations Subcommittee in 1955. But Zwicker was confirmed with only two dissenting votes, McCarthy and his diehard Nevada supporter, George Malone. All other right-wing Republicans deserted him.

Zwicker retired from the Army as a major general in 1963.

JOSEPH NYE WELCH, whose charming style and skillful interrogation of the McCarthyites made a great hit with the national television audience in 1954, soon retired from his Boston law firm and enjoyed a brief second career as a movie actor. He was cast as the trial judge in *Anatomy of a Murder,* which also featured James Stewart, Lee Remick, Ben Gazarra, Arthur O'Connell, and Eve Arden. Voted the "Father of the Year" in 1956, he died on Cape Cod at the age of sixty-eight.

FREDERICK FISHER, Joe Welch's law firm associate who was the subject of a brutal McCarthy attack, suffered little. He told me in 1981 that immediately after the McCarthy attack, he had experienced a warm surge of sympathy everywhere. Interest in the incident quickly sub-sided, and his life returned to normal. Fisher continued with the Bos-ton law firm, and in 1973–74 he served as president of the Massachusetts Bar Association. He is now sixty years old.

G. DAVID SCHINE finished out his Army service in Alaska. In 1955 he returned to New York, married a former Miss Universe, and rejoined the Schine organization. He has spent the subsequent years in various hotel and entertainment enterprises in New York, Florida, and Califor-nia, and in 1971 produced the highly successful movie, *The French Connection.* He lives in Los Angeles.

FRANCIS P. "FRANK" CARR left the McCarthy committee in the summer of 1954 and became an executive of a major trucking and transportation company located in his native state of Rhode Island. The Society of Former Agents of the FBI advises me that Carr is deceased, but they have no record of the date of his death.

ROY COHN resigned from the committee in the summer of 1954 and returned to New York where he became a very successful courtroom lawyer and a powerful figure in his own right. He was indicted by federal grand juries three times on charges ranging from wire fraud to extortion and was acquitted each time. Cohn attributed the indictments to a vendetta against him by then U.S. Attorney Robert Morganthau, as well as the late Robert Kennedy, who had been attorney general when the first indictment occurred.

At a testimonial dinner for Cohn in 1973, six state Supreme Court judges, various political leaders, a city councilman, and the mayor-elect attended. The New York *Times* criticized the public officials for attending the function, which it called a "major non-event."

He remains today what he was in 1954, a bright, aggressive, and energetic fighter. His causes might not be my causes, now any more than they were in 1954, but it is obvious that at the end, whoever has been his adversary will know he has been in a fight. Cohn is now fifty-three years old.

ROBERT T. STEVENS served as secretary of the army until the autumn of 1955. He then returned to his family textile business, where he continued an active leadership role until age seventy, when he retired permanently.

In the last months of his textile company employment, he came to Washington to call on three of "my boys" who had gone on to other government assignments. They were Ken BeLieu, who had been his senior military aide during the McCarthy conflict, and who was then serving as one of President Nixon's congressional liaison aides; Fred Weyand, who had been a military aide along with BeLieu, and who later became the last U.S. field commander in Vietnam and finally Army Chief of Staff; and me. I was then serving as a Republican member of the U.S. Civil Aeronautics Board.

While visiting my office, he spoke with pride of a May 1968 speech he had delivered at the invitation of Senator Karl Mundt at the dedication of a small Mundt library at General Beadle College in Madison, South Dakota, a year earlier. He gave me a copy of that speech in which he reminisced

> . . . The duty of blocking the whole attack was mine . . . The accusing word swept over the innocent as well as the guilty. . . . Guilt by association was proclaimed. The harm done to a person so affected was rarely ever lived down. . . . It temporarily . . . became a force utterly at variance with the very purpose of the Bill of Rights. . . .

Even before I left the Pentagon I learned that intense publicity and notoriety were unmarketable commodities, at least in the business and legal communities. So I became for three years a "Fifth Street lawyer," the Washington legal community's definition of one who practiced alone near the courthouse, taking whatever cases came along. It was not a productive venture; in the first three months I grossed twenty-five dollars.

My tarnish was still evident in June 1958 when the White House asked various senators if I would be acceptable as a commissioner of the Interstate Commerce Commission. Styles Bridges, the senior Senate Republican, sent word to Chief of Staff Sherman Adams that he would block any presidential appointment for me which required Senate confirmation because "John wasn't very nice to Joe McCarthy." Nonetheless, with the help of my old South Dakota friend, former Senator Chan Gurney, I became a senior attorney at the Civil Aeronautics Board, where I stayed for thirteen years, the last six of them as one of the five board members. I was appointed to one of the two Republican seats by President Lyndon Johnson in 1965. By now the Senate had forgotten me, and I was confirmed unanimously. My term expired in 1970, and it did not suit the Nixon administration to reappoint me. By then, however, seventeen years had elapsed, and my "past" was obscure. I was able to join a strong Washington law firm with a respectable Connecticut Avenue address. I stayed there for five years and then joined with a friend in a two-man operation from which I gradually phased out as I became absorbed in this book.

JOE MCCARTHY died in May 1957 at the age of forty-nine of an acute liver infection. About five thousand people passed by his body at Gawler's Funeral Parlor, one block from the White House. Later, the Senate held a memorial service for him. At McCarthy's second funeral at Appleton, Wisconsin, the next day, the funeral home stayed open all night before the funeral, and again thousands filed past the casket. He was buried in St. Mary's Cemetery, beside the graves of his parents, on a bleak hilltop overlooking the Fox River.

Acknowledgments

I wrote a four-hundred-fifty-page first draft of this narrative in the summer of 1954, immediately following the Army-McCarthy hearings, while I was still serving as Army counselor, and still had access to the Army's files and records, and to McCarthy's executive transcripts of the Fort Monmouth travesty. Having kept that draft in my possession has assured accuracy in dates, places, and persons present at incidents I now describe.

At intervals of about five years since 1954, I have tried to revise and complete my first attempt, but the entire 1954 experience had been so repugnant to me that I was unable, through the years, to discipline myself sufficiently to keep at the project.

In 1978, after repeated pressures from my wife and daughter, and by many of my twenty-eight nieces and nephews, all of whom were either small children or as yet unborn when McCarthy frightened the world, I decided to write for them and their contemporaries the complex story I had never theretofore been able successfully to set down on paper.

Working from the 1954 document, I wrote a 1,000-page revised version in 1978, a 590-page revision to that document in 1979, and a new 510-page revision in 1980, which W. W. Norton & Company, Inc. was interested in publishing.

When I advised them that I wished to withdraw and rewrite that version, Eric P. Swenson their vice-chairman and executive editor, who is also my editor for this book, introduced me to Evan Thomas, III, a reporter in *Time* magazine's Washington bureau. His work in recasting and rewriting my earlier manuscripts resulted in this book.

I am grateful also to Eric Swenson and his colleagues at W. W. Norton & Company, Inc., for their belief that this is a story worth telling.

Many of my former colleagues in the Army Counselor's office through the years have urged me to write this story, as have many others with whom I had contact during that difficult period, and to all of them I am grateful.

My friend Julia Walters suffered patiently and with continued good humor through the preparation of the 2,100 pages which constituted the 1978, 1979, and 1980 versions, and she has my thanks, as does also my friend and neighbor, Barbara Goff, who helped me with the manuscript which finally was sent to the publisher.

But it is to my own small family that I owe the most special thanks, and for whom I have the most gratitude.

My dear Margaret remains the same sweet and gentle Virginian she was when we first met. Through the bitter McCarthy experience she was my most loyal friend and supporter, as she has always remained. Since 1954 when she first urged me to write this narrative, she has sympathized with and understood the aborted efforts which occurred periodically for over twenty years until this final effort bore fruit. And I am particularly grateful for her forbearance and continued encouragement in the past three years it has taken to complete the effort.

Rebecca, our colic-plagued infant of the 1953–54 era, an only child, is now herself a lawyer. While reading the manuscript in 1981, she paid her parents the ultimate compliment when she observed that all of her remembrances of her small childhood and as a primary school girl are happy ones, and that she never sensed any of the turbulence and family distress which resulted from McCarthy's attacks on me in 1954, and the problems her parents faced with my professional career for many years after the McCarthy experience.

Bibliography

My primary source for this book was, of course, my own experience. I began recording it almost as it happened, with my diary that became the Army's "Chronology of Events" at the Army-McCarthy hearings. And in the summer of 1954, I began writing the narrative that became this book more than twenty-five years later.

In recent years, I have found other source documents in government records. The transcripts of McCarthy's Fort Monmouth hearings I located in the Army's Suitland, Maryland, warehouses in the retired files of the Signal Corps. These were the same executive transcripts turned over to the Army in the autumn of 1953 while we were "cooperating" with McCarthy. They have been declassified and are publicly available. However, those transcripts, still on file at McCarthy's old committee, the Senate Permanent Subcommittee on Investigations, as of 1979, are still labeled "secret."

In the National Archives I found the October 1953 memo, now declassified, prepared in the Army counselor's office and sent to Secretary Stevens, describing the status of fifty-nine Fort Monmouth "lepers."

By making a direct request to Senator Henry Jackson, who still sits on the Investigations Subcommittee, I succeeded in getting access to certain executive transcripts of closed sessions of the Army-McCarthy hearings that I had never seen, or in some cases had not even known about. Prior to his intervention, I had been denied access by the subcommittee.

The sixty-nine-page Army brief, prepared in the Army counselor's office in 1954 but never submitted to the Senate, is on deposit at the National Archives as an unclassified document.

Under the Freedom of Information Act, in 1979 I received from the FBI the Hoover-to-Bolling letter that formed the basis for the famous "Purloined Letter." All thirty-five names, as well as all the information about them, had been blacked out, even though all the names appear in various unclassified documents made available in the National Archives.

Over the years, I have discussed many of the events in this book with the participants, including Senators Karl Mundt, John McClellan, and Charles Potter; Sherman Adams, Gerald Morgan, William P. Rogers, General Lucius Clay, Lieutenant General Walter Weible, Major General Ralph Zwicker, Major General Jerry Persons, Anna M. Rosenberg Hoffman, Phil Potter, Anthony Lewis, Murray Marder, Joe Alsop, Robert T. Stevens, Struve Hensel, Lew Berry, Charles Haskins, Mel Dow, John Simon, Norman Dorsen, Joseph N. Welch, James D. St. Clair, Ken BeLieu, Robert F. Kennedy, Reverend Francis B. Sayre, James Juliana, Tom LaVenia, and Aaron Coleman.

Invaluable to me was a scrapbook of almost every New York and Washington daily newspaper and every weekly news magazine clipping about the Army-McCarthy hearings and the events that immediately led up to them. The book was compiled by Angie Shinebarger, a secretary in the Army Counselor's office at the time. Equally essential, of course, was the transcript of the hearings themselves:

U.S., Congress, Senate, Committee on Government Operations, *Charges and Countercharges Involving Secretary of the Army Robert T. Stevens, John G. Adams, H. Struve Hensel and Senator Joe McCarthy, Roy M. Cohn and Francis P. Carr: Hearing on S. Res. 189*, 83d Cong., 2d sess., Apr. 22–June 17, 1954, 2,980 pp., and S. Rept. 2507, 130 pp.

And the various Senate investigations in which McCarthy was involved provide remarkable insights into his career:

U.S., Congress, Senate, Committee on Banking and Currency, *Study of Reconstruction Finance Corporation. Lustron Corp.—Transportation Contract: Investigative Hearing.* 81st Cong., 2d sess., Jan. 16–Mar. 14, 1950, and Special unnumbered report.

U.S., Congress, Senate, Committee on Armed Services, *Nomination of Anna M. Rosenberg to be Assistant Secretary of Defense: Hearings on Nomination,* 81st Cong., 2d sess., Nov. 29–Dec. 14, 1950, and Executive Report No 16.

U.S., Congress, Senate, Committee on Foreign Relations, *State Department Employee Loyalty Investigations: Hearings of S. Res. 231.* 81st Cong., 2d sess., Feb. 22, 1950 et seq., S. Rept. 2108, 281 pp., and 34 pp. of minority views.

U.S., Congress, Senate, Committee on Rules and Administration. Subcommittee on Privileges and Elections, *Maryland Senatorial Election of 1950: Hearings on S. Res. 250.* 82d Cong., 1st sess., Feb. 20, 1951, et seq., 1222 pp., and Report 647.

U.S., Congress, Senate, Committee on Rules and Administration. Subcommittee on Privileges and Elections. *Investigation of Senator Joseph R. McCarthy. A Resolution to Investigate Senator Joseph R. McCarthy to Determine Whether Expulsion Proceedings Should be Instituted: Hearings on S. Res. 187.* 82d Cong., 1st sess., Sept. 28, 1951, and May 12–16, 1952. Unnumbered report (The Hennings Report) December 31, 1952, 400 pp.

U.S., Congress, Senate, Committee on Rules and Administration. Subcommittee on Privileges and Election, *Investigation of Senator Joseph R. McCarthy and William Benton: Hearing on S. Res. 304.* 82d Cong., 2d sess., July 3, 1952. Unnumbered report (The Hennings Report) December 31, 1952, 400 pp.

U.S., Congress, Senate, Select Committee to Study Censure Charges. *Hearings on S. Res. 301.* 83d Cong., 2d sess., Aug. 28–Sept. 16, 1954, 399 pp., and Report No. 2508, Nov. 8, 1954, 68 pp.

Of the secondary sources, I consider the best book written about McCarthy to be Richard Rovere's *Senator Joe McCarthy* (New York: Harcourt Brace, 1959, 280 pp.). The book has a pronounced point of view, however; in 1970, William F. Buckley wrote that it was "romantic . . . confused . . . disingenuous . . . evasive . . . frivolous."

Two particularly thoughtful books about McCarthy and his period are:

Fried, Richard M. *Men against McCarthy.* New York: Columbia University Press, 1976, 426 pp.

Griffith, Robert. *The Politics of Fear.* Lexington, Kentucky: University Press of Kentucky, 1970. 362 pp.

Jack Anderson did a good bit of investigative reporting and is very detailed on McCarthy's early years in Wisconsin.

Anderson, Jack, and May, Ronald W. *McCarthy, the Man and the Ism*. Boston: The Beacon Press, 1952. 430 pp.

For vivid pictures of the McCarthy era, I recommend:

Cook, Fred C. *The Nightmare Decade*. New York: Random House, 1971. 626 pp.

Manchester, William. *The Glory and the Dream*. New York: Little, Brown, 1973. 1397 pp.

Thomas, Lately. *When Even Angels Wept*. New York: William Morrow, 1973. 654 pp.

Michael Straight's book on the Army-McCarthy hearings was useful in helping me recreate the day-to-day drama of the hearings.

Straight, Michael. *Trial by Television*. Boston: The Beacon Press, 1954. 282 pp.

The only book on McCarthy's censure is that of Senator Watkins, who was chairman of the censure committee. It is a very well-told story, with particular emphasis on the inner workings of the Senate.

Watkins, Arthur V. *Enough Rope*. Englewood Cliffs, N.J.: Prentice-Hall, and The University of Utah Press, 1969. 202 pp.

For a very thorough examination of the Loyalty-Security program and its flaws, see:

Brown, Ralph S. *Loyalty and Security*. New Haven, Conn.: Yale University Press, 1958. 524 pp.

As I finished this narrative in the fall of 1981, a superb book on McCarthy and the press was published. In careful detail, it documents how McCarthy used the press, and how easily the press was used by him.

Bayley, Edwin R. *Joe McCarthy and the Press*. Madison, Wis.: University of Wisconsin Press, 1981. 270 pp.

As this book was being readied for printing, a new biography of McCarthy appeared. It is the most detailed and comprehensive biography yet published, and it debunks some of the myths about McCarthy. Where my own experiences are involved, however, I disagree with some of his facts.

Reeves, Thomas C. *The Life and Times of Joe McCarthy—a Biography*. New York: Stein & Day, 1982. 899 pp.

For Roy Cohn's version of events, see his *McCarthy*. New York: New American Library, 1968. 292 pp.

BIBLIOGRAPHY 273

In his memoirs, Ray Jenkins devotes a chapter to his role as special counsel at the hearings. Though Jenkins had done his best to help McCarthy at the hearings, after twenty-four years' reflections, he is highly critical in his book.

Jenkins, Ray H. *The Terror of Tellico Plains.* Knoxville, Tenn.: East Tennessee Historical Society, 1978. 199 pp.

McCarthy's own book is a hundred-page paperback of his speeches and debates.

McCarthy, Joseph R. *McCarthyism, the Fight for America,* New York: Arno Press, 1952. 100 pp.

Other books:

Bean, Louis. *War Jobs Parity McCarthy—Influence in the 1954 Mid-Term Election,* Washington: Public Affairs Institute, 1954. 54 pp.
Belfrage, Cedric. *The American Inquisition 1945–1960.* Indianapolis: Bobbs-Merrill, 1973. 316 pp.
Buckley, William F., and Bozell, L. Brent. *McCarthy and His Enemies,* Chicago: Henry Regnery, 1954. 413 pp. Published again in 1970 by Arlington House, New Rochelle, N.Y. 425 pp.
Crosby, Donald F. *God, Church and Flag,* Durham, N.C.: University of North Carolina Press, 1978. 307 pp.
DeMello, Duane. *The McCarthy Era 1950–1954.* New York: Scholastic Book Service, 1968. 95 pp.
Evans, Medford. *The Assassination of Joe McCarthy.* Belmont, Mass.: Western Islands, 1970. 303 pp.
Ezell, Macel D. McCarthyism: *Twentieth Century Witchhunt.* Austin, Texas: Steck Vaughn, 1970. 41 pp.
Freulicht, Robert S. *Joe McCarthy and McCarthyism—the Hate That Haunts America.* New York: McGraw-Hill, 1972. 160 pp.
Goldston, Robert C. *The American Nightmare.* Indianapolis: Bobbs-Merrill, 1973. 202 pp.
Griffith, Robert and Theoharis, Allan. *The Specter.* New York: New Viewpoints, 1974. 368 pp. Original essays on the Cold War and the origins of McCarthyism.
Hirschfeld, Burt. *Freedom in Jeopardy.* New York: Julian Messner, 1969. 192 pp.
Latham, Earl. *The Meaning of McCarthyism.* Lexington, Mass.: D.C. Heath, 1973. 198 pp.
Lattimore, Owen. *Ordeal by Slander.* Westport, Conn.: Greenwood Press, 1950–71. 236 pp.
Lokos, Lionel. *Who Promoted Peress?* New York: Bookmailer, 1961. 219 pp.
McCarthy, Joseph Raymond. *Major Speeches and Debates of Senator Joe McCarthy.* New York: Gordon Press, 1975. 354 pp.
McCarthy, Joseph Raymond. *America's Retreat from Victory: The Story of George Catlett Marshall.* New York: Devin Adair, 1951.

Mandlebaum, Seymour J. *The Social Setting of Intolerance*. Chicago: Scott Foresman, 1976. 176 pp.

Matusow, Allen J. *Joseph R. McCarthy*. Engelewood Cliffs, N.J.: Prentice-Hall, 1970. 181 pp.

O'Brien, Michael. *McCarthy and McCarthyism in Wisconsin*. Columbia, Mo.: University of Missouri Press, 1980.

Oshinsky, David. *Senator Joe McCarthy and the American Labor Movement*. Columbia, Mo.: University of Missouri Press, 1976. 206 pp.

Potter, Senator Charles E. *Days of Shame*. New York: Coward-McCann, 1965. 304 pp.

Reeves, Thomas C. *McCarthyism*. Hinsdale, Ill.: Dryden Press, 1973. 139 pp. Kreiger, 1978. 139 pp.

Rorty, James and Deckter, Moshe. *McCarthy and the Communists*. Westport, Conn.: Greenwood Press, 1972 (1954). 163 pp.

Theoharis, Athan G. *Seeds of Repression*. Chicago: Quadrangle, 1971. 238 pp.

Williams, Edward Bennett. *One Man's Freedom*. New York: Atheneum, 1962. 344 pp.

Index

Hensel investigated by, 148–49
informants concealed by, 181–83, 217–18
as Investigations Subcommittee chairman, 38–39
as judge, 12
libel protections for, 67
Loyalty Boards abused by, 98–100, 110–13, 115
Malmedy massacre charges by, 18–19
marriage of, 47, 48
Marshall attacked by, 36
McCormack press support for, 62
monitored phone calls feared by, 219
newspapers attacked by, 23, 62–63
officials' criticisms of, 100–101
officials' support for, 58, 100
office of, 51–52
Pearson attacked by, 50–51
in Peress investigation, 117–22, 124–27, 128–29, 251, 252
personality of, 103–4
popular support for, 94–95, 140, 242, 248
power of, 38–39
press manipulated by, 23, 27, 61–62, 232
"pseudo events" created by, 61–62
in "Purloined Letter" investigation, 48, 49, 71–73, 181–84
Reber attacked by, 165–66
at Republican Convention of 1952, 36
in Rosenberg accusations, 34–36
Schine's relations with, 59, 60, 77, 84–85, 86, 114–15
as senator, 18, 20
soybean investments made by, 21, 28
spies employed by, 28, 213
State Department accused by, 22–23, 24–25, 100
Stevens cross-examined by, 169–70, 172–75
subpoena powers used by, 67
in Tydings committee hearings, 24–25

Tydings's defeat engineered by, 30–31, 32
underground network of information for, 28
Wheeling speech by, 22–23
in World War II, 12
Zwicker attacked by, 127, 128–29, 131, 134–35
McCarthyism:
Army-McCarthy hearings as true reflection of, 232–33
broad influence of, 36–37
Buckley on, 27
destructive force of, 101–2, 193
European views on, 37, 41
executive branch processes blocked by, 236–37
first reference to, 62
ingredients of, 25
as political liability, 242
popular fears expressed in, 94–95
Thomas on, 257
Truman's criticism of, 104–5
McCarthyism: The Fight for America (McCarthy), 62–63
McClellan, John, 111–12, 166, 206
in Army-McCarthy hearings, 154–55, 164, 194, 206, 218
on Investigations Subcommittee, 154–55, 251
in Peress promotion investigation, 251, 252
McCormack, Robert, 62
McGrory, Mary, 127, 173, 188, 190
McLaurin, John, 244
McLeod, R. W. Scott, 37
Mesta, Perle, 212
Milton, Hugh, 142
Milwaukee *Journal,* 62
Monroney, Mike, 249
Morgan, Gerald, 112, 113, 191, 196, 197, 198
Morganthau, Robert, 264
Mundt, Karl E., 93, 133, 134–35, 136, 235
Army-McCarthy hearings chaired by,